The Gilded Beaver
AN INTRODUCTION TO THE LIFE
AND WORK OF JAMES DE MILLE

James De Mille

THE GILDED BEAVER

*An Introduction to the
Life and Work of
James De Mille*

PATRICIA MONK

ECW PRESS

Copyright © 1991 by Patricia Monk

All rights reserved.
This book may not be reproduced in whole or in part, by
photocopy, or other means, without permission of the publisher.

CANADIAN CATALOGUING IN PUBLICATION DATA

Monk, Patricia, 1938-
The gilded beaver : an introduction to the life and work of James de Mille

Includes index.
ISBN 1-55022-104-3 (bound). – ISBN 1-55022-106-X (pbk.)

1. De Mille, James, 1833-1880 – Biography.
2. Novelists, Canadian (English) – 19th century – Biography.*
I. Title.

PS8457.E452Z75 1991   C813.4   C89-094653-1
PR9199.2.D452Z75 1991

This book has been published with the assistance of a grant
from the Canadian Federation for the Humanities, using funds
provided by the Social Sciences and Humanities Research
Council of Canada. Additional grants have been provided by
the Ontario Arts Council and The Canada Council.

Design and imaging by ECW Type & Art, Oakville, Ontario.
Printed and bound by The Porcupine's Quill, Inc., Erin, Ontario.

Published by ECW PRESS, 307 Coxwell Avenue, Toronto M4L 3B5.

IN MEMORIAM
Kathleen Gardin Monk
1908–1989

. . . biography has to rely heavily on some evidence but a great deal on speculation, unless there are diaries and family papers to provide firmer ground. But biography at its best is a form of fiction. The personality and sympathies of the biographer cannot be sifted out of what is written.

— *Robertson Davies,* The Lyre of Orpheus

TABLE OF CONTENTS

    List of Illustrations 8
    Preface 9
    Acknowledgements 10
    A Note on the Citation of Research Materials 12
    Introduction 13

    PART I
1. The Family History of the De Mills 19
2. James's Early Life, 1833–51 32
3. At Brown University, 1852–54 57
4. The Uncertain Years, 1855–65 80
5. At Dalhousie College, 1865–80 110

    PART II
6. De Mille's Occasional and Light Verse 153
7. De Mille's Early Fiction 175
8. The Satirical Romances and the Novels of Sensation .. 198
9. *A Strange Manuscript Found in a Copper Cylinder* .. 228

    Conclusion 250
    Appendix A: Contributions to the *Christian Watchman* . 257
    Appendix B: Contributions to the *Christian Visitor* ... 261
    Selected Bibliography 262
    Index 284
    Permissions 293

LIST OF ILLUSTRATIONS

James De Mille	*frontispiece*
Elizabeth Tongue (Budd) De Mill, James's mother	28
The De Mill house on the Bay Shore	34
Horton Collegiate Academy Residence	38
The *Elizabeth Bentley*	44
Brown University in De Mille's time	64
Emily, an unknown person, Alice, Frederick, Eliza	88
Acadia, First College Hall	94
Elisha Budd De Mill	98
Frederick, Eliza, Emily, and Alice in the grounds of the house on the Bay Shore	104
Dalhousie College	112
The Rev. Dr. John Pryor	130
De Mille's Grave in Camp Hill Cemetery	138
Illustrated manuscript page of "Class Poem — 1854," describing the Junior Burial	154
Eliza, Emily, Frederick, Mrs. De Mill, Alice	196
Illustrated manuscript page of "Eggs Eggs Eggs," which later appeared in *The Dodge Club* as "A Nightmare"	200
Arthur De Mille, James's youngest brother, and Alice	212
An engraving from the first edition of *A Strange Manuscript Found in a Copper Cylinder*	230
Annie De Mille, at the wedding of her youngest son, Frank	254

PREFACE

Two points of spelling should be noted. To begin with, the spelling of James De Mille's surname presents considerable hazards. His own branch of the family, from their arrival in Canada, spelled it De Mill or DeMill, but American branches spelled it variously as Demill, DeMill, De Mille, DeMille, De Mil, and De Milt. James himself adopted the spelling De Mille on entering Brown University, and thereafter used it in his literary work. This spelling is now generally considered to be official, but in all documents concerning his professional career at Dalhousie, it was spelled De Mill. In other documents and early critical and biographical references, the spelling varies according to the writer (and occasionally the printer). In this biography, I have adopted the spelling De Mille for all my own references to James, and the spelling De Mill for family members of his own generation or earlier, but not for his children or his youngest brother, Arthur, who followed his usage. In quoting from other writers, I have retained their spelling.

Similarly, the name of the city of his birth is now officially Saint John, with the first word always written in full. This convention was not always followed by earlier writers, and in quotations I have always copied the usage of the writer concerned.

ACKNOWLEDGEMENTS

This book would not have been possible without the help of a great many people. In particular, I am grateful for the incomparable encouragement and assistance of my colleague, Dr. Malcolm G. Parks, who was always ready to listen to me on the subject of my problems and pleasures with James De Mille's life and work. I also very much appreciate the moral support, helpful suggestions, and constant good humour of Dr. Laura Groening.

I owe much also to the willing help of Mrs. Martha L. Mitchell, university archivist of Brown University; Mrs. Patricia Townsend, university archivist of Acadia University; Dr. Charles Armour, university archivist of Dalhousie University; Ms. Karen Smith of the Dalhousie University Killam Library Special Services; and Mr. Allan Dunlop of the Public Archives of Nova Scotia.

Many other individuals have given me the benefit of their advice, among them Dr. Barry Moody of the Department of History at Acadia; Dr. Peter Waite of the Department of History at Dalhousie; Dr. Thomas B. Vincent of the Royal Military College in Kingston, and the Reverend Philip Griffin-Allwood.

A source of special pleasure and gratitude was the interest expressed in the project by Mr. Noel James De Mille, grandson of James De Mille, and his wife, on a visit to Halifax in 1985. 1986

For their generous permission to refer to and to quote from manuscripts and other documentary sources in their possession or care, I would like to acknowledge the courtesy of many institutions and people. For official records, I am grateful to the president and Board of Governors of Acadia University; the Board of Governors of the Andover Newton Theological School; the president and Board of Trustees of Brown University; and the president, Board of Governors, and Senate of Dalhousie University. For permission to make use of their holdings of letters and other documents by and about De Mille, I am grateful to Acadia University Archives, Dalhousie University Archives, the National Archives of Canada, the Public

Archives of Nova Scotia, the New Brunswick Museum, the Saint John Regional Library, the National Library of Scotland, the Beinecke Rare Book and Manuscript Library of Yale University, the Butler Library of Columbia University, the Historical Society of Pennsylvania, Miss Edith Creighton of Halifax, Mr. A.D.H. Burpee of LaHave, the pastor of the Old Cambridge Baptist Church of Cambridge, Massachusetts, and the pastor of the Leinster Street Baptist Church in Saint John, New Brunswick.

I am additionally grateful to Dr. D.M.R. Bentley for permission to include in chapter 8 material that has previously appeared in *Canadian Poetry*, and to Dr. M.J. Edwards of the Centre for Editing Early Canadian Texts of Carleton University, for permitting me to consult the bibliographical checklist of De Mille's works compiled by the staff of the centre.

I am also very grateful for the courtesy and help offered by the staff of the following libraries and institutions in consulting their collections: the Archives and Special Collections Division of the Harriet Irving Library of the University of New Brunswick, the Archives and History Division of the West Virginia Department of Culture and History, the Cincinnati Historical Society Library, Harvard University Archives, the Legislative Library of Nova Scotia, the Library of the University of British Columbia, the Massachusetts Historical Society Library, the New Brunswick Legislative Library, and the New York Historical Society.

I would like to acknowledge the financial support of the Social Sciences and Humanities Research Council of Canada in the form of a Leave Research Fellowship for 1982–83, when much of the initial research for this project was completed. This book has been published with the help of a grant from the Canadian Federation for the Humanities, using funds provided by the Social Sciences and Humanities Research Council of Canada.

These expressions of indebtedness would be sadly lacking if I failed to acknowledge the work of three scholars whose earlier efforts to present James De Mille to the world were a constant source of encouragement and assistance. Sir Archibald MacMechan, Lawrence J. Burpee, and Dr. R.E. Watters were all forced by circumstances to leave their work on De Mille incomplete. In bringing my own work to completion, I have endeavoured to the best of my ability to produce a study that would meet with their scholarly approval.

Last, but by no means least, during these last stages of turning the manuscript into the book, I have much appreciated the firm, tactful, and good-humoured collaboration of my editor at ECW PRESS, Mary Williams.

A NOTE ON THE CITATION OF RESEARCH MATERIALS

This book has a selected bibliography instead of a list of works cited. This bibliography has been divided into a number of sections, and each section has been given a letter that has been included at the end of each parenthetical reference in the text, so that citations may be located with relative ease. For example, the parenthetical reference (Archer, *Canada* 2; G) refers to page 2 of *Canada: A Short History of the Dominion of Canada* by Andrew Archer, which may be found in the selected bibliography section G, "General References: Published Material," listed alphabetically under the name Archer. Some bibliography sections have several parts: thus, the reference ("In Barbary"; B2) refers to an entry in section B —"Manuscripts and Papers of James De Mille" — part 2 — "Verse." A number of frequently cited periodicals are not assigned a bibliographical section in parenthetical reference, because the full publication date of each citation is given in the text.

Introduction

The Gilded Beaver, the name of the ship in which James De Mille's forbears originally came to the New World, offers a curiously apt comment on the man himself. It suggests not only his dyed-in-the-wool Canadian personality (the beaver), but also the layers of misinformation (the gilding) that envelop him and almost hide the real man from view. Consequently, it functions admirably as the title of a biographical and critical introduction that attempts to present the "real" James De Mille, to strip away the misinformation, and to reveal a Canadian writer of considerable personal and literary interest.

From the beginning, as a result of missing records and personal papers, this elusive Canadian personality has accumulated a gilding of myth, legend, gossip, libel, and sheer confusion. His brother Alfred, who might have helped biographers, was too anxious to preserve James's status as a gentleman and a scholar to be helpful. For example, it was probably Alfred who was responsible for the report that De Mille was being considered for the Chair of Rhetoric at Harvard at the time of his death, a report that Harvard's records reveal to be quite false. De Mille's colleagues and students at Dalhousie University gave Archibald MacMechan, the first person to attempt a biography, wildly conflicting descriptions of De Mille's person and personality, apparently according to whether they liked or disliked him. MacMechan either could not or would not attempt to reconcile the discrepancies, since he subsequently abandoned his project.

De Mille's work attracted a similar critical gilding from critics who either liked or hated it. On the one hand, some of them, such as the editorialist in the *Acadian Recorder* who reported that eminent authorities (unnamed) had declared *Cord and Creese* to be the equal of anything by Wilkie Collins, lavished extravagant praise on him. In doing so they were attempting to boost De Mille's importance as a Nova Scotian writer (some early Nova Scotian critics found it convenient to forget that he had been born in New Brunswick) far above anything he would have claimed for himself. On the other hand, even MacMechan, in an article he published about De Mille, made it clear that his opinion of most of De Mille's work was not very high, and H.P. Scott, in a lecture on De Mille reprinted in the *Dalhousie Gazette*, described him as "a thorough hack" (136; F). Elsewhere, Albert Coldwell, in his Vaughan Prize essay on Acadia College alumni published in an early history of the college, sums up De Mille's career as a writer by describing him as the author of "various contributions to light literature" (114; G), and the description manages to be both snobbish and inaccurate in its implications of a casual dilettantism. During a relatively short life, De Mille wrote at least 26 books, including children's books, and a number of short stories, quite apart from his nonfiction and verse. The qualification "at least" is necessary when counting the novels because of the confusions and problems about his corpus which arose as a result of the scattering of his papers after his death in 1880. Under this impressionistic biographical and critical treatment — a covering at least as opaque as the usual literary gilding if not as uniform in nature — De Mille himself has almost disappeared.

Fortunately, however, he has not disappeared altogether: there is some information still to be gleaned about the man and about his work. The first part of this study is intended to examine the evidence about the man and reveal him as clearly as is possible, setting him against a background of his time and place, as an individual, as a family man, as a writer, and as a teacher. In the second part, a similar attempt is made reexamine the evidence and to straighten out the problems and confusions that surround his work, discussing the general characteristics of the corpus thus established, but without offering a detailed reading of any single novel, except *A Strange Manuscript Found in a Copper Cylinder*.

An intriguing human being, albeit a rather shadowy one, does emerge, as a result of these examinations, to reward the investigator's efforts.

INTRODUCTION

Moreover, although in the jigsaw puzzle of nineteenth-century Canadian — especially Maritime Canadian — literature, De Mille's life and work constitute only a single piece, if that piece can be seen clearly, its precise importance in the whole picture can properly be estimated and that whole itself becomes a little clearer.

PART I

CHAPTER 1

The Family History of the De Mills

In May 1658, *De Vergulde Bever* (*The Gilded Beaver*), carrying emigrants from the Netherlands to New Netherland, the Dutch settlement in North America, arrived in New Amsterdam (later New York City). On board were "Anthony de Mis from Haerlem, and Wife and two children" (O'Callaghan 3: 52; De Boer; G, H). The misspelling of the family name was only one of many that were to persist among Anthony's descendants, but the family historians, chief among them Richard Mead Demill, claimed to be able to trace from Anthony the descent of all the De Mills, Demills, Demilts, and De Milles in North America. Seven generations later, in a letter dated 12 October 1882, Alfred Henry De Mill, James's younger brother, describes to Richard Mead Demill his own unsuccessful attempt to trace the family history before Anthony in the Netherlands. Even more recently, Noel James De Mille, James's grandson, was successful in tracing the family's roots in France,[1] before they settled in the Netherlands.

Anthony and his wife Elizabeth, James's great-great-great-great-grandparents, settled in New Amsterdam, where to the family of two daughters, "Maria and Anna, aged three and one years respectively," who had accompanied them (De Boer; H), they later added four more children: Isaac,

Pieter, Sarah, and Anthony. According to Richard Demill's "Family Record," completed in 1864, Anthony senior appears to have been a successful and important member of the community, a property owner, and to have survived the changes in the community's political fortunes comfortably, for his name first appears in the city records on 13 October 1664 in a list of "ye names of such inhabitants of New York, &c., as took the oath to be true subjects to his Majestie [King Charles II] . . . after the surrender of New York Fort" to the British (3; H).[2] On 17 August 1673, however, after the city had been recaptured by the Dutch and renamed "New Orange," Anthony was "appointed *Schout* [Sheriff] . . . for the term of *one year*" (6; H). Nevertheless, he again held office under English rule when, in 1687, he became the "Assistant Alderman, Dock Ward" in what was by then New York City. Judging from items from the inventory of his estate at his death, which included

> among other things, 10 pictures valued at £2.10s. — 40 (?) "Reading Bookes greate & small," £3. — 1 "Flower Booke" 3s. — Ground in Beaver St. £22. — "1 Small Silver Cup & 3 pr Buttons 1 Tumbler 4 Silver Spoons 1 do Mostard & teeth picker," £5.4s. — other Silver Spoons, etc., and "1 box old bookes." (Demill 14; H)

he was financially comfortable by the standards of his times. He died in 1689.

Pieter (or Peter) was Anthony's fourth child and second son, born in 1661 (the date of his baptism is given as 12 October, so that he was probably born earlier that month). On 4 August 1687, he married Maria van de Heal, and they had nine children. He was a political survivor like his father, for he began as a member of the "Committee of N.Y., a Council of War" in support of Jacob Leisler, and took part as "Ensign of Foot" in Leisler's rebellion against the Crown in 1691. After Leisler's overthrow, however, he was commissioned as "Lieutenant of a foot Company belonging to the regiment in the City and County of New York" by the new governor, Richard, Earl of Bellomont. In 1700–01, he served a one-year term as sheriff of New York City. Soon after this, he purchased property in Stamford, Connecticut, and moved there in 1715, with his wife Mary. He died on 10 September 1722, survived by four of his children: Peter, Mary, Hannah, and Anthony (Demill 16–29; H).

Peter, whose birthdate is not known, was the eldest of Pieter's surviving children. He married Abigail Banks. They had nine children. Peter and Hannah, the two eldest, both died in childhood. They were followed by Abraham, Mary, and another Peter, who, Richard Demill writes, "according to my grandfather . . . was murdered at the age of 20, and his murderer hung on Gibbett Island." Richard's grandfather was Joseph, the next youngest to the murdered Peter, and there were three younger children: Elizabeth, Abigail, and yet another Peter. Only three of the nine (Abraham, Joseph, and Elizabeth) survived their father, who died in Stamford in 1774 (Demill 41; H).

Abraham, Peter's third child and second son, was born on 21 December 1735. He was "the ancestor of the branch of the family, residing in St John, New Brunswick" (Demill 41; H). On 5 October 1756, he married Mary King, and their first and apparently only child, John (James's grandfather), was born the following year. Mary died of smallpox in 1759, when her son was two years old (Demill 42; H). Abraham seems to have left home about this time, for he was apparently no longer living in Stamford at the time of his father's death. Richard Demill notes that he is not mentioned in his father's will, and adds that "the inference would naturally be that he was dead also" (that is, like the other children who are not mentioned and are known to have died before their father). Demill then goes on to speculate that

> possibly, he may have been far away, and his father, not knowing whether he were alive or dead, and considering him, if living, in no need of assistance, may have confined himself to such a provision as would secure the respectability of his [Abraham's] son *John*'s appearance. (43; H)

Demill then quotes a "Letter of Alfred H. De Mill Esq," James's younger brother, describing the belief among the members of the Saint John branch of the family that Abraham

> was a merchant in the India trade and sailed in his own ship. At the breaking out of the Revolution he was on his way home from Calcutta, and, not liking the movement, he put in at one of the Dutch West Indies, sold out, took a second wife, sister of the Governor of the Island — a fat widow, with a fat plantation — settled down as a planter, and there died. (42–43; H).

The original of the letter from which Demill is quoting is not among Alfred's surviving correspondence, but in his own unfinished history of the family, largely derived from Demill's, Alfred De Mill repeats this information, discreetly omitting the remark about the "fat widow, with a fat plantation," and adds that Abraham "sent for his son when the war was over; but the latter had married and removed to St. John NB," and that the date of Abraham's death is "supposed previous to 1790" ("De Mill Pedigree"; H).

John, Abraham's son and Peter's grandson, was born at Stamford, on 26 August 1757. At the time of his grandfather's death, when a bequest of "wearing apparel" was left to him, he was 17 years of age, and was "either at school or an apprentice" (Demill 43; H). Since, according to Esther Wright's study of the New Brunswick Loyalists, on John De Mill's arrival in Saint John at the close of the American War of Independence, his occupation was listed as "carpenter" (Wright 276; G), it is more likely that he was an apprentice than a student at 17. Alfred De Mill says that John was educated in New York, that he "went . . . into a Regiment of Royal Volunteers on the breaking out of the Revolution" in 1776, and that during the war he served under Cornwallis in Virginia ("De Mill Pedigree"; H). Alfred also appears to have thought at one point that John's regiment might have been the King's American Regiment, but later he seems to become uncertain about this, supposing that John was in the same regiment as Nathan Smith, whose daughter he married. If Alfred is correct in this supposition, then John was in the First Battalion of Delancey's Brigade, which Wright gives as Smith's regiment although she does not actually identify John's (329; G). John Fortescue's account of the campaign in the Carolinas and Virginia during the war indicates that Cornwallis had one "Provincial corps" under him at the battle of Camden (near Charleston), and that two others were among reinforcements sent to him under the command of Major General Leslie, but he does not mention them by name (Fortescue 324, 337; G).

At some point during the war years, John met and married Elizabeth Smith, daughter of Dr. Nathan Smith, a surgeon in the First Battalion of Delancey's Brigade. The date and place of the marriage remain uncertain ("probably in New York," according to Alfred De Mill, who offers no date), but the couple's first child, Abraham (who died in infancy), was born in New York on 23 May 1782. In 1783, John, accompanied by his wife (and by their son if he survived so long), came to Saint John with the Loyalists. He drew a city lot in Saint John (then Parrtown), but later sold it and moved out to Hampton, where he took up farming. In Hampton, John and Elizabeth De Mill had nine more children in addition to Abraham, of whom the youngest was Nathan Smith, James's father (Alfred De Mill, "De Mill Pedigree"; H).[3] Elizabeth died in 1819 and John in 1825.

Nathan Smith De Mill was born on 14 October 1804 in Hampton, and named for his mother's father, the army surgeon. Unlike his father, he does not seem to have found farming attractive, and according to another family historian, Muriel De Mill Raymond, as a youth he became interested in ship-building activities which were going on at Hampton Ferry and along the Norton shore of the Kennebecasis River. Eventually he went to St. John where he took up that sort of work" (59; H). According to the obituary notice of Nathan that was sent to the *Christian Visitor* by the members of the Leinster Street Baptist Church, he first came to Saint John in 1818 (Obituary; G).[4] Although an interest in shipbuilding may have propelled him from Hampton to Saint John, it was in business that he established himself. In 1825, he was listed among the "Freemen" of the city in the "Register of Voters" of Saint John, and was described as "Clerk" (Saint John, Register; H). (The list was simply a list of business licenses, costing "Five Pounds," issued in the city.) By this time, Nathan was prospering to such an extent that on 15 August 1828 he was able to purchase from John Owens "a certain ship or vessel now building . . . by estimation Three hundred and forty Tons Together with all and singular appurtenances" for "one thousand pounds of lawful money of New Brunswick" (Saint John County, [Property]; H). In the same year, he was described as "merchant" on the certificate of his marriage to Elizabeth Budd (Trinity, Marriage; H).

Although no portrait of him has survived, and even a reliable description is lacking, we can get some idea of Nathan's personality from the impression he made on other people, and from what is revealed of him in those of his own letters that have survived. Among Archibald MacMechan's research notes for his projected biography of James De Mille is the record of his interview of a Mrs. Fay:

> Father Demill . . . big man, keen face, dark eyes & florid complexion, *vegetarian.* with two girls Kate? clever broad forehead & Rose? both remarkably fine complexions, with them in boarding-school. kept no servant, mother retiring, never saw her. Father had a fish-commission business at the wharf. "Face like Abraham Lincoln." (MacMechan; H)

Since James's sisters were named Elizabeth, Emily, and Alice, since his mother was active in the church, and since there is no other evidence that Nathan's business included a "fish-commission business," Mrs. Fay's memories of Nathan's appearance should be regarded with some caution. Lawrence Burpee, who was the eldest son of Nathan's youngest daughter, Alice, and prepared a study of James's life for publication in the early nineteen hundreds, describes Nathan as follows:

> a man of stalwart frame and even more stalwart character, as impulsive and daring in his undertakings as he was inflexible in seeing them through. Unyielding as granite in what he conceived to be the right, a Puritan in religion, in business one whose word was always as good as his bond, intolerant of hypocrisy, hiding under a stern exterior a warm and generous heart. (Lecture 1; H)

All Burpee's writing about James undoubtedly draws heavily on his mother's memories of her family.[5] Since the Burpees lived in Ottawa, and Lawrence was born in 1873, it is impossible that he should remember Nathan personally, and unlikely that he would remember James. But he certainly could have obtained additional information on visits to his mother's family as a child and as an adult.

What is revealed of Nathan Smith De Mill in his business correspondence (two letterbooks covering the years 1833–47 and 1847–51, respectively) suggests, however, that Burpee's portrait may be slightly idealized. Certainly Nathan appears to have been quite aggressive in pursuing his interests. In a letter of 20 June 1839 to his chief trading partners in England, Messrs Cannon Miller of Liverpool, he writes:

> I beg to call your attention to a case [of] Indigo shipped per *Samuel*, on which I had to pay £9.11.7 (nine pounds, eleven shillings, and 7d) in foreign duty in consequence of not having a British Character. I would thank you to attend to this matter, and cause the duty to be returned. I beg also to call your attention to the oakum [shipped] per *Westmorland* which I cannot sell from its very bad quality. Let me know what I am to do with it. I received a letter from Mr Todd stating the oakum shipped by your house could not be used and ordered a lot to be shipped from this port for his ship. (Nathan De Mill; H)[6]

He was also shrewd enough to be severe about what he deemed to be unnecessary extravagance on the part of the shipmasters in his employment, as the same letter indicates:

> When the ship *John Bentley* left this port, I furnished her with a full supply of Stores (bread excepted) for the purpose of leaving more means in your hands, not expecting the disbursements would amount to over £400, but to my very great surprise I found on receipt of her account that over £700 was expended. What I expect at your hands is a strict control over the disbursements of any vessel I may consign to your house and wish you to say to Captain Geach that I expect he will sail the ship *John Bentley* on as cheap a scale as Captain D. Robertson.

If his employees were recalcitrant, he could be ruthless. Evidently Captain Geach did not heed the instructions that were passed on to him, for on 9 October Nathan writes to Cannon Miller again about him: "I am disappointed with Captain Geach and shall un-ship him on the *John Bentley*'s arrival here." His emphasis on being careful with the "disbursements" (expenses) is, from time to time, sufficiently emphatic as to suggest meanness rather than shrewdness. In a letter to Captain George Hunt, dated 24 December 1839, he writes: "As the ship *Elizabeth Bentley* will be under your sole direction whilst in London, I beg you will make her disbursements as light as possible. I have every confidence in you that your disbursements will be as moderate as possible." In keeping with this regard for money, he was usually well insured against disaster, as he points out in a letter of 23 January 1837 to another of his trading partners, Messrs. Wilder, Pickersgill, describing one of the terrible Saint John fires:

> You no doubt will have heard of the dreadful conflagration with which we have been visited . . . 118 merchants have been turned out of doors by this visitation and the writer of this included, but am happy however in stating that I succeeded in rescuing all my goods except a very small amount say £40 which was insured.

He must therefore have been very chagrined by the fire of 1841, when he suffered a fairly heavy loss and had to request, in a letter of 27 November, an accommodation from one of his creditors, Messrs. Joseph Parratt and Sons:

> On the night of the 15 [November] this City was again visited by a very extensive fire. . . . Having occupied what was called a fireproof Brick store that on trial was found insufficient. . . I have lost a large amount of goods uninsured, having placed too much confidence in the building. Under the circumstances I hope you will bear with me until spring.

Since, on the other hand, he was extremely generous in supporting his church, to which "he gave largely of his means," and was "ardent in his support of every religious or benevolent work" (Obituary; G) possibly he was averse not to spending money but to spending it unnecessarily. Caution, in fact, characterizes all the business activities revealed in the letterbooks, and there is nothing in them to support Burpee's characterization of Nathan as "daring" in business matters.

Burpee is probably more accurate, however, when he calls Nathan "a Puritan in religion" (Lecture 1; H), for this is clearly at the root of Nathan's widely known aversions to alcohol and to literature (or at least, to novels). Nathan had been brought up, like his father John, in the Church of England, and indeed married and had his first five children baptized in that faith:

> for many years, he belonged to the Church of England, for whose tenets in their evangelical form he showed the most ardent attachment. . . . When quite a young man, his attention was arrested by the spread of Intemperance and the evils arising therefrom. . . . [He] associated himself with a few others, and established a Total Abstinence Society here. (Obituary; G)

It is reasonable to assume that the aversion to alcohol was in part why he left the Church of England for the Baptist church, since the former took no very firm position on abstinence. The *Christian Visitor* describes his decision as follows:

> In the year 1840, he was deeply agitated by doubts in reference to the doctrines of the church to which he belonged. Too honest to remain when his conscience was at all dissatisfied, and too deeply attached to the church of his fathers to leave her without great cause, he passed many months in the deepest anxiety, and in the most careful examination of the points in doubt. At length he was convinced that

it was his duty to join the Baptist Church, and accordingly he was baptised in April 1842. (Obituary; G)

It is also reasonable to assume that this aversion to intemperance was fostered by observation and experience of its effects in a rowdy nineteenth-century seaport. He describes these effects in a letter of 20 May 1835 to Cannon Miller:

> At the time of the brig [*William*] being at Cocagne Mr Cutler informed me that the Master & Mate were drunken characters, and that the Master would go through the Street with a Bottle of Rum in his pocket — very many of your Captains, when they get on this side of the Atlantic, indulge in habits of intemperance. I have known the Master of a ship lying drunk for a week or more in his cabin and the consignee had no power to turn him out. (Nathan De Mill; H)

Apart from the offence to Nathan's temperance principles, the cost to the merchant would have been considerable, since the ship would have been lying idle for the week of the captain's drunkenness because nothing could be done without his authority. To Captain Hunt, therefore, Nathan writes in his letter of 24 December 1839: "If Freight should offer, do not allow any kind of intoxicating liquor to come on board." Moreover, shrewd businessman that he was, he did not overlook other practical benefits of running his ships "on the temperance plan," as he describes it to his New York agents, Messrs. Thomas Irvin and Company in a letter of 14 January 1835. Accordingly, he instructs his agents on 20 April 1836:

> Captain Robertson informed me [that] whilst at Savannah he forwarded you a certificate that no ardent spirits had been used on board said vessel during the year past, consequently you will be able to obtain the 5/Cent discount of the amount of premium.

His aversion to alcohol was very well known in the Saint John business and shipping communities, and earned him the nickname, among those who did not share his views, of "Cold Water De Mill" (Burpee, Notes; H). The popular story, that this nickname was bestowed upon him on the occasion when he discovered a barrel of rum aboard one of his vessels and personally threw it overboard, is, apparently, purely apocryphal.

Elizabeth Tongue (Budd) De Mill, James's mother

So, apparently, is the story that, on receiving a consignment of novels, he burned them all. There is an actual incident, however, that may have given rise to this story. Such a consignment did arrive, but as his stiff letter of 28 March 1846 to John S. Pratt, the merchant who consigned it to him, reveals, his response was less dramatic:

> Your favors of 10 December and 16 [February] I have received, the former with a case of Books received a few days since.
> I have not Been able to Sell to our Booksellers and have Been compelled to Send the entire lot to an auctioneer with Directions to Sell them in lots as requested.
> The Books for this Province to Sell are Religious Books, including those in the Sunday School Departments, Moral Subjects including Works on the Temperance Cause or the Total Abstinence Principle, [and] Travels and Voyages. Those Works you have sent are nearly all Novels and such as I do not like to Sell for I consider them in the devil's department. However as you have sent them to my care I shall attend to the Sale and remit as soon as I am in funds.

Like his aversion to alcohol, therefore, his aversion to literature had both a practical and a religious aspect: novels were both the "devil's department" and a commodity that was unsalable locally. Moreover, just as his aversion to wasting money was balanced by his generosity to "religious or benevolent work," so his aversion to novels was balanced by a tolerance for literature in his own household. His wife, Elizabeth, shared with their son James a liking for literature, and Mrs. Gaskell's *Cranford* and the novels of Charles Dickens are included among the works that Burpee says they discussed ("Biographical" 2a; "Appreciation" 1; E).[7]

Elizabeth De Mill is less easy to characterize than her husband. Born Elizabeth Tongue Budd, she was the daughter of a Loyalist family of Digby, Nova Scotia, that was no less distinguished than the De Mill family, although it has not been traced in the same detail by any of the family historians. Her father, Elisha Budd, according to Raymond in her account of the De Mill family, "was of New York; an ensign in the King's American Regiment. At the peace he went to Digby, where he became a merchant, and Justice of Common Pleas" (59; H). By the end of hostilities, Elisha Budd had been promoted, for when he married Mary Ann Bonnell in Digby on 15 August 1789, his marriage certificate described him as lieutenant (Wilson 359; G).

His wife was one of the daughters of Isaac Bonnell, formerly of Connecticut, who served with the Prince of Wales's American Regiment and settled in Kingston, New Brunswick (Raymond 59; Wright 261; H, G). Elizabeth was born, according to Raymond, on 16 June 1807 (59; H), and the records of baptism of Trinity Church, Digby, show that "a female child of Elisha Budd Esq. named Elizabeth Tongue" was baptized on 2 August 1807 (Trinity, "Notitia" 98; H). Elizabeth was named after her mother's sister Elizabeth Budd, who married William C. Tongue of Windsor, Nova Scotia. Burpee describes Elizabeth Tongue De Mill as "a sweet-faced and sweet-natured gentlewoman" (Lecture 1; H). Pictures of her taken later in life show her as dark-haired woman, with an oval face, and of medium build.

Nathan Smith De Mill and Elizabeth Tongue Budd were married on 9 July 1828, in Trinity Parish Church (Trinity, Marriage 72; H) and returned to Saint John to live. Nathan's office was on Water Street (Nathan De Mill flyleaf; H), but he also, according to Burpee, owned a house on Charlotte Street ("Biographical" 2a; H). This latter was the home in which the couple raised their family.

NOTES

1 Described in conversation with the author, 26 May 1986.

2 Richard Mead Demill's carefully organized and documented "Family Record" supplies most of my information about the early history of the family up to their removal to Canada. It is not paginated, but organized in numbered paragraphs, and parenthetical references to it are therefore by paragraph, not page number.

3 The other children were John (born on 16 February 1784 and died in infancy), Mary (born on 5 March 1786 and died young), another Abraham (born on 3 May 1788), Fanny (born on 21 November 1790 and died young), Henry (born on 21 November 1792), William (born on 21 September 1795), Thomas (born on 24 February 1798), and Rufus (born on 14 August 1802).

4 The unsigned and untitled obituary notice begins with the information that it was "Approved at the meeting of the Leinster St. Baptist Church on Friday evening, Dec. 30" (Obituary; G). If James was able to return to Saint John at the time of his father's death, it may well have been composed by him.

5 Alice Susanna De Mill was born on 25 October 1847; she married Lewis Johnston Burpee, by whom she had six children, on 5 June 1872, and died in Ottawa on 20 October 1926 (Raymond 64; H).

6 Two of Nathan De Mill's letterbooks have survived. These letterbooks, as letterbooks commonly did in business of this period, consist of manuscript books into which a copy clerk would each day copy the date, address, and text of the day's business letters before the originals were dispatched, as the official records of the business transacted. In quotations from the letterbooks, I have regularized irregular punctuation and spelling, and expanded abbreviations, since these, which seem to be the results of the copy clerk's haste, make the letters very difficult to follow. Cannon Miller was a shipping company in Liverpool, England, and one of De Mill's most regular trading partners.

7 "Biographical" and "Appreciation" are the two separately paginated sections of Lawrence Johnston Burpee's typescript titled "James De Mille," a short unpublished book manuscript, apparently prepared for the Ryerson Press. Mention of James's literary discussions with his mother occurs in both parts.

CHAPTER 2

James's Early Life, 1833-51

James De Mille was born on 23 August 1833, in Saint John. No birth or baptismal record exists, since many of the records of Trinity Church, Saint John, which his family was attending at this time, were destroyed in the fire of 1877, so that the year of James's birth was for a long time in dispute, being given variously as 1833, 1834, 1836, and 1837. Raymond, usually the most reliable of the De Mill family historians, however, claims it is 1833 (59; H), and this agrees with the fact that in registering at Brown University in February of 1852, James gave his age as 18, meaning that he had reached his eighteenth birthday in August 1851 (Brown, Register 54; H). He was Nathan and Elizabeth's third child, two boys having already been born to them: Elisha Budd De Mill (named for his maternal grandfather, and usually referred to in the family as Budd), on 13 April 1829; and William John De Mill (known as Will, named for two of his father's brothers), on 7 April 1831 (Raymond 59; H).

James was perhaps fortunate in having this particular position in the family. His years of babyhood were extended beyond the two allowed by chance to Budd and Will because, although Elizabeth gave birth to a fourth child, Charles Frederick, on 28 March 1836, he died at the age of 16 months, leaving Elizabeth, at least until the birth of Alfred Henry on 20 May 1838 (Raymond 59; H), with more time to devote to her three-year-old toddler, James, than might normally have been expected in a family that was eventually to consist of nine children. In later years, certainly, the attachment between James and his mother, as recorded by Burpee from family recollections, was very strong:

> But to his mother alone did he reveal his inner self, his thoughts on religion, on literature, on life, his hopes to turn that which was in him to some worth-while purpose. "They would walk for hours" says one of his sisters "up and down the garden paths, discussing Swedenborg or Goethe, laughing over some memorable passage in Dickens' latest novel, or quoting bits of *Evangeline*." ("Biographical" 2a; H)

The sister concerned is almost certainly Burpee's mother, Alice. Burpee also reports about James as a child that his "Memory [was] noticeable[;] when a child [he] could repeat anything after hearing [or] reading [it] once or twice," and he adds among his notes about James's adult years that his memory was "astonishing — seemed to retain without effort any fact or statement to which he ever gave a moment's thought" (Notes; H). One of James's younger brothers, Frederick, notes that "Mother says he had a strong temper but kept it sternly under control."[1]

Nathan appears to have been a good Victorian father. This at least is the view of the members of the Leinster Street Church, whose memorial notice says that "In his family, his management was firm, yet gentle" (Obituary; G). The management may have seemed more firm than gentle to the managed, for when James, by then an adult in business for himself, writes on 24 February 1856 to the schoolboy Alfred at Horton, his letter shows a concern that Alfred should not apply directly to their father for extra money at that time because the consequences could be unpleasant:

> If you squeeze yourself this way a little you can go to Brown next term with flying colors but if Father takes it into his head that you are not economical he wont want to let you go.... And now Alf be careful... dont write home for money or father will be sending you a serious letter. (B3)[2]

The De Mill house on the Bay Shore

He repeats this caution in another letter to Alfred the following year (on 12 October 1857): "The money you have had thus far has come from me and father has not paid it yet. He is unapproachable on the subject of money" (B3). These remarks argue at least a healthy respect for Nathan's temper in his grown-up son, although, since it was written at a time of financial crisis, the response James expected of his father may not have been typical. Nevertheless, Nathan, in the opinion of the Leinster Street Church members, was a good family man, for they continue their notice:

> He sought to bring up his household in the fear of God, and in obedience to the dictates of honor and morality. For thirty-seven years he maintained family worship both morning and evening, and to those who watched him most closely, and knew him best, he proved most plainly the profound sincerity of his christian [sic] profession. (Obituary; G)

Nathan's severity, which could not have escaped the notice of the community of which he was a well-known and important member, was therefore clearly acceptable and, indeed, no more than his duty by their standards.

During James's early years, the family was living, as I have already mentioned, on Charlotte Street, in what Burpee describes as "the old house in the city, a roomy place with a huge attic" (Lecture 5; H). At some point after marrying, however, Nathan had also begun purchasing land outside the city, although the date of the initial purchase is not known, and he built a summer home

> on the Bay Shore in Carleton, on the other side of the harbour. The family spent their winters in the city and their summers on the Bay Shore. It was a lovely spot. . . . The house had some fine timber behind it, through which an avenue ran to the main road. In front, the ground sloped down, in a series of green meadows, to a beach of sparkling pebbles. (Biographical 2a–3; H)

James's childhood, both in the city house and at the summer home — assuming the purchase and construction of the Bay Shore House to have been made as early as Raymond suggests — is clearly comfortably middle-class.[3]

His early schooling was probably at the old Saint John Grammar School, but although MacMechan and Burpee agree on this, it is not absolutely certain. Frederick De Mill seems to have given J. S. Knowles differing information. In correspondence with Frederick about James in preparation for an essay he was writing, Knowles asks "What school did he attend here? Mills or Duval?" (Knowles, Letter; H). The relevant paragraph in the finished essay, however, mentions two completely different names:

> The first school James attended was kept by a man named Fitzgerald, who like other old-time pedagogues, did not hesitate to apply the "birch" liberally, according to Solomon's rule. "Fits" as the boys called him while severe was a clever teacher. He afterwards, went to Mr. Hartt, father of the late Charles Hartt, the celebrated naturalist and geologist . . . ". (Knowles, "Professor" 1; H)

The information in this essay, in fact, has to be regarded very sceptically. Even granting the accuracy of Frederick's understanding of what he was told about events that happened before his own birth (when he was born in 1845, James was already 12), Knowles himself, where he can be checked against other sources, is hopelessly muddled. All four names mentioned (Mills, Duval, Fitzgerald, and Hartt) were presumably those of the owners and instructors of schools in Saint John in the early nineteenth century, although they have not been identified as such. If James did attend any of these four schools, it would not rule out attendance at the Saint John Grammar School altogether, for he could have attended any of them before going there, particularly if they were like the English dame schools, which took very young children and taught only reading, writing, and arithmetic. Or he could have started there and been removed to one of these others in 1842, when he was nine years old (which was when Nathan moved from the Anglican church to the Baptist church), since it seems unlikely, although not impossible, that James would continue to go to a Church of England school after his father's change of religious affiliation. But if he left the Saint John Grammar School in 1842, he could not have gone immediately to the Baptist Horton Collegiate Academy, because Horton records show that he did not arrive there until 1847.

If James did go to the Saint John Grammar School, there is, as a result of the Saint John fire that also destroyed his baptismal record, no record of his attendance there. In his history of the Saint John Grammar School, John Bowes describes "the queer old building which for seventy years stood on the corner of Germain and Horsfield streets" (2; G). The school had been established by "an act of Assembly passed March 5, 1807" as an Anglican foundation of which the rector of Trinity Church was always to be, *ex officio*, the president of the board of directors (Bowes 2; G). If James attended the school, he probably did so from 1840 when he would have been seven years old, although Bowes does not indicate at what age boys could begin their education at the school, so that he might well have been younger.[4] At this time, the preceptor, or principal, would have been James Patterson (later Dr. Patterson), "a gentleman of the University of Glasgow" who had been engaged as preceptor to start on 1 December 1818, and who remained as principal until 1857 (Bowes 7, 18; G). During this period, the school offered the standard curriculum of classics, mathematics, and English, for an annual fee (as of 1838) of six pounds, in sessions of "six and a half hours daily attendance . . . during the summer and six hours daily during winter" (Bowes 9; G). Until 1847, the school had no library (Bowes 10; G), so that James would have been dependent on home sources for his earliest reading, if, after six or six and a half hours school of classes and some additional preparation time, he had time left to do anything except the required reading. But he would have been well enough prepared by his classwork for more advanced study in due course.

James, following his older brothers, Elisha and William, began attending Horton Collegiate Academy at the beginning of the fall term in August 1847.[5] This date has again been disputed, notably by Burpee (Notes; H), but James cannot, in fact, have started at Horton earlier than this, for in the "Report of the Institutions of the Nova Scotia Baptist Education Society at Horton" for 15 February 1847, the schedule of students in Horton Academy in the past year does not include his name (Crawley, *Memorials* 238–40; G).[6] Moreover, he cannot have started later than that if he matriculated from Acadia in 1849.[7] Douglas McLeod's assertion, that James entered Horton in 1847, aged 14 going on 15, is therefore correct (McLeod 7; F).

Horton Academy was, at this time, already a flourishing institution. In his history of Acadia University, Ronald Longley describes how the establishment of a "suitable Seminary of learning" was approved by the Baptist Association of Nova Scotia in 1828 (21; G). According to the prospectus issued by the association, "a principal object to be observed" was "to place the means of instruction as much as possible within the reach of all persons," and "to attend to those branches of Education which are

Horton Collegiate Academy Residence

of more general use. . . . the usual branches of English Literature, and of scientific, classical, and other studies, which usually comprise the course of education at an Academy and College" (Longley 145-46; G). The prospectus provided for religious instruction so that the students could be "led to a knowledge of the true relation of man to his Creator," but it was to be nonsectarian, and the seminary was to be "open to children and persons of any religious denomination," although it was directed, "That of the Committee and Board of Directors, that part who shall be members of Baptist Churches, in connection with the Nova Scotia Baptist Association, shall have the sole regulation of the Theological Department in the Seminary" (Longley 146; G). It was also to "be conducted upon a principle of the most strict and simple Economy," and the fees for tuition and board were to be set "at as low a rate as possible."

The committee of management struck by the association set to work, and as described in the various accounts of the beginnings of the academy, they did so with the utmost economy. According to D. G. Whidden, "In February 1829 they purchased a farm consisting of 50 acres of upland and 13 1/2 acres of dyke from James Graham for £550" (G). Cramped and plainly furnished, according to E. A. Crawley's account, the old farmhouse soon needed to be expanded, and in 1831,

> A more commodious building than the old farmhouse was soon erected, containing a residence for the principal, and needful rooms for a pretty large boarding school, to which two large additions were subsequently made. A year or two after the erection of the first building an edifice of the form of a graceful Greek temple of the Ionic order was constructed from a plan furnished by a Boston architect. This building provided ample space for a large academy hall and several small rooms for recitation. ("The Rise" 31; G)

The "boarding school" with its additions was still in use in James's year at the academy, but the "graceful Greek temple" of the academy hall had been incorporated only two years before his arrival into the first college hall.

Living conditions at Horton Academy were austere, but not unpleasantly so. The prospectus required the "diet and dress of the Scholars to be of the plainest kind," and the residence or "boarding house" for the students to be run economically (Longley 146; G). The boarding house was run by a steward (under the direction of the principal), and, if the list of the "Steward's Duties" drafted by the trustees is to be relied upon, the students were adequately, if plainly, fed on a diet that included whole milk, wheat bread, meat, fish, and large quantities of vegetables, in return for whatever they paid (Acadia, Horton Academy Documents; H). There is no record of how much was charged for meals in 1847, but initially, the Trustees had said that "Boarders at the Academy table shall pay at the rate of seven shillings and sixpence a week" (Acadia, Horton; H). The students' laundry and mending were also taken care of, for the trustees instructed that "the clothes[,] bedlinen, and towels of the Boarders must be washed thoroughly and carefully . . . The Steward will also do all minor repairs . . . such as mending socks[,] sewing on buttons, etc.," and "the bedlinen [shall be] changed every week" (Acadia, Horton; H). According to an advertisement for the academy, this service cost "8s.6d. per week," with the boarders being required to provide their own "beds, bedding, and towels" (Acadia, *Catalogue*, 1861–62 back cover; H). Students were also to be provided with "hot water every morning or evening in such quantities as may be requisite for cleanliness," and a good fire was to be "provided and maintained by the Steward" in the dining rooms of the boardinghouse, in the seminary itself, and in the study hall (Acadia, Horton; H); fuel for the small stoves heating the students' rooms was paid for by the students at the rate of "2s. 6d. per Term" (Acadia, *Catalogue*, 1861–62 back cover; H). The students and faculty worked and ate by candlelight when daylight was insufficient, with "good mould candles" provided by the steward for the academy study hall "at the rate of one candle to every four boarders," and for the boarding house itself (Acadia, Horton; H). Much of the students' comfort would, of course, depend on the goodwill and competence of the steward in carrying out the trustees' instruction that "the scholars shall be made as comfortable and cleanly as they could be in the best and most carefully regulated home" (Acadia, Horton; H). But judging from the warmly drawn pictures of Horton Academy provided by James in later years in both fiction (as Grand Pré School, in his series of books for boys beginning with *The "B.O.W.C."* [A1]) and reminiscences (such as "Horton Sketches" [A4]), we may conclude that conditions (at least during his attendance there) were not unbearably spartan.

Discipline, too, was probably not unbearably strict. It was governed by considerations of what was proper behaviour: "every boarder shall behave in the same quiet and orderly manner that he would in a well conducted home" (Acadia, Horton; H). It stressed punctuality, tidiness, quiet and sedate behaviour, and obedience to the rules. This obedience, moreover, was to be a cooperative effort, and the trustees, through their regulations for the conduct of the boarders (which were to be read to the students at school assembly once a month), required that each student should "not only himself observe the above regulations . . . but he shall also endeavour to the utmost of his power to enforce their observance on others." Pupils were required to attend prayers daily, and on Sunday to attend a "place of worship" chosen by their parents or the principal, and to spend one hour of Sunday afternoon, "or as near that time as the length of the days will allow in reading the Bible" (Acadia, Horton; H).

The curriculum was in keeping with the aims set out in the prospectus, and provided the standard fare for the period. The work in classical studies in 1846-47, for example, was described by the acting principal, E.A. Crawley, as having included Homer, Xenophon, Greek Testament, Valpy's *Delectus*, Fisk's *Greek Exercises*, *Greek Trees and Grammar*, Horace, Virgil, Caesar, and Ellis's *Latin Exercises and Grammar*. In mathematics, it included algebra, Legendre's *Geometry*, Euclid's *Elements*, navigation, surveying, practical geometry, mensuration, and arithmetic. In the "English Branches," which seem to have covered a great deal of territory, were included the history of England, the history of Rome, the history of Nova Scotia, declamation, English composition, English grammar, natural philosophy, geography, bookkeeping, reading, spelling, and writing (Crawley, *Memorials* 242; G). Class hours were supplemented by "hours for study in preparation for school" (Acadia, Horton; H). The classes themselves, much of which would be in the form of recitations of previously learned material, started at nine in the morning and ran through until late afternoon, with a break at midday.

Religious matters played a more important role in the life of the academy than the curriculum itself admits. In the winter of James's year there, a movement of religious revival was current in Nova Scotia and in the early months of 1848, it reached Wolfville and Horton Academy. James subsequently wrote an account of the effect of this revival among the students in three of his "Horton Sketches" published in the *Christian Watchman* in February and March of 1861, under the pen name "Gamma." Although he neither gives names nor speaks directly in the first person, it can be inferred from the account that James himself was one of the students who was converted (that is, who made a public profession of personal faith in

Christ) during the days when the revival was at its height in the academy, and that he was subsequently baptized. The memorial notice for Nathan Smith De Mill in the *Christian Visitor* seems to support such an inference (Obituary; G).

At the end of one year at Horton, James entered Acadia College in the fall of 1848. The transition would not have been difficult for him, for the academy and the college were closely interlocked. When the act to set up Acadia College as a degree-granting institution was passed in 1841, in fact, academy and college were sharing the same building, but increasing enrollment soon required larger and distinct accommodation for the college students. A new college hall was therefore constructed, incorporating the old academy building, and brought into use in 1845:

> The whole edifice thus completed comprised . . . a president's residence, a museum of considerable size, containing also the philosophical apparatus, a library of good dimensions, three recitation rooms, twenty-six or twenty-eight studies and dormitories, and a large bell tower of fair appearance and good height. (Crawley, "The Rise" 39; G)

James's life as a college student, therefore, would have differed very little from his life as an academy student. The routine was firm but not severe:

> [Students] arose at six o'clock each morning and a short time later presented themselves to a monitor in one of the class rooms to attend prayers. After breakfast classes began and continued, with an interval of an hour at noon, until four o'clock when they met again for prayers. The evenings were generally devoted to study by light of a candle or lamp. In winter the rooms were heated by the use of small stoves. (Longley 74; G)

This description is actually of the college in the years immediately after 1855, but it is highly probable that the routine was similar in the earlier period when James was there. The curriculum for the academic work of the students would also have changed very little between the academy and the college. Students entering their first year at Acadia were on probation as candidates for matriculation, and on completion of that first year, were required to take the matriculation examination. They were examined right across the curriculum in English grammar, mathematics, history, geography, and Latin and Greek literature, and on passing they signed the matriculation book and were admitted as matriculated students to the upper-year classes of the college. James successfully passed his exams and matriculated in 1849 (Acadia, *Catalogue,* 1861–62 20; G).

Having completed his first year at Acadia successfully, James is generally assumed to have done a second year there, starting at the beginning of September 1849 and ending just before he and Elisha left for Europe. There is, however, reason to doubt this, since his name does not appear again in the records. He may have been at home that year as a result of illness. It is known that there was illness in the family in August and September of 1849, for on 25 September of that year Nathan writes to Cannon Miller that Will has just died: "I have just met with a very severe visitation in the sudden death of my son in the 19th year of his age which took place yesterday morning after a month['s] illness" (H). Eleven months later, on 20 August 1850, Nathan writes again to Cannon Miller announcing that Elisha and James are sailing to England on the *Elizabeth Bentley,* and he gives as one of the reasons for the trip that "My son James has had very weak eyes for a year and has been advised to take a sea voyage" (H). The weak eyes would in themselves be sufficient for someone to avoid concentrated study for a year, regardless of what caused them, but the implied sudden onset a year previously, or just about the time Will died, suggests that they were caused by illness — perhaps the same illness that caused Will's unexpected death. There is no mention anywhere of what the illness was. Measles (*rubeola*) seems a likely candidate since it fulfils the criteria of being a potential killer (encephalitis and meningitis are among the complications) and it can, although it does not commonly do so, have "eye complications" (Thomas 864; G). In any sort of convalescence, however, a period of rest away from study would doubtless be necessary, and a sea voyage an obviously desirable way of achieving it.

Although the *Elizabeth Bentley* did not leave from Quebec City until the middle of August, Elisha and James must have left Saint John in early July in order to get to Quebec City in time via the route described by Burpee. Because there was no direct rail route through New Brunswick, they

> had to take a very roundabout route, by steamer to Portland, by rail to Boston and thence to Burlington, thence by steamer down Lake Champlain to St Johns [St.-Jean, Quebec], where they again found themselves on British territory. From St Johns to La Prairie, opposite

The Elizabeth Bentley

Montreal, they travelled on the first railway constructed in Canada, the Champlain and St Lawrence Railroad, built in 1835. . . . After a short stay in Montreal . . . they spent three weeks in and about the ancient capital. ("Biographical" 6–7; H)

Burpee does not explain why they did not travel by ship from Saint John to Quebec, which might have been more straightforward since Nathan himself had ships sailing between Saint John and Quebec City and Montreal. The *Elizabeth Bentley*, with Elisha and James on board, finally cleared Quebec on 17 August 1850.

The trip was an important event for both young men, and both of them kept journals describing it. Unfortunately, James's journal, described by Archibald MacMechan as consisting of "nine chapters altogether; four . . . devoted to England, Scotland, Wales, and France, and five to Italy," has not survived, except for some brief excerpts cited by MacMechan himself in his article "James De Mille, the Man and the Writer" in *Canadian Magazine*. MacMechan, who saw the journal when he first contemplated writing a full-length biography of De Mille soon after arriving in Halifax, also comments that the journal was "a very interesting MS account of his travels which throws much light on this period and on his own character. Unfortunately it was written some time after his return, and has not the freshness of first impressions jotted down as they are made" ("James De Mille" 406; F). Elisha's journal has survived, but Elisha, it must be admitted, is a dutiful rather than an inspired diarist: he records patiently but rarely brings a scene vividly to life, and even more rarely does he introduce his brother directly as a participant in their activities. Nevertheless, he manages to provide a fairly good picture of their travels.

The ship arrived in Liverpool, according to Elisha's opening paragraph, "on Sunday morning the [15] September after an exceedingly pleasant passage of 29 days from Quebec" (Elisha De Mill; H).[8] MacMechan quotes James as saying that the voyage was one of "uncommon enjoyment" because they were "well supplied with books both for reading and studying" ("James De Mille" 409; F). He suggests that much of the studying was of French and Italian, by means of which James and Elisha "managed to pick up enough French and Italian on the voyage to serve all traveller's purposes while on the continent" ("James De Mille" 409; F). Once they had disembarked at Liverpool, they went first to a hotel, and then in the afternoon to one of the local churches, where they wished to hear a Dr.

45

Veil preach but were disappointed. When they got back to the hotel, the son of Mr. Miller of Cannon Miller was waiting for them, and took them home with him. Nathan De Mill had made arrangements with Mr. Miller in his letter of 20 August: "You will be so kind as to advance them some money as travelling expenses and also procure them some letters [of introduction] to places they may visit as they may never have another opportunity to see the Old Country" (H). In addition to complying with this request, Mr. Miller invited them to stay with him as long as they were in Liverpool. After several days in Liverpool, where Elisha "was particularly struck with the Nelson monument" in front of the Exchange (Elisha De Mill; H), they took a steamer round the coast to Caernarvon and made a short walking tour of the area, taking in Snowdon, the Pass of Llanberis, and Beddgelert, and getting soaking wet more than once.

On returning to Liverpool, they decided to go next to Scotland, and took a steamer up the coast to Glasgow. For Elisha the trip was not particularly pleasant:

> When we left for Greenock there was every prospect of a storm. The wind blew very strongly. The vessel pitched about so that many of the passengers were quite sea sick — Although not subject to sea sickness the motion of the steamer made me feel quite uncomfortable so that I retired to my berth at an early hour and was soon asleep.

But he was clearly not so uncomfortable that he lost interest in his surroundings, for he continues: "I was awakened in the morning by my brother who called me up to see Ailsa Cra[i]g. I was on deck just in time to get a pretty good view of it." They spent the rest of September and most of October in Scotland. From Glasgow they went through parts of the Highlands to Edinburgh, where Elisha found "the palace of Holyrood . . . venerable rather than magnificent," and then turned south again, coming through Dalkeith, Galashiels, and Abbotsford, to Carlisle, where they "visited objects of interest" and "walked out to the curiosities and antiquities in the vicinity of Penrith," and then made their way back to Liverpool (Elisha De Mill; H).

From Liverpool they turned their attention to the rest of England. They spent a few days travelling from Liverpool to Bristol, where they arrived at the beginning of November, and then went on to Bath (where they stayed less than a day), and finally to Oxford, where they arrived late on a Saturday evening, having been "delayed two hours on the road" (although Elisha does not explain the cause of the delay). The next day being a Sunday, he says, "we took a short walk about the town and not knowing exactly where to go concluded to attend the University Church." The next morning they spent "looking at the Colleges," although, he adds perhaps regretfully, "we could not see the whole of the Bodleian Library" (Elisha De Mill; H). In the afternoon they left for London.

Elisha's description of their visit to London is a synopsis, not a sequence of dated entries. Writing at the end of their stay there, he says, "As I have neglected writing a regular journal of London I must trust a great deal to memory. I find it difficult to keep a journal of the day's proceedings in such a large city" (Elisha De Mill; H).[9] The account is not particularly vivid, or even very clear, but they saw all the sights that they wanted to see and seem to have enjoyed their visit.

They left London after only two weeks, on 18 November, and travelled to Dunkirk "by a screw-steamer." In Dunkirk, they received their first taste of a truly different culture in one of the sidewalk cafes:

> We called for cafe [and] the waiter brought us a little cup of coffee without milk and a petit verre of Cognac. As we did not desire brandy we drank rather slowly our little cup of coffee. While we were drinking an Englishman came and after talking about a variety of things he told us that when we wanted coffee with milk we must call for cafe au lait. For our little taste of coffee without milk we paid a franc. (Elisha De Mill; H)

From Dunkirk, where "there is little . . . to detain the passing stranger," they went through Lille and Amiens to Paris, arriving almost a week later. They stayed in Paris for two weeks, where Elisha was able to keep a more regular journal than in London. Their initiation into Continental culture continued:

> We now began to think of looking out for another place of residence[;] we soon found one that suited us and returned to our hotel for the things which we had left there. We were now initiated into a few of the customs of Paris. As we had not told of our intended departure we were charged for the two nights. And in adition [sic] to the charge made in England for boots, waiter and chambermaid we found

another interesting item viz bougie 1 franc apiece. It seems to me that at a hotel we pay to be furnished with lights to go to bed by. And it is rather an imposition to charge a franc for half an inch of candle. Determining not to be bougied again I left for my new abode — Our room was rather small but much more convenient than the other. (Elisha De Mill; H)

On the first Sunday morning of their stay, they "went to the Cathedral of Notre Dame," and in the following days they visited the Louvre, the "Hotel des Monaies," the Observatory, the Luxembourg Palace Gardens, and the Church of St. Eustache, and made an excursion to Versailles. Before they left Paris they needed to obtain their visas for Italy, and Elisha is uncharacteristically irritated by having to waste not one but two days trying to get this done: "Another day was to be spoiled with these abominable passports," he writes tersely (Elisha De Mill; H).

When they had their visas, they went south from Paris, travelling by *diligence* (stagecoach). They briefly visited Orléans, where Elisha "was much disappointed" because he "expected to find more antiquities," and thought the streets "dirty, narrow and crooked." They then continued through Nevers, Mâcon, and Cleremont (he seems to mean Clermont-Ferrand), where "we had not time to look around us," to Lyons. After two days in Lyons, they continued on to Avignon, where they met with a more specific disappointment "in not being able to see the old palace of the popes. We wished very much to see the inquisition and its relics, but the guard would not admit us without a permit" (Elisha De Mill; H). As in many places, however, it is impossible here to tell from Elisha's account how strongly either he or James felt about the disappointment. From Avignon they went to Arles, where they spent only half a day, and continued on to Marseilles.

From Marseilles they sailed for Italy, no doubt extremely excited about their visit, for they were arriving during one of the most stirring periods of Italian history. The protracted struggle of Italian patriots against the domination of Austria and towards national unification, the Risorgimento, had kept Italy in a political, social, and cultural ferment since 1816, and it was by no means over. Of particular interest to James would be the effect of the still rising tide of the romantic movement — the legacy of the English visitors Byron and Shelley, in particular — and of the cultural nationalism of such leading poets as Foscolo, Manzoni, and Leopardi, in literature, and of such composers as Rossini, Donizetti, and Verdi, in music.

Their voyage from Marseilles took them to Leghorn, via Genoa. Elisha's sense of humour shows briefly again in his description of their vessel as "the oldest and the slowest of all the steamers that ply in the Mediterranean." Since it took them the best part of two days to reach Genoa, he was probably correct. His exasperation must have been considerably aggravated when, after all his trouble about passports, on arriving in Genoa, he found that something was wrong: "Owing to some question about my passport, I was not permitted to land and all day had the satisfaction of looking at Genoa without being able to go on shore. It was too bad. "They arrived in Leghorn on the following morning and left immediately for a two-day stay in Pisa, where they "went to see the wonders . . . the leaning tower, the Sacred Baptistry and Campo Santo" and were "very comfortably housed . . . I like one thing in the Italian hotels — there is plenty of water" (Elisha De Mill; H). From Pisa they went to Florence.

They arrived in Florence at about six on a Saturday evening. Either for lack of opportunity or from a lingering sense of tourism being inappropriate on the Sunday, Elisha records that "the next day being Sunday we spent the greater part of it in our rooms." After visiting the "royal gallery" on Monday, they spent two more days in Florence and visited "a splendid monument . . . erected in memory of Dante, although his bones are in Ravenna," before returning through Arezzo to Leghorn, where "we found a steamer going to Civita Vecchia the same afternoon and by five o'clock we were on our way to the *Eternal* City." The emphasis on "Eternal" is Elisha's own, and is the only clue to what must have been a very considerable excitement on his part.

At seven o'clock on 29 December 1850 (one of Elisha's few precise dates), the two young men entered Rome. Having found somewhere to live, they went out next day for their first sightseeing walk, which they enjoyed immensely. "In the evening," Elisha writes, "we went home to our cheerless little room and began in earnest the study of Italian. This with our journal of the day occupied the time until quite late" (Elisha De Mill; H). Language study apparently occupied most of their evenings during the weeks of their stay in Rome, and Elisha reports on their progress three times. On New Year's Day, 1851, he writes:

> In the evening we spent our time at home studying Italian. We have begun to make ourselves understood by signs and a dialect composed

of French and Italian. A great number of the people understand French. Almost everyone knows a little of that language, so that I find no difficulty in making known my wants." (Elisha De Mill; H)

Within a week, however, he was able to record an improvement: "We make some progress in Italian [and] can form a pretty good idea of what is said to us and can manage to ask any ordinary questions. I like Italian much better than French. It is more regular, more sonorous and much . . . easier of acquisition." Two weeks later, he reports a considerable increase in their ability to communicate: "We are getting along pretty well . . . and have little difficulty in making ourselves understood" (Elisha De Mill; H). It is possible that their liking for the language helped them to acquire it more easily than French.

James and Elisha stayed in Rome for four weeks, and even Elisha's sedate prose style manages to capture their enjoyment as they began their round of sightseeing with visits to monuments, art galleries, libraries, museums, and what Elisha describes simply as "antiquities." They visited, among other things, the Capitol, the Colosseum, the Trevi Fountain, the galleries of the Vatican, "the manufactory of mosaics in the Vatican" (which Elisha describes as "exceedingly interesting"), the Etruscan museum, the Villa Borghese, and the gardens of the Quirinal. He records briefly a visit to "the Basilica of San Sebastian with the catacombs beneath" (which James was later to draw on for the setting of *The Martyr of the Catacombs*):

> One of the monks went with us as a guide. It is a dark rough gloomy place, a perfect labyrinth. One cannot enter these catacombs without a feeling of solemnity. Here are the ashes of the early Christians. The tombs of many a martyr — In such a place as this the early professors of the faith sought refuge from the violence and cruelty of their persecutors. (Elisha De Mill; H)

They also visited a number of churches, including the Church of Santa Maria Degli Angeli. The pace of their visit was obviously quite hectic, but they do not seem to have become jaded.

One enthusiasm in particular shines through. In Rome they did not feel it necessary to stay in their hotel rooms on Sunday, for on the first Sunday of their stay "in the afternoon we went to see St Peters." It is clear that St. Peter's was the building they liked above all in Rome, for not only did they both go back again the following day, but on the day after that, Elisha records: "we did not visit many places today, it being Epiphany . . . in the afternoon James left me to take another look at St Peters." The following Sunday morning, too, they heard "some delightful music in St Peters," and two weeks later, just before leaving for Naples, they paid "a farewell visit to St Peters."

Leaving Rome on 27 January 1851, having joined up with a group of four other travellers, they started for Naples. The party travelled by what Elisha refers to as the *vetturina* (stagecoach), and Elisha apparently liked it very much: "This mode of conveyance is very slow but we have the . . . time to spend upon the coach and another thing, the vetturina furnishes the dinner and bed. In Italy I would rather travel by vetturina than by any other mode" (Elisha De Mill; H). On the second day, their journey took them through the Pontine marshes where, Elisha notes, "the road is excellent." When they arrived in Naples, three days later, the first thing Elisha did was attend to their travel documents: "Today has been spent in walking about the city getting our passports signed etc." Once this chore was done, however, they were free to enjoy themselves. They began with a slight setback: "This morning we intended to go to Pompeii but missed the trains and then concluded to go to the Museum." The following week they did go to Pompeii, about which Elisha was extremely enthusiastic: "Today we visited Pompeii. It has been one of the most pleasant and interesting days of my life." He found it too confusing to remember the names of all that they saw there, but he took time to record one famous landmark: "Near the city gate is a stone sentry box in which was found the skeleton of the sentinel." After the visit to Pompeii, they made excursions to Baia and to Sorrento, where they visited "the house in which Tasso was born . . . [and] the church of San Martino." They also made a special excursion to Vesuvius, hiring a guide and ponies, scrambling up to the rim of the crater over the lava, and even rather recklessly going down into the crater itself to look into "the horrid gulph. This is almost circular and the sides are quite precipitous all around preventing any further descent even if the flames of sulphur constantly ascending [abated]."

After this excursion, the whole party returned from Naples to Rome. During their stay in Naples, Elisha received a letter from home, and his record of it is one of the few really personal glimpses we obtain of him:

This morning I received a letter from home. I had since I left home a strong desire to visit the Holy Land, and for some time after the reception of my letter . . . was in a state of great confusion. At last taking into consideration the lateness of the season, the places still to be seen in Europe and finally the state of our funds I concluded to let Palestine remain unseen and to return to Rome for the carnival and . . . not to look upon those scenes hallowed by associations of such intense interest.

Perhaps his disappointment was stronger than he permits himself to express in the journal. Certainly, from this point on he writes with less enthusiasm, and he begins to find his companions difficult to get along with. He records an argument about the way they should travel, in which, he mentions in passing, "James and Dr G. were neutral"; and later, in describing another visit with the party to the catacombs, he says flatly, "I began to get tired of some of our company." The offender was an American, whose fictional portrait, doing exactly what Elisha complains about in his journal (comparing St. Peter's Basilica unfavourably with churches in America), is one of James's best comic portraits in *The Dodge Club*.

At the beginning of March, the party left Rome for Perugia, stopping for the night at Civita Castellana, and then going on to Spoleto and Foligno before reaching Perugia itself. They remained there only a short time before leaving for Florence, where they spent six days. Elisha does not record anything about these six days, possibly because he and James had already visited Florence before going to Rome. From Florence they travelled rapidly through Bologna, Ferrara, Padua (where they "proceeded at once to visit the objects . . . most worthy of attention"), and Venice, where they "first went to get our passports visa'd" for Milan. From Venice, they went first to Verona and then on to Milan.

From Milan they were to go to Geneva, but when they got as far as Domodossola they were unable to proceed immediately through the pass because it was blocked by snow. The difficulty caused Elisha some concern because he was receiving conflicting advice about the relative accessibility of the Simplon and the St. Gotthard passes, but after a day in Domodossola, they were able to proceed as far as Iselle, where they arrived at "six o'clock [in the evening]" and heard that "the road was not yet passable." Next morning, Elisha continues, "we were awakened at an early hour and after a light colation [sic] prepared for our passage across the Simplon with the prospect of being obliged to spend the night on the summit of the pass." This gloomy expectation was not, however, fulfilled, and they were able to get through the pass to Brig, in Switzerland, where (so Elisha records with a faint note of impatience) they spent the morning "waiting for the diligence which was delayed . . . cause unknown." On the way to Geneva, they made a stopover that James and Elisha made the most of by walking out to visit the Castle of Chillon.

The following day, the whole party left by steamer for Geneva, where they arrived on 31 March. From Geneva they went through Lausanne, Berne, and Basle without spending very much time in any of them, and crossed into Germany. They travelled just as quickly through Germany into Belgium, and by the end of the week they had reached Brussels. Here they stayed long enough to make a day's excursion to Waterloo: "The next morning at 7 o'clock the carriage was before the door and in a few minutes we were on our way to the blood stained field." From Brussels they went to Antwerp, and from Antwerp, after an overnight stay, they returned to Paris, where they remained for another month, sightseeing and studying. Elisha records that he was "reading and writing but making very little progress in la Langue Francaise," and he adds, "I can read French pretty well but cannot speak it as readily as Italian" (Elisha De Mill; H).

Finally, however, they started their journey back to England. They landed in Southampton on 9 May 1851, and promptly started for London, where they arrived "by three o'clock" and "immediately engaged lodgings for a week in the Strand." The following morning, a Sunday, Elisha records, with something of the air of one returning to civilization after time in the wilderness, that "This morning we went to Exeter Hall and heard a very good sermon" (Elisha De Mill; H).

It is not quite clear how long they remained in London, for this is where Elisha's journal ends. They might have sailed directly from London, whether on one of their father's ships (for Nathan's own vessels did call at London, although rarely) or on one of some other Saint John merchant's vessels, or they might have gone back to Liverpool and sailed from there. The whereabouts of the *Elizabeth Bentley*, on which they had travelled on their outward voyage, are not mentioned in Nathan's correspondence until a letter of 16 September 1851, to Cannon Miller, in which he writes: "The *Elizabeth Bentley* arrived at Shippigan on the 1st [September] — all well" (H). If the "all" of "all well" refers to Elisha and James as passengers, then they were clearly in England, if not London, until at least the beginning of August (assuming the return trip from Liverpool to Shippigan took the same amount of time as the outward voyage of 29 days). If James and Elisha were in England until August, it is curious that Elisha records nothing in his journal for that period, but it is simply not possible to reach a definite conclusion about their departure date.

Once they were safely home, however, it was time for each of them to move on to the next stage of his career. For Elisha, this was perfectly straightforward: having completed his B.A. at Acadia, and his graduate work at Brown, he was ready to proceed with his vocation as a minister. At the beginning of October 1851, he went to the Newton Theological Institution in Massachusetts, where on 6 October he was "examined for admission to the Inst[itute] Junior Class," and admitted (Andover; H).[10]

For James, things must have seemed equally straightforward: he would return to Acadia and resume his interrupted programme of studies for his B.A. But his student days at Acadia were over. MacLeod suggests that James was not sent back to Acadia because of its financial situation (MacLeod 20; F). Certainly there were serious problems at Acadia in 1850 and the early part of 1851 as a result of the resolution passed at the Maritime Baptists Convention in June 1850 "that the Convention must accept state aid for the Academy only, not the College," and the effect of this decision, combined with "the sudden termination of the English campaign," had brought about "a financial crisis" (Longley 64; G). But enough money had been scraped together to survive the immediate crisis, and the new president, Dr. J.M. Cramp, had been installed before the convocation of 1851 (Longley 66–67; G). The situation was already improving, therefore, by the time James was ready to resume attendance at the beginning of the fall term, although it may still have been somewhat uncertain. But whether or not the situation was improving, it is unclear why a decision was not made immediately, to avoid the loss of a term's work. When James did resume his studies, he resumed them at Brown, and when he did return to Acadia, after an interval of 10 years, he did so not as a student, but as the newly appointed professor of classics.

NOTES

1 Frederick Edward De Mill was born in Saint John on 24 June 1845 (Raymond 59; H); he died on 24 October 1923 also in Saint John, where he is buried in the family plot in Fernhill Cemetery (Fernhill; H). The note is contained in a small notebook now in the possession of A.H.D. Burpee, of East LaHave, Nova Scotia.

2 All James's surviving letters to Alfred are among James's papers, and unlike his business correspondence, at least one of them is humorously illustrated with a portrait of the recipient (12 Oct. 1857; B3).

3 Raymond suggests that this initial purchase was as early as 1830, for between her statement of the date of Elisha's birth in 1829 and William's in 1831, she inserts the note that "At some time Nathan S. DeMill bought from Michael McCarthy a lot on Bay Shore, and built there a home in which the family lived," but the only transactions I can find between Nathan De Mill and a Michael McCarthy in the Saint John County records are dated after 1854 and do not appear to refer to the purchase of this land. The two other purchases Raymond mentions are "1850, June 27 . . . Nathan S. DeMill bought from Samuel Robins 24 acres at Bay Shore" and "1853, June 14 . . . Nathan S. DeMill bought from Henry Nice 35 acres at Bay Shore, adjoining the 24 acres mentioned above" (Raymond 59; H). By the time of Nathan's death in 1864, the family's home in the city was on Coburg Street (*Morning News* 28 Dec. 1864: 3).

4 The notice advertising a similar primary school, the Baptist Seminary at Fredericton, which appears on the back cover of the Acadia Catalogue for 1863–64 (H), sets out tuition fees for children "under 10 years of age," but again no minimum age is given.

5 According to the Acadia catalogue for 1861–62, the Horton Academy's fall term ran from the beginning of August to mid-December, and the winter term from the beginning of January to mid-June (H).

6 The names Budd DeMill and Will. DeMill appear in this schedule and in the accompanying schedule of students in Acadia College there is an entry for "W. DeMill*." The asterisk, according to a note, indicates "a pupil who subsequently entered college," and it appears against other names. Clearly it is William John De Mill, James's older brother, who is meant, and not James himself (Crawley, *Memorials* 239; G).

7 In the absence of any evidence to the contrary, I take the matriculation date of that period to refer to the date the student *has* matriculated, or finished his first year of college work successfully, not as the date he *is* matriculating, or starting his matriculation year. If, therefore, James matriculated from Acadia (that is, if he completed his first year there successfully) in 1849, as indicated in the "List of Matriculated Students" (Acadia, *Catalogue* [1861–62]: 20; H), he must have started his work at Acadia at the beginning of the previous fall term (in September of 1848), having left Horton Academy in mid-June of 1848.

8 Elisha De Mill's journal consists of three unpaginated manuscript volumes. Citation by page number for any particular quotation is therefore impossible, and citation by date often so, since the entries are not systematically dated. I have given dates for dated entries and for undated ones where I have been able to calculate them. I have also regularized place-name spellings, and inserted occasional punctuation.

9 The last date before the description of what they did and saw in London is

55

Tuesday, 5 November, the day they arrived there. The description takes up the remaining pages of this volume, and the next volume begins with an entry dated 18 December in Dunkirk, on the north coast of France.

10 Since Elisha's days there, the institution has undergone some changes, including a change of name. Documents concerning the earlier Newton Theological Institution, such as the faculty minutes for 1851–52, which record Elisha's attendance, are in the Franklin Trask Library at Andover Newton Theological School, as it is now called.

CHAPTER 3

At Brown University, 1852-54

James De Mille entered Brown University, in Providence, Rhode Island, at the beginning of the second term of the academic year 1852–53. He was entered in the register on 20 February, spelling his own name and his father's with the final "e," naming Nathan as his "parent or guardian," and giving (as already mentioned) his age as 18 (Brown, Register 54; H). He had been admitted to the second (sophomore) year of the four-year "A.M." (master of arts) degree programme. James was entering a very different kind of student environment from the one he had been accustomed to at Acadia.

Brown University, according to its historian, Walter C. Bronson, had been founded in 1764 by the Baptists of Rhode Island in order to provide a suitable institute for, in the words of Brown University's "Petitions for a Charter," "cultivating the Moralls and improving the Knowledge of the rising Generation upon which Foundation the Harmony good Order and Reputation of Society depend" (Bronson 493; G). Like Acadia College, however, Brown imposed no religious test upon entering students, although the "Directions for Students" published in the university catalogue for

1851–52 include the statement that "Candidates for admission are required to present to the President adequate certificates of unquestionable moral character" (Brown, *Catalogue, 1851–52* 48; H), and it accepted students from other Christian denominations. From small beginnings, the university had by 1852 grown to a respectable size, having a faculty of 14 (including the librarian and the registrar), and a student body of over 200. Its reputation had also increased from purely local to national: when De Mille arrived in 1852, for example, there were students from 17 states other than Rhode Island, as well as one from the Ionian Islands, and one from Burma (Brown, *Catalogue*, 1851–52 20; H). De Mille, a Canadian, is not included in the count because the catalogue came out at the beginning of the first term of the academic year, and he did not arrive until the second.

At the time James entered Brown, the academic programme had recently undergone considerable revision. Under the new system, as it was called, set out in the catalogue, the candidate for the master of arts had to have "obtained certificates of proficiency" in Latin and Greek (two years work in each), one modern language (one year), mathematics (two years), natural philosophy, English language and rhetoric, chemistry and physiology, history and political economy, and intellectual and moral philosophy (a single subject), and "the Evidences of Christianity." Some substitutions, such as "one Modern Language for a year in an Ancient Language, or for a year in Mathematics," were permitted. Before graduating, students were also required to pass final examinations in "the Ancient Languages, in Natural Philosophy, and in three other studies of the course to be selected by the Faculty" (Brown, *Catalogue*, 1851–52 26–27; H). James's programme was slightly unusual because he was given credit for work done at Acadia: he took half a year each of mathematics, Latin, and Greek, one year of rhetoric, one year of history, one year of chemistry and physiology, one year of intellectual and moral philosophy, one year of natural philosophy, one year of German, and half a year of French. If strict equivalence was enforced (although there is no evidence one way or the other on this point), he was given credit for a year and a half in one ancient language, a year in the other, a year in mathematics, and, under the rules for allowable substitutions set out in the catalogue, was permitted to take half a year of French as a substitute for the missing half year of one ancient language.

The new system was controversial from the beginning, and many people continued to think it unsatisfactory. Bronson argues that "There are two additional pieces of evidence that the New System had done little or nothing to raise the intellectual tone of the college," of which the first is the lack of candidates for the various prizes that had recently been introduced. "The other evidence," he continues,

> comes from a student's journal of the junior and senior years. The student was a bright young man, vivacious and witty, with intellectual interests in several fields; he was elected a member of Phi Beta Kappa in his junior year, and received the salutatory honor at graduation. Yet though he was above the average of his class in ability and scholarship, his journal shows a schoolboy worrying and shambling through his lessons, not a university man out on intellectual quests. To the last he is forever making hasty preparation for the next recitation, often in another class the hour before, writing the required essays in a rush, and doing almost no reading as a supplement to the textbooks. Both he and his classmates are constantly calculating their chances of being "called up" to recite, and are full of schoolboy hilarity when a class exercise is omitted. On December 31, 1854, he truly diagnoses his case as follows: "On the whole, I fear most of this year has been wasted. I have managed to work through my College duties; but have done nothing beyond the text-books & what I have done has been listlessly." (Bronson 292; G)

The system was still being tinkered with while De Mille was there, so that by the beginning of his final year some amendments had been made to the requirements that had been in force when he arrived. The requirement for Latin and Greek, for example, had been cut to a year and a half of each, that for mathematics to one year; the requirement for natural philosophy was stated specifically as one year, as were those for rhetoric, chemistry and physiology, history, and intellectual and moral philosophy. Additional courses (electives) were now required and had to be selected "from the courses in Political Economy, Geology, Didactics, a second Modern Language, or from advanced courses in any of the other departments" (Brown, *Catalogue, 1853–54* 25; H).

In his descriptive poem of student life at Brown, the "Class Poem–1854," De Mille describes the class he entered as "the fun-loving class Sophomore" (line 84; A3). Fun loving it may have been, but the material to be covered in his four courses (Latin, Greek, mathematics, and French) was substantial. This workload, together with his unfamiliarity with Brown, ensured that he had to be fairly hardworking simply to keep up.

In Latin language and literature, his professor was John L. Lincoln. Lincoln, who in Robert Brown's compilation of student memories is described by Samuel Thurber of the class of '58 as giving the impression of "perfect competency as a Latin scholar and as a disciplinarian" (Brown 123; G). In his Latin class, De Mille was expected to complete "sometimes six, and never less than five, exercises a week," and the set books (or required texts) were "The *Germania* and the *Agricola* of Tacitus, (Tyler's edition)" and Juvenal. Recommended as well as required texts were listed: "the Latin Grammar used is Andrews' and Stoddard's. Zumpt's is recommended as a work for reference. Other books recommended are Riddle and Arnold's *English-Latin Lexicon*, Smith's *Dictionary of Antiquities* (the 2d edition, English, is the best) and Becker's *Gallus*" (Brown, *Catalogue*, 1851–52 36; H). "Exercises" included both written and oral translation of portions of the text. For the latter, the students were called upon in turn to recite and perhaps to parse. The experience of one student, however, illustrates the embarrassing pitfalls of this method of instruction. Edward Hicks Magill (class of '52) recalls that in one of Professor Lincoln's classes

> a careless fellow whose lessons were rarely, if ever, well prepared, rose to recite the familiar ode of Horace in which he congratulates himself on finishing a book of his odes, with the well-known words, "Exegi monumentum aere perennius" ("I have raised a monument more lasting than brass"), and mistaking the *egi* of *exegi* for a part of the verb *edo*, "to eat," he began briskly, "I have eaten a monument harder than brass," whereupon the professor quickly but courteously remarked, "That will do. You may sit down and digest it." (Brown 101–02; G)

The written translations were corrected and handed back, with explanations, in the modern manner.

De Mille took Greek from James O. Murray, in the temporary absence of Professor James R. Boise. The set text for this term was either Homer's *Iliad* or a work by Aeschylus, not named in the catalogue, but probably *Prometheus Bound*. De Mille's own recollection of this class, which not only describes the method but also mentions *Prometheus Bound*, is part of his "Class Poem." What he says about *Prometheus*, in his usual punning style, supports the idea that this is the work he himself studied in the class:

AT BROWN UNIVERSITY, 1852-54

> When the lecture-bell summoned each student away
> To spend at reciting, the best of the day,
> When the hall for reciting with wide open door
> Stood dingily, drearily, coldly before,
> Where the ever remorseless professor began
> To call on each tremulous, cowering man
> To arise, and the difficult lesson recite
> Which he'd wholly forgotten, the previous night —
> "Oh!" we cried with fully many a shudder and frown —
> "That the classical tongues could do nought but perplex us —
> "That Demosthenes ne'er could get into the Crown —
> "That Prometheus was bound to eternally vex us!" (lines 143–54; A3)

"On the Crown," one of the orations of Demosthenes, the Athenian statesman and orator, was studied in the second-year Greek class in 1853–54, but, judging by the catalogue was not part of De Mille's course. In second-year classes not only were "essays . . . required on subjects connected with the authors read," but there were "generally five and sometimes six exercises [in translation] a week," and, as in his Latin class, in addition to the required texts, recommended texts were specified: "The Greek Grammar used is that of Kühner. The Lexicon that of Liddell and Scott. As works for reference: Smith's *Dictionary of Antiquities* and Becker's *Charicles* are recommended" (Brown, *Catalogue*, 1851–52 41–42; H).

It is not clear if the method was the same in his mathematics class, and the workload, too, is harder to assess. Much may have depended on how well the student was prepared by his school, for the mathematics course was the only one that laid out the precise preparation required for entering it:

> any person who intends entering upon the foregoing Mathematical course, should bring with him to the University a thorough knowledge of Arithmetic and the Elements of Algebra, including the first four chapters of Davies' Bourdon, or what is equivalent. (Brown, *Catalogue*, 1851–52 30; H)

The particular topic for the term in which De Mille was enrolled was "Analytical Geometry," with the textbooks being "Davies or Church" (Brown, *Catalogue*, *1851–52* 30; H). De Mille's professor in mathematics was Alexis Caswell, who had come to Brown in 1828 from Halifax where he had been the first pastor of the Granville Street Baptist Church, and one of the men instrumental in the foundation of Horton Academy (Longley 18–19; G). Samuel Thurber (class of '58) describes him as a man with "urbanity, patience, [and] geniality" in his dealings with students, among whom he was apparently very well liked (Brown 122; G).

De Mille's fourth class in his first term was French, which he took with an instructor in modern languages, a Mr. Verdi (Brown, Faculty 38; H). The set work for the second term in the class was either Bossuet's *Discours sur l'histoire universelle* or Michelet's *Précis de l'histoire de France*. The language work continued from the first term "with oral and written exercises" (Brown, *Catalogue*, 1851–52 38; H).

The daily pattern of student life during De Mille's years at Brown is nowhere set out in detail, although it can to some extent be reconstructed. It had certainly changed somewhat since the "pure and simple" academic life of the "early days," as recollected by Albert Harkness, who graduated in 1842:

> The students lived together in the college, dined together in the Commons Hall. The hours for devotion, for study and for recitation, the same for all, were regulated by the college bell with the precision of clock-work. The entire academic body, officers and students, was expected to attend chapel service at six o'clock in the morning and again at five in the evening . . . Every student was required to meet his teacher in the class-room directly after prayers in the morning, at eleven a.m., and at four p.m. From seven to nine in the evening it was his bounden duty to be at his books in his own private study. (Brown 68; G)

But it had not changed completely. From the timetable set out in the faculty records for De Mille's first term, it can be seen that students still had a fairly long day. In this particular term the brave souls who were taking Advanced Physiology were up earlier than everybody else, for it was offered at 6 a.m. (fortunately only twice a week). Usually, however, the first classes of the day began at 8:30 a.m., by which time the students would already have attended chapel and eaten breakfast, and the last classes of the day sometimes finished as late as 5:50 p.m., just in time for normally scheduled evening meals. De Mille himself would have been in his Greek class for an hour and twenty minutes, starting at 8:30 a.m. (six days a week, Monday through Saturday), followed immediately by another hour and twenty minutes in his Latin class, starting at 10 a.m. (five days a week, Monday through Friday). In the afternoon his French class met from 2:30 to 3:30 p.m., five days a week, and his mathematics class (analytical geometry) met at 3:30 p.m., five times a week, for an hour and twenty minutes (Brown, Faculty 38; H). The evening study hours were strictly enforced, and students' rooms were checked by professors (a system that caused much resentment among the students).

At this period, classes might be held in any of three of the four college buildings of the time (the fourth, Manning Hall, contained the library and the chapel). The largest of them, University Hall, was the original university building, and was almost certainly beginning to show its age and the effects of having been used as an army barracks in 1770 during the War of Independence, although it probably had not reached the state in which Anthony McCabe, the university's steward for many years, first saw it:

> At this period (1877) University Hall looked more like a well-battered relic than an institution of refinement and culture. . . . The low ceilings and poor ventilation, combined with suffocating gases from the ancient furnace and lack of sufficient heat in the recitation rooms, would often cause the class to "cut." The classroom furniture consisted of large iron chairs screwed to the floor, each one having the right arm large enough to hold a blank-book and inkwell for examination purposes, and once each quarter of a century they would receive a coat of paint. . . . In those days the temperature of the lecture-room in winter very frequently went below sixty degrees and the iron chairs were a source of much discomfort and chilliness. The thoughtful student soon learned to carry his heaviest overcoat into the lecture-room and with it carefully pad these dreaded ice-cold chairs. . . . A long, narrow and very high walnut table instead of a desk stood on a low platform. When the professor was seated at the table very little of him could be seen except his feet and legs. (Brown 308–10; G)

De Mille puts what may be a reference to this seating problem into his "Class Poem": "Those lecture room forms were too stiff and too hard / Although we had often a pleasant dis-cushion" (lines 253–56; A3). He may,

Brown University in De Mille's time

in addition, have found in the contrast between the discomforts of this "battered relic" and the relatively comfortable new buildings of Horton and Acadia an ironic sidelight on the price to be paid for a good education.

The level of comfort in the domestic arrangements at Brown similarly contrasted with those at Horton. Until just before De Mille's arrival, students and single members of faculty living on campus ate in the Commons Hall, and James Angell recalls it as it was in his student days:

> Most of us took our meals in Commons Hall . . . on the first floor in the middle of the east side of University Hall. Each class had its own table. If the fare was not very sumptuous, it was not costly, and the conversation was lively. Occasionally it became so boisterous as to stir the amiable steward, Mr. Elliott, known familiarly to us as "Pluto," to bring down his big bread-knife with a loud resounding whack on his table, and to shout with his husky voice, "Order, order." I cannot say that the usages in Commons Hall were conducive to elegant manners. But the plain meals were spiced with the flavor of excellent companionship. (Brown 91; G)

McCabe notes that "the tables were bountifully spread, considering the low price paid by the students, one dollar per week," although beyond mentioning Mrs. Elliot's "famous Brown pies" and the breakfast fare of "hot brownbread, crackers and milk," he does not describe what was actually served. Although it seems a sensible and efficient arrangement, "Commons were abolished in 1850" (Bronson 250; G) and replaced by a system under which students who were lodging in the college boarded (that is, took their meals) in private homes, where the quality and quantity of the food served must have been quite variable.

Most students were accommodated in single or double rooms in University Hall or Hope College, with a few having both board and lodging in private homes around the edge of the campus. De Mille was among the former, occupying a single room on campus for his first term, for which he paid $9 in rent. In his junior and senior years, however, he shared a room (for which the rent was $4.50 per term), and, although his roommate in his junior year is unknown, in his senior year, he shared with Henry Wentworth Johnston, from Wolfville, Nova Scotia.[1] In both years, De Mille and Johnston were in University Hall, of which the fourth storey was nicknamed "Pandemonium" because of the rowdy behaviour of its occupants, although it is not possible to judge for certain from the room numbers (37 and 31, respectively, for the two years) whether De Mille was one of the rowdies or one of the sufferers from noisy neighbours. Each of the student rooms, according to McCabe's description, was equipped with "a large closet, one half used for coal and the other half for a clothes-press," and the furniture

> consisted of a bedroom set, generally of pine or ash and occasionally of walnut. Many of the rooms had three and four carpets—as the old one became worn a new one would be nailed down above the old, thus avoiding labor which the students regarded as useless. (Brown 310, 312; G)

The coal was required for the stoves that heated the rooms, and these were, as one student (Whitman Bailey, class of '64) recalls them a few years after De Mille's time, a considerable hazard:

> Everyone had a stove, and ashes were cast into the halls, whence they were now and then removed. It was a mercy that no disastrous fire ever occurred. We all devoutly believed that the buildings were fireproof. (Brown 203–04; G)

McCabe concurs: "It must have been through the aid of divine Providence that this ancient structure never caught fire from this source" (Brown 312; G). Washing water was also an individual problem, for, according to McCabe, "University Hall did not have any water supply until about 1880. . . . Each student was supposed to provide water for himself at the old pump at the east of Hope College" (Brown 313; G), and Bailey describes the very casual method of disposing of it: "Basins were generally emptied from the windows of the dormitories, with or without the warning cry, 'Stand from under!' Indeed, the propulsion of the liquid and the cry of alarm might be simultaneous" (Brown 203–04; G). The sanitary facility, "a small brick building known among the students as 'Sprague Hall,' " was situated on the far side of a garden just outside the south entrance of University Hall (Brown 314; G).

De Mille did not, however, have to spend all his time working. In March, a few weeks after his arrival, he was proposed as a member of the Philermenian Society of Brown. Originally founded, in 1794, as the Misokosmian Society, the society, as described by Bronson, "held fortnightly meetings, for debates, speeches, declamations, and the reading of essays and poems" (147; G). In the minutes of the meeting of 27 March 1852, after the vote on the new admissions, the secretary recorded the names of the "gentlemen . . . appointed as committees to inform the newly elected members of their election," and among them Bancroft was to inform De Mille (Brown, Philermenian Society, Minutes; H). De Mille, after the expiry in the fall term of his probationary period in the society, took an active part in the debates. In an article on De Mille, H. L. Koopman mentions that in 1853 De Mille was elected "the poet of the society," and says of him that "he was a favorite speaker, and those who were near the society's rooms when a meeting was going on, always knew when De Mille was up by the applause that followed his sallies of wit" (Koopman 28; E).[2] In addition to its debating and social function, according to Bronson, the society "began in 1798 to collect a library," which

> gradually increased, until in 1821 it contained 1594 volumes, including such works as *Tom Jones*, *Tristram Shandy*, and Byron's poems; the books were kept in the college library-room until 1823, when they were removed to the society's quarters in Hope College. (Bronson 180; G)

During De Mille's years at Brown, the meetings of the Philermenian Society were held on Saturday afternoons in these same quarters. The library, however, was as important to De Mille as the meetings, and he was soon borrowing from it on a regular basis.

Brown did, of course, have a library at this time, which the society's library supplemented, rather than substituted for. In 1851, the university library was located in Manning Hall, and it contained "upwards of 24,000 well selected volumes" (Brown, *Catalogue*, 1851–52 44; H).[3] It was open daily for four hours under the supervision of the librarian, Professor Reuben A. Guild (who combined this position with his teaching of the theory and practice of agriculture) and his assistant, William H. Mills (Brown, *Catalogue*, 1851–52 8; H). On occasion, it operated a reserve system for textbooks, such as those for the first half of the class in intellectual and moral philosophy, a class for which the description lists the required books, and then continues: "copies of the above works, in sufficient number for the use of the class, are placed in the Library" (Brown, *Catalogue*, 1851–52 29; H). Students paid a fee of $1.50 each term to use the library: the entry, "For Use of College Library [$]1.50," appears on the account sent to De

Mille's father (Brown, Accounts 44; H). Students could be fined for having overdue books.

De Mille began borrowing from the university library shortly after the May recess. During the remainder of the term, he borrowed (and presumably found time to read) the three volumes of Washington Irving's *A History of the Life and Voyages of Christopher Columbus*, the two volumes of John Lloyd Stephens's *Incidents of Travel in Central America, Chiapas, and Yucatan*, the second volume of the same author's *Incidents of Travel in Yucatan*, Irving's *Bracebridge Hall* and his *History of New York* (by "Diedrich Knickerbocker"), and a book, shown in the borrowing register as Wycherley's *Dramatic Works*, that cannot be identified from the library's catalogue for the period. De Mille did not borrow from the Philermenian Society library at all during this term.

The term ended on 15 July 1852. De Mille's account for the term, as sent to his father, shows the various fees required: "For Tuition, $12.00; For Room Rent, $9.00; For Use of College Library, $1.50; For Registrar's Salary, $2.00; For Servants' hire, $3.50; For Public Fuel, $1.25; For Repairs [unspecified], $1.25; For Private Damage—" (Brown, Accounts 44; H). His academic standing is also shown here for three of his four classes: Latin (14.3 out of 20, or 72 percent), Greek (18.5 or 93 percent), and French (11.4 or 57 percent) (Brown, Accounts 44; H). His grade in mathematics does not appear, but it is given elsewhere as 18 (90 percent) (Brown, Record 4; H). The low grade in French is unexpected, suggesting that he may have shared the difficulties with the language that Elisha experienced and recorded in his journal on 10 April 1861 as he and James passed through Paris on their way home (Elisha De Mill; H). James's general performance, however, is fairly good considering his midyear arrival in a strange academic setting.

De Mille returned to Brown on 3 September 1852 for the beginning of the fall term. He was now an "undergraduate of three years standing" beginning his junior year. His three courses for the year were natural philosophy, chemistry, and rhetoric and English literature.

Natural philosophy covered what is now called physics. De Mille's instructor was probably Professor Henry Day (Brown, *Catalogue*, 1852–53 7; H). According to the description of the class, the year's work introduced the students to "Mechanics, Hydrostatics, Pneumatics, Optics, Acoustics, and Astronomy" (Brown, *Catalogue*, 1852–53 36; H), although there is no indication of how this list of topics was divided between the two terms. For its time, the class was quite advanced in offering demonstrations ("the instruction is by illustrated and experimental lectures") that De Mille may have found enjoyable, but they were "accompanied by daily examinations on previous lectures, and exercises in application of the principles taught" (Brown, *Catalogue*, 1852–53 36; H). The recitation of previously learned material was also required, which probably accounts for De Mille's comment in his "Class Poem" that

> The demands of the study of Physics, I fear,
> From us ever gained but reluctant complyings;
> And 'twas thought from the grumblings that any might hear
> That we gained from the sciences nothing but sighings.
> (lines 173–76; A3)

The textbooks required were Olmstead's *Natural Philosophy*, Jackson's *Optics*, Pierce's *Treatise on Sound*, and Norton's *Astronomy* (Brown, *Catalogue*, 1852–53 36; H). De Mille's grade for the first term was 19 out of 20 (95 percent), but dropped sharply in the second term to 8.5 out of 20 (42 percent) (Brown, Accounts 63, 285; H).

De Mille's second class that year was chemistry and physiology, taught by Professor George I. Chace. The first term covered "Chemistry proper, Heat, Electricity, Galvanism and Magnetism," and the second covered "animal and vegetable Physiology, including classifications of Plants and Animals." The description adds that "In that part of the course relating to the Anatomy and Physiology of man, particular reference is had to the laws of health and regimen," and there were "weekly exercises in themes" (Brown, *Catalogue*, 1852–53 30; H). The work was again both practical and theoretical, and more advanced students were allowed, if they wished, "to pursue the science by the aid of the knife and the microscope," but there is no evidence that De Mille was among them. Amasa Eaton (class of '61) recalls that "the chemical laboratory was then in the basement of Rhode Island Hall. The hot-air furnace was in the middle of the laboratory, and pipes running through the room carried heated air to the lecture rooms above" (Brown 188; G). The effect of this arrangement on the students is reflected in the "Class Poem," in which De Mille writes of "The horrible lecture room scorching and burning, / Amid which the result was a curious one— / For like Ephrahim's cake we were all underdone!" (lines 185–86; A3). The reference is to the biblical declaration in the book of Hosea that

"Ephraim is a cake not turned" (7.8), and hence "underdone" because cooked on one side only; the students were "under" Professor Dunn not because he was teaching the class, but because his class in rhetoric and English literature was held in room above the laboratory. Whitman Bailey (class of '64) recalls in addition that

> Somewhere in the building were secreted the human skeleton and the manikin [presumably some kind of model of the human body showing musculature and internal organs], which were subject to periodic and more or less lengthened [sic] disappearances that to this day are not wholly accounted for. (Brown 202; G)

De Mille's chemistry grades show a pattern similar to those in his natural philosophy class: for the first term, he received 17 out of twenty (85 percent), but in the second term he dropped to just over 15 (75 percent), although obviously this drop is by no means as sharp as the one in natural philosophy.

Rhetoric and English literature, his third class for the year, is probably the most important in terms of De Mille's later development. The class, almost always taken in the student's third or junior year, was designed "to enable the pupil to write and speak his own language with correctness and elegance, and to cultivate in him a literary taste, and to import to him a knowledge of the English language and its literature." In the first term, the students studied "the formation and combination of sentences, the nature and use of Figurative Language, the qualities of Style and the composition of Essays," and in the second term, "Logic, and the higher branches of Rhetoric and Criticism, and the History of the English Language and Literature." The work in both terms included "Regular Exercises in Composition and Declamation" and "written themes on . . . leading topics" (Brown, *Catalogue*, 1852–53 31–32; H). The class was taught by the professor of rhetoric and English Literature, Robinson P. Dunn, of whom Samuel Thurber (class of '58) says, "he was affable, kindly, cultivated in manner, easy and fluent of speech, a genuine example of good rhetoric, himself more potent as a lesson than the books we repeated to him verbatim" (Brown 122; G). John Tetlow (class of '64) also recalls Robinson's teaching methods with appreciation:

> Of course we had no daily themes, and, except during the preparation of essays for the "junior exhibition" and the "commencement

exercises," we had no personal conferences with the professor for suggestion and criticism. But we took down from dictation lectures on the "many qualifications which make a good writer" . . . and wrote essays and original speeches at frequent intervals and received them back with unmistakable evidence that they had been attentively read by a competent critic. (Brown 227; G)

De Mille was, therefore, fortunate to have had the attention of a good teacher for this class, and, since he was one of the orators at the Junior Exhibition that year, he presumably had the particular advantage of personal conferences on his contribution. Nevertheless, his grades in this class show the familiar drop between the first term (18 out of 20, or 90 percent) and the second (14 out of 20, or 70 percent).

It is probably not possible at this distance to know exactly why all three of De Mille's grades drop between the two terms of the year, although we can certainly speculate. It should be noted, first of all, that in the latter part of the second term De Mille missed a considerable number of classes as a result of illness, and that he was excused from others for unspecified reasons. These absences certainly affected his classwork and his performance in the examinations. Koopman, considering the point, suggests also that "his mind was evidently too active along its own lines to conform to the routine of college studies" (Koopman 27; E). There is, moreover, evidence that De Mille was not simply wasting time during this year but was developing intellectually, if not academically.

His contributions to the Philermenian Society debates are part of this evidence. His probationary period was up in October 1852, and at the meeting of 30 October, De Mille was among the students "enrolled on the list of members" (Brown, Philermenian Society, Minutes; H). During the year he took part as a principal speaker in two debates: on the Fugitive Slave Law and on the advisability of the purchase of Cuba from Spain by the United States (Brown, Philermenian Society, Minutes, 4 Dec. 1852; 12 Mar. 1853; H). He was also presumably attending the other meetings, although this cannot be verified because attendance records were not kept.

His reading outside the set texts for his classes offers more evidence of his independent development and demonstrates a wide-ranging intellectual curiosity. During the year, his borrowings, from both the university library and the Philermenian Society library, included a wide range of fiction and nonfiction: more of Washington Irving's novels; Frederick E. Forbes's *Five*

Years in China; Lorenzo Sabine's *American Loyalists*; *Voyages and Travels of Sir John Mandeville*; Longfellow's *Poets and Poetry of Europe*; *Don Quixote* (twice); three volumes of Boccaccio's *Opere*; Isaac D'Israeli's *Curiosities of Literature* (twice); Swedenborg's *Heaven and Hell*; George Sale's *Koran* (a translation); John Gibson Lockhart's *Ancient Spanish Ballads, Historical and Romantic*, two volumes of what are described as "Jeffries' *Contributions*";[4] Dickens' *Pickwick Papers*; Giovanni Rosini's *Monaca di Monza*; one or more of the 40 volumes of Sir Walter Scott's Waverley novels; a volume of selections from Sir Thomas More's works; Thomas N. Talfourd's *Miscellanies*; four volumes of Hazlitt's literary criticism (*Lectures on the English Comic Writers*, *Table Talk*, *Lectures Chiefly on the Dramatic Literature of the Age of Elizabeth*, and *Spirit of the Age*); Schlegel's *A Course of Lectures on Dramatic Art and Literature*; Magnus Björnstjerna's *Theogony of the Hindoos*; a volume of Longfellow's poems; and James Fenimore Cooper's *Red Rover* (Brown, Library; Brown, Philermenian Society, Library; H).

One of the highlights of the academic year at Brown was the Junior Class Spring Exhibition. This is recalled by Robert Brown (class of '71) as

> The most graceful and enjoyed event of the year. . . . At this exhibition the best original speeches of the junior year work were delivered by their authors, and it was a higher honor to speak at junior exhibition than was the perfunctory appointment for commencement, which was strictly according to marks. The junior exhibition speaker, however, had no halo about his head, for while he was trying to prove the greatness of his soul or his proficiency in oratory very likely the audience was reading comments about him, full of sarcasm, ridicule, and abuse . . . . for the wicked sophomores had been busy for weeks preparing mock programmes. (Brown 270; G)

Bronson, however, calls the humour of these mock programmes "almost as coarse as it is dull" (297; G). De Mille, as already noted, was one of the students chosen to take part in this year. According to the official programme of the event, his contribution to the proceedings, which were held on Saturday, 21 May 1853, was an oration in English on the subject of "Arabian Fiction." His text, unfortunately, has not survived, but it may well have contributed to the article "Imagination and Fancy Among the

Arabs," which he published in *Godey's Lady's Book* in 1861.

This contribution is the first suggestion of any particular literary leaning to be noticed in De Mille, and its topic is certainly in keeping with the exotic subjects of some of his reading. From his junior year, however, a few scattered pieces of his early writing have survived. One is a piece of nonsense verse entitled "The Brunensian Hippodrome," written for inclusion in a manuscript collection of verse by members of Psi Upsilon (B2). The other, one of his two contributions to the Junior Burial, is a mock dirge to the tune of "Auld Lang Syne" ("Song" ["Ye Whimpering Coves"]; A3).

The Junior Burial, unlike the exhibition, which was official and academic, was a purely student activity. These mock funerals, in which copies of the rhetoric texts for the year were buried in Narragansett Bay, had begun several years before De Mille's junior year. They became more popular and elaborate in the 1850s, according to Bronson, as a part of the general increase in "Pranks of various kinds," which reflected the agitation stirred up a few years earlier that had culminated in the so-called rebellion of 1851 (297; G).[5] The programme for the "Burial of Whately & Campbell by the Junior Class of Brown University. July 5, 1853," in De Mille's junior year, is fortuitously but fortunately the earliest to survive (Brown, Junior; H). It is hard to tell from the programme whether there is any residue of the kind of hostility Bronson describes as having taken place during the rebellion, but certainly there does not seem to be anything but good-natured fun in De Mille's recollection of the occasion.

Two days later, the spring term ended, and De Mille returned home for the vacation. During this vacation, his first professional publication, an article entitled "Acadie, and the Birth-place of Evangeline," appeared in *Putnam's Monthly* (A4), and it was probably but not certainly written, in view of the time required for his participation in the Junior Burial at the end of the term, in the early days of the vacation. It is not unlikely that he also spent some time visiting Elisha, who had been ordained on 1 July, after leaving theological college, and had begun work as pastor of the Baptist church at Amherst, Nova Scotia. Moreover, since his father had a reputation for disliking idleness, it is possible that he also spent some time working in his father's office (MacMechan; H).

At the beginning of September 1853, De Mille returned to Brown to begin his senior year. He was then one of the "Undergraduates of Four Years' Standing" (Brown, *Catalogue*, 1853–54 9; H), and among those who "sustained their examinations upon the studies pursued last term" (Brown, Faculty 2 Sept. 1853;). He enrolled in his three final-year classes, intellectual philosophy and moral philosophy, German, and history and political economy. Since no long absence is recorded towards the end of October and the beginning of November, he apparently cannot have interrupted his work to attend Elisha's wedding to Emma Pryor Johnston, which took place on 3 November 1853 in Wolfville, at the home of the bride's father.[6] De Mille was absent from lectures four times (that is, from four individual classes) in the last week of October and from prayers twice, but this would mean no more than one day's total absence, and it would have taken him longer than this to travel to Wolfville to attend the wedding and return to Providence.

The class in intellectual and moral philosophy consisted of a half class in intellectual philosophy in the first term, and a half class in moral philosophy in the second term. Both parts were taught by President Francis Wayland himself. Students attended five lectures a week, one of which was a review class of the previous week's lectures. James Burrill Angell, a student at Brown in the late 1840s (class of '49), and subsequently both a professor and the university's president, describes the method of instruction in this class (and in his history class) as follows:

> The recitations were conducted in a manner which furnished a remarkable training to the memory. The first man called on was asked to give an analysis of the lesson assigned; the second man then took up the discussion as given in the textbook or in the lecture of the previous day; the third, when called on, without prompting followed the second, and so on with the rest. It was believed by the students that a pretty exact verbal reproduction of the text was credited with the highest marks, consequently the best scholars cultivated the verbal memory so that they gained great facility in reproducing a text. I think that when in our junior year we had from twelve to fifteen pages of Smythe's Lectures on History as a lesson, at least half a dozen men in the class would in two hours prepare themselves to recite the whole of the lesson with substantial fidelity to the text. I think this practice was carried to excess. At the same time the power thus acquired has been of great service in life to many men. I ought not to leave the impression that ideas were not esteemed of more worth than words. The utmost freedom of asking questions and of

discussion was permitted in the classroom, unless it was obvious that the liberty was abused. (Brown 89; G)

The quality of memory that Burpee records as having been noticeable in De Mille as a child must have been of considerable help in such classroom practices. Moreover, the exercise provided for it in the classroom must have contributed, as Angell suggests it did for many other Brown graduates, to its continuing strength in his later life — an effect that Burpee also records (Notes; H). The students also wrote weekly essays. The textbooks listed for the first term are "Locke on the Understanding, Reid's and Stewart's Works, Cousin's Psychology, and Abercrombie on the Intellectual Powers," and no additions are made for the second term (Brown, *Catalogue*, 1853-54 27; H). De Mille's comments in his "Class Poem" suggest that he rather enjoyed these classes:

> Metaphysical learning was pleasant indeed—
> We found genius in Stewart and something to Reid,
> And we learned with delight this most excellent rule,
> That each his existence might pleasantly pass if he
> Would stick to the men of the "Common-sense school,"
> And properly scorn all Fichte-tious philosophy. (lines 247–56; A3)

De Mille's grades for the classes certainly support the notion that he enjoyed them: for intellectual philosophy he obtained 15.84 out of 20 (79 percent) and for Moral Philosophy 16.59 out of 20 (80 percent) (Brown, Record; H).

The record of De Mille's German class, taught by the newly appointed professor of modern languages, James Burrill Angell, is rather confused. He is not shown on his student account as having enrolled for it in the first term, but in the record of student standing he is shown as having completed two terms, with a grade of 13 out of 20 (65 percent) in each (Brown, Accounts 272; Record; H). The work for the class in both terms consisted of "oral and written exercises" from Woodbury's *Eclectic German Reader*, lectures on the history of the German language and literature, and the reading of Schiller's *Wilhelm Tell* and Goethe's *Iphigenia* (Brown, *Catalogue*, 1853-54 35–36; H). De Mille's grade suggests that he might have been thinking of his own achievement, both here in his German class or earlier in his sophomore-year French class, when he comments "Could a foreigner hear it his heart would be wrung / At the sound of his language all mangled and broken" ("Class Poem" lines 291–92; A3).

De Mille's third class that year was history and political economy, with Professor William Gammell. The class description announces that "The course in History commences with the fall of the Roman Empire, and embraces a general survey of the organization of European Society, and its progress in Mediaeval and Modern times," and it included "the Colonial and Revolutionary history of the United States, together with the theory of the American Government, the history of its formation and the outlines of its successive administrations." The textbooks used were "Guizot's *History of Civilization*, Hallam's *Constitutional History of England*, Weber's *Outlines of Universal History*, Bayard and Story on the *Constitution of the United States*" (Brown, *Catalogue*, 1853–54 32; H). Whether De Mille's account, in "Class Poem," of the fate of students in the History class reflects the professor's sense of humour or De Mille's own is not clear:

> In the History courses we met with a fate
> Which all would most willingly, eagerly, shun,
> For the class was most fearfully pressed by the weight
> Of many an awful Historical pun.
> For Oh! with what feelings of woe, did we hear
> "That a serfeit of slaves might be found at the South —"
> And when people complained — that provisions were dear —
> "That the dreadful complaint was in everyone's mouth!"
>
> (lines 257–64; A3)

Given De Mille's own propensity for punning, one might consider this a case of poetic justice. De Mille's marks for this class throughout the year, judging by his "weekly reports," were generally high (16, 17, or 18 out of 20), and for the first term his grade was 17.66 out of 20 (88 percent). In the second term, although, with a couple of exceptions, his weekly marks continued high (Brown, Accounts 272; H), he failed the final examination. In the minutes of the faculty meeting held to discuss the students' standing, it is noted, without any reason for the failure being suggested, that "De Mille having failed in his examination in History his rank is withheld" (Brown, Faculty, 30 June 1854; H). This failure brought his final grade down very sharply, although it did not prevent him from graduating.

During this year, he had continued to be active in the Philermenian Society. As a full member, he participated in the formalities of electing new members, and the minutes of an early fall meeting record that "Committees were appointed to inform [new members] of their election . . . To Johnston [Henry Wentworth Johnston, new to Brown this term, and De Mille's roommate] & Bullock, De Mille." He participated as polemicist in a debate on the motion "that the Theatre should not receive the support of a Christian community," and he was a "disputant" in the debate in support of the motion that "the establishment of the secret ballot would be beneficial." In June 1854, he was on the list of members whose membership was being considered for cancellation for nonpayment of dues, but his name was removed from the list after discussion (Brown, Philermenian Society, Minutes, 1 Oct. 1853, 12 Nov. 1853, 10 Dec. 1853, 11 June 1854 [respectively]; H).

De Mille continued to use the University library throughout the year, but the number of volumes he borrowed fell. In addition to books placed "on reserve" for his philosophy class, he borrowed Björnstjerna's *Theogony of the Hindoos* (again), *Christian Revelation*, Martin's *Nova Scotia* (twice), Mallet's *Northern Antiquities*, and volume 23 of *Blackwood's Magazine*. All his recorded borrowings are in the first term (Brown, Library; H). There is no record of borrowing from the Philermenian library (Brown, Philermenian Society, Library; H).

But whereas the amount of his reading drops, the amount of his writing, as evidenced by his publications, increases sharply. Beginning with "The Maranon" (a poem) in the January 1854 issue of *Gleason's Pictorial Drawing-Room Companion* (A3), he published 16 short stories and another poem over the next eight months. It might be considered a promising beginning for a professional writer, however little he may have been paid for them (or if he was paid at all, since there are no records of this).

The spring term of De Mille's senior year ended on 13 July 1854, and he returned to Saint John for the summer. Since he had been appointed "Class Poet" for the class of 1854, it is reasonable to suppose that he spent some time composing his offering. After the summer vacation, he returned briefly for his graduation ceremony.

The eighty-fifth annual commencement of Brown University was celebrated on 6 September 1854. It took place in the First Baptist Meeting House of Providence, and the "Order of Exercises" shows music, prayer, the delivery of orations on various topics by students, the award of "Premiums" (prizes), and the conferring of degrees. Twenty-three students, including De Mille, were awarded the degree of master of arts (Brown,

Commencement; H). The following day, De Mille took part in the equally traditional class day of the graduating class. Bronson states that

> the records of the class of 1841 show that one of the main features [of Commencement], the class supper — or dinner — had already become a well-established custom, for the dinner is there called "a venerable relic of the past." It was held in the City Hotel, on the day after Commencement, and lasted from 3 to 6 p.m. Toasts were drunk, and songs sung . . . and the class ode [delivered]. (237; G)

It was at this dinner that De Mille delivered his "Class Poem."

When commencement and class day were over, De Mille's student days were also over. He presumably returned directly to Saint John, ready to look for a career, although there is before this point no indication of what direction he might take. As things turned out, it was to be some time before that direction was finally settled.

NOTES

1 Henry Wentworth Johnston was the son of Dr. Lewis Johnston and his wife Theresa, and brother to Emma Pryor Johnston, Elisha Budd De Mill's first wife (Kirkconnell 3; G). James De Mille and H.W. Johnston were therefore brothers-in-law as well as roommates. Some years later, Judge John Wentworth Johnston, Lewis's brother and Henry's uncle, was to be involved in Dr. Pryor's confrontation with the Granville Street Baptist Church in Halifax.

2 Koopman does not give a source for this information, but it is quite possible that he could have acquired it, in the course of his work on *Memories of Brown* (Brown; G), from former students who knew De Mille personally at Brown. Although De Mille died young, many of his contemporaries would have been only in their seventies at the time Koopman was carrying out his research, and they could easily have provided him with such information. He also records a description of De Mille at this time, as "large and burly . . . decidedly a man's man," and says that De Mille was known to his friends at Brown as "Jim De Mille" (Koopman 29, 27; E).

3 The catalogue description goes on to say that "a large proportion of these [books] have been purchased within the last few years, with special reference to the wants of gentlemen engaged in literary and scientific pursuits. [The library] is constantly increasing from the proceeds of a permanent fund of $25,000, established for this purpose

in 1839," and records the combined number of volumes in the Philermenian Society and the United Brothers (a second similar student society) as 7,000 (Brown, *Catalogue* [1851–52] 44; H).

4 This entry is not clear. On the one hand, it could refer to *Contributions* (4 vols., 1844) by Francis Jeffrey (editor of the *Edinburgh Review* from 1802–29), with the name misspelled by whoever wrote it down, since this explains the annotation "2 vols." against the entry. On the other hand, it could refer to John Jeffries's *A Narrative of the Two Aerial Voyages of Doctor Jeffries with Mons. Blanchard; with Meteorological Observations and Remarks. The first Voyage, on the Thirtieth of November, 1784, from London into Kent; the Second, on the Seventh of January, 1785, from England into France* (1786), which is in Brown's 1843 catalogue, although it is only a single volume. De Mille might have been particularly interested in the latter, however, since "Jeffries was a Boston physician, who removed to Halifax with Lord Howe's troops" (Mitchell, 3 Feb. 1983; H).

5 According to Bronson's account,

> Professor A.L. Koeppen, formerly of the University of Athens, who had been granted the use of a college room for a course of lectures the year before, was for some reason denied a renewal of the privilege. . . . Action seemingly more opposed to the spirit of the New System can hardly be conceived. Professor Koeppen secured a hall, and invited the university students to attend his lectures free of charge, as they had done the previous year. Some members of the Faculty excused the students from evening study hours that they might go, while others held to the rules.

In response, Bronson continues, Brown's executive board put its foot down and insisted that students remain on campus and that faculty should check that they were actually in their rooms during study hours:

> There followed the so-called rebellion of 1851, during which the students "used the most abusive epithets towards the President and Faculty," and made disturbances in chapel. In January the President conferred with the Executive Board on "the insubordination of last term," and laid it chiefly to the lack of unanimity in the Faculty about the enforcement of discipline. A committee having confirmed his opinion, the board voted that it was "expedient" that Mr. Greene and Professors Porter and Norton "should terminate their connexion with the University." The three resigned forthwith. (296; G).

6 "At Annandale, Wolfville, on Thursday evening, the 3rd inst., by the Rev. A.R. Crawley, the Rev. E.B. Demill, of Amherst, to Emma Pryor, daughter of Lewis Johnston, Esq., M.D." (*Christian Messenger* 10 Nov. 1853: 355.) Arthur Crawley, the officiating clergyman, was a son of the Reverend E.A. Crawley, and a former classmate of Elisha and James at Horton Academy.

CHAPTER 4

The Uncertain Years, 1855-65

When De Mille returned to Saint John in the fall of 1854 after the Brown commencement, the possibilities of employment were limited. He was certainly well educated, but he had no practical training, and apparently no aptitude or preference for any particular profession. The provincial economy was on a downward swing, and business in Saint John was not flourishing. Some years later, in the early pages of the *Christian Watchman*, Elisha De Mill gave it as his opinion that "ever since the 'cholera year' [1854] the general business of the province has been in miserable condition" (2 Jan. 1861: 2).

De Mille's first job was more or less in keeping with his literary bent. At the beginning of 1855, he became assistant editor of the *Christian Visitor*, under the editorship of the Reverend I.E. Bill. The *Christian Visitor* (it was spelled "visiter" in the first few issues) had been set up in October of 1847 by a committee, which included Nathan De Mill, "appointed by the N.B. Baptist Association, at its late Session, to attend to the preliminaries for the getting up of a new paper," which was to be "the organ of the denomination in this Province." It was to be "devoted to Religious and General Intelligence," and, among other topics, "The Cause of Temperance

... shall command due attention" (20 Oct. 1847: 2). The paper appeared weekly, usually on Wednesday, the number of pages per issue varying throughout its life. Towards the end of 1854, Bill announced a number of changes in the format of the *Christian Visitor*, and mentioned that "in this connection we are happy to say that Gentlemen of acknowledged literary attainments and of elevated religious principle have engaged to render all needful assistance in perfecting our plan" (1 Dec. 1854: 788). If these "gentlemen" included De Mille, this announcement may have served as a hint of what was to follow.

In the last issue of the year, under the heading "Assistance in the Editorial Department," Bill announced his "very great pleasure in being able to inform the readers of the 'Visitor' that he [himself] has been able to secure the valuable aid of Bro. James De Mill, graduate of Brown University" (20 Dec. 1854: 320). De Mille's name first appears on the masthead (where it is spelled "DeMill") in the first issue of 1855 (3 Jan. 1855: 1). Very little can be determined about his duties, although it is probable that he wrote some of the contributions to the paper as well as getting the material ready for the press. The rather romantic fable "Faith, Hope, and Love," about the archangel Israfel, which appeared almost immediately after he had joined the paper (21 Feb. 1855: 29) under the pen name "Aleph" (later attached to one of De Mille's likely contributions to the *Christian Watchman*),[1] is very probably his, and the series "Encourage Your Minister" may be his, at least in part.[2] De Mille's name continued to appear on the *Visitor*'s masthead up to and including the issue for Wednesday, 18 April 1855. In the following issue it has disappeared, and Bill includes on the editorial page a note saying that De Mille had left the paper:

> It is not probably known to our readers that our beloved friend and assistant Mr. James DeMill, has been in the United States for the last two months. He fully expected when he left home to return before the first of May, but unexpectedly circumstances have arisen to render his continuance in that country necessary for some time to come. Having counted upon his valuable assistance in conducting the "Visitor," we cannot but deeply regret that he has decided not to return. We shall not however, be altogether deprived of his aid, for we have good reason to hope that he will be our frequent correspondent furnishing such information fresh from the neighbouring republic as shall deeply interest our readers. His timely assistance

hitherto demands an expression of our heart felt gratitude to him, and earnestly do we pray that prosperity and success may attend his pathway wherever God in his providence may direct his footsteps! (*Christian Visitor* 25 Apr. 1855: 66).

De Mille, then, had left some time before the note appeared, probably about the end of February. The reason for his journey to the United States, and the circumstances that, according to Bill, prevented his return to Saint John, will probably never be known in detail. If he was not paid for his work at the *Visitor*, as is more than likely, then an opportunity for paid employment in the United States must have seemed very attractive.

It is not likely, however, that he set out with the deliberate intention of not returning at the beginning of May. For one thing, he cannot have relied upon finding work in the United States, and for another, his brother's wife was seriously ill. According to an announcement in the *Christian Messenger*, Elisha, as previously noted, had married Emma Pryor Johnston, daughter of Lewis Johnston, at her parents' home, Annandale, in Wolfville on 3 November 1853 (10 Nov. 1853: 355). In September of 1854, Emma gave birth to a daughter, Louise Pryor (*Christian Messenger* 15 June 1854: 187), who was named after her mother's cousin, Annie Pryor's older sister, Louise (or Louisa) Pryor, who had died in Cambridge in June 1854. At the time of her daughter's birth, Emma was already suffering from consumption (tuberculosis), and afterwards she became even more seriously ill. A letter from John Francis in the *Christian Visitor*, written from Elisha's parish of Amherst on 23 May 1855 mentions that "Mrs. DeMill seems much better" (23 May 1855: 82),[3] but a few weeks later the prognosis was clearly not good, for Francis writes again saying that "You will be glad to learn that Mrs. Demill was sufficiently recovered to justify the attempt to remove her to Wolfville, she having anxiously desired to visit the home of her childhood once more, whether it should please the Lord to restore her to health or otherwise" (20 June 1855: 99).[4] Although Emma reached home without suffering any apparent ill effects from the journey, her condition was irreversible, and she died "the victim of that fatal disease consumption, and after many months of sufferings" on 3 August 1855 in Wolfville (*Christian Visitor* 8 Aug. 1855: 127). Louise survived her mother by less than a year, and died on 29 April 1856 (*Christian Messenger* 30 Apr. 1856: 139).

The job that detained De Mille in the United States at this time of crisis for the brother who was also his "closest friend" (Burpee, Notes; H), was that of bookkeeper in the office of the West Columbia Mining and Manufacturing Company in Cincinnati, Ohio. How he got this job is a rather involved story, going back to the crisis of 1851 in the financing of Acadia College. In the aftermath of this crisis, in 1853, the Reverend E.A. Crawley had been appointed president with the responsibility of securing additional income for the college. At President Crawley's suggestion (Longley 72; G), the board of governors of the college decided that it was "advisable to invest £2000 in the stock of the West Columbia Mining and Manufacturing Company" (Acadia, Board, 19 Apr. 1854; H). The investment was made, but in December of that year, Crawley, then in Boston, "received information respecting the state of the Company which induced [him] to visit West Columbia, in order to prosecute further inquiries on the spot" (Acadia, Board, 13 July 1855; H).[5] The board received letters from him, dated 10 and 29 January 1855, reporting "difficulties" in the affairs of the company, and at the board meeting on 28 March they were informed of a letter announcing that "it was quite uncertain when he would be able to return, as he had been elected President of the Company on the resignation of the late President and was engaged in attending to its affairs" (Acadia, Board, 28 Mar. 1855; H). According to the published statement by the board, the "difficulties" resulted from insufficient capital, extravagant expenditures, unjustified payment of dividends, and general mismanagement (Acadia, Board, 13 July 1855; H). Whether it was salvageable and, if it was, whether Crawley was the man to salvage it remain debatable, but Crawley stayed there, and his resignation from the presidency of Acadia was accepted by the board in 1856, when at one of their meetings "A letter was read from the Rev. Dr. Crawley, dated 'July 1856,' tendering his final resignation as President of Acadia College" (Acadia, Board, 20 Sept. 1856; H). There is no sign that the Acadia Board of Governors ever recovered their investment.

Precisely when De Mille became involved in this business and took up his job as bookkeeper is unknown. If Bill's statement in the *Christian Visitor* of 25 April 1855, that De Mille had been gone two months, is accurate and if it took him two to four weeks to get to Cincinnati, then he would have arrived in Cincinnati somewhere between the middle and the end of March. On 24 September 1855, his father mentions that he is working there in a letter to John Miller of Cannon Miller: "My son James . . . with nothing in prospect but loss and disappointment went to the United States and engaged as a clerk . . . in Cincinnati" (Nathan De Mill; H). On 9 November,

John Francis, who was travelling in the United States collecting donations for the church, wrote to the *Christian Visitor* from Nashville that

> On my way here I passed through . . . Cincinnati, where I had a sweet interview with Dr. Crawley and Mr. Jas. DeMill. They looked exceedingly well, and I am inclined to think God will overrule their removal to that City for good. There is hope yet for the funds of the College. (28 Nov. 1855: 190)

Whereas his father describes him as a "clerk," the Cincinnati city directory that covers 1855 records that "Demill Jas. b.k. [book-keeper]" was living at "13 W[est] 3d," which was also the residence of H. van Bergen, agent of the West Columbia Mining and Manufacturing Company, and hence possibly also the company office (*William's* 69, 289; G).[6] The work probably combined general clerical duties and actual bookkeeping. Since it is unlikely that De Mille would go as far as Cincinnati for employment without good reason, it is probable that he originally went there as a messenger from the Acadia governors (including Dr. John Pryor, De Mille's future father-in-law) to Dr. Crawley (a close friend of Dr. Pryor) and was encouraged to stay as a clerk or secretary by Crawley, who as company president might be supposed to have enough influence to find a job for De Mille, and would clearly require some trustworthy assistance in his attempts to turn the company's affairs round.

The result of this series of events (or of one similar to it) for De Mille was the bookkeeping job. But although MacMechan's mention of the boys working in their father's "counting-house" (MacMechan; H) and Nathan's own mention in his letter of 24 September to John Miller "that I had promised [James] a share of my business" (Nathan De Mill; H) suggest that De Mille had some experience of clerical work before this job, bookkeeping, which (again according to MacMechan) he "learned on the way out," can hardly have seemed very attractive to him (H). Nor could the prospects of advancement have seemed attractive or secure in a company that was in serious financial difficulties. It is therefore not surprising that, by the beginning of January 1856, De Mille had already resigned and left Cincinnati. Crawley, in writing to Pryor on 30 January 1856 about the company's state, asks: "Where is Jas Demill now: Will any body give him my very kind regards[?]" (Crawley; H). The enquiry suggests that the parting had been amicable on both sides.

THE UNCERTAIN YEARS, 1855-65

Since the precise date of his quitting the job is not known, it is not clear how much time elapsed between his leaving Cincinnati and his return to Saint John. Prompted by this uncertainty, and by the story, in his novel "The Minnehaha Mines," of a young man's adventures in the Midwest, including a disguised version of the West Columbia Mining and Manufacturing Company's problems, rumours arose that he had done a number of other things during his stay in the United States. He would certainly have travelled on a river steamboat, since this was virtually the only way to move about that area of the United States at the time with any degree of ease; but given his defective eyesight (the aftermath of the illness suffered before he went to Europe), the suggestion of recurrent illness during his final year at Brown, and his lack of experience in any kind of physical labour, he could hardly have travelled as anything but a passenger. The incident in chapter 12 of "The Missionary's Son," another story serialized in the *Christian Watchman* but apparently never published as a book, in which, after a brief interview with a steamboat captain, "in a quarter of an hour more Willie was steaming down the Ohio River" as a crew member is pure fiction, although what Willie saw on his travels might well have been what De Mille himself observed (20 Mar. 1861: 4). Among the obituary notices about De Mille, collected by his brother Frederick, the one in the *Morning Herald* reported the very widespread rumour that during this stay in the United States, De Mille "was in Ohio holding a Professorship in a Female Seminary, and also in West Virginia as Secretary to Rev. Dr. Crawley" (*Morning Herald* 29 Jan. 1880). The confusion here is twofold. The sudden introduction of West Virginia into the story arises from the fact that although the office of the West Columbia Mining and Manufacturing Company was in Cincinnati, Ohio, the mining operations themselves were located in nearby West Columbia. There are, however, two other places in the United States named West Columbia — one in Texas, and one in West Virginia — and the obituary writer inadvertently selected this last one. The confusion about the "Female Seminary" arose from the fact that Dr. Crawley did, in fact, set up such a seminary — which he first mentions only as "a seminary now projected here," in a letter to W. Hare dated 15 March 1856 — at least a month after De Mille had arrived back in Saint John (Crawley; H).[7] The timing, therefore, makes it quite clear that De Mille was never a teacher in the seminary, for he had returned to New Brunswick long before it opened.

He was back in Saint John early in 1856. On 24 February 1856, he wrote from Saint John to Alfred at Horton about one of the latter's frequent requests for money, and this letter establishes the latest date by which De Mille could have arrived in Saint John. In the letter, however, he uses the phrase "ever since I came home," which suggests that at least a couple of weeks had elapsed, placing him in Saint John as early as mid-January (Letter to Alfred De Mille, 24 Feb. 1856; B3). On his arrival, he discovered that the "miserable condition" of the economy referred to later by Elisha was already well established.

The year 1854 was even at the time recognized as one of economic crisis with long-term consequences. The economic situation of Saint John in particular, and New Brunswick as a whole, at the end of 1854 had been summed up by an editorial in the first issue of the *Christian Visitor* for 1855:

> So great is the change which has taken place within one year that it is painful to look back. — The dawn of eighteen hundred and fifty four was hailed with rejoicing, and for months we were in a feverish dream. Never was the city so prosperous; never was wealth so abundant. Indeed the greatness of our prosperity was only equalled by the greatness of its fall. When the plague came among us it was the first check which our progress had received, it found us unprepared, and even in its presence all unsuspicious of the calamity following closely behind. For the Cholera[,] though terrible, was the forerunner of moral woes of an equally terrible nature; and scarcely had it disappeared from our midst, before the glutted European timber market joined with the effects of the Russian war, had brought upon us a commercial crisis, such as we had never before experienced, one not confined but universal in its extent.
>
> Our present condition is most melancholy. The Banks refuse discount, and the scarcity of money is felt by all. The timber trade is ruined, and the price of all wood goods has fallen to a frightful degree. Freights are unprecedently low, and ships at any price are unsaleable. (3 Jan. 1855: 2)

Although the De Mill family was fortunately left untouched by the cholera epidemic, Nathan De Mill's business was hard hit. He had, for example, taken delivery of two new ships in 1854,[8] which would have involved a considerable capital outlay, and the recovery of this investment by syndicating shares in them to other people would have been seriously affected by the slump in the economy. As both a shipowner and a merchant largely, but not solely, concerned with the timber trade, he was doubly in difficulty, although the diversity of the remainder of his freight handling was enough to keep him in business on a somewhat reduced scale.

De Mille, therefore, could not look to his father for continued support, even had he chosen to do so. Nathan was still not in a position to offer him the "share of my business," mentioned in his letter of 24 September 1855 to Miller (Nathan De Mill; H), and there were still five younger and completely dependent children in the household. There was barely enough money to allow Alfred, who (according to the same letter) in the fall of 1855 had been working in his father's office, to go to Horton Academy to continue his studies. The previously quoted letter from De Mille, written shortly after his arrival back in Saint John, to Alfred, who had requested money to be sent to him for life at Horton, explains that Nathan "feels sore yet about money matters" and that "in fact prospects are very discouraging" (24 Feb. 1856; B3). Another letter, written late the following year and again in response to a request for money from Alfred, makes it clear that the continuing and escalating financial crisis was still pressing Nathan De Mill hard. Affectionately, but firmly, De Mille makes it clear to Alfred that his request is inappropriate:

> I rec'd your letter day or two ago & am sorry you are blue. Don't let yourself be troubled too much about money. Just now it's the scarcest thing in the world. The best men in the country are tight & the strongest houses in the States are crumbling to pieces everywhere. The Philadel[phia], Baltim[ore] & Washington banks have suspended, all the Western Banks have done likewise & it is expected that Boston & New York will follow. St John feels the effects and Father is squeezed into the smallest compass. He let a note of his be [dishonoured] last week for the first time in his life. Whether he'll get thro[ugh] or not is more than I can say. I can only hope. You must make up your mind to be tight. The money you have had thus far has come from me and father has not paid it yet. He is unapproachable on the subject of money. These 10/- are from your ma. Little driblets of money will continue to go to you. Budd will send 20/- soon & so on. Don't be discouraged, neither be stuck up with an idea that father's rich for he is in as much danger now as it is possible[.] (12 Oct. 1857: B3)[9]

Emily, an unknown person, Alice (in front), Frederick, Eliza

Alfred was in fact disappointed in his hope of going from Horton to Brown, as James and Elisha had done, as a result of the financial crisis, and he instead went to Acadia College, from which he graduated in 1860. (Frederick and Elizabeth, the two next youngest children after Alfred, received no formal schooling beyond day school in Saint John, although by the time the two youngest girls, Emily and Alice, were ready for boarding school, money was found to send them to the "female department" at Horton Academy.)

Mrs. De Mill, too, was worried about her husband's business affairs. In a letter to Alfred at Horton, she writes, "Your father will not have any business to do this Winter all the timber trade appears to be broken up. . . . what a long tedious time your father has had" (Elizabeth De Mill; H).[10] Alfred continued to ask for extra money throughout his academic career even up to the point of his graduation, although there is nothing in the letters to show why Alfred needed the money, and nothing in the descriptions of the town, the academy, or the college to show how or when he could have spent it. De Mille continued to send it to him, nevertheless, although accompanying the gifts with hints about their father's (and his own) financial situation that Alfred seems to have been unable to take: "I send five Pounds. What ever more you may want write at once & I'll send it along in time. I'd have said this before but couldn't. Father's hard up. I'm hard up" (Letter to Alfred De Mille 19 May 1860; B3). It should be noted that Nathan De Mill's difficulties may have been with the cash flow in his business, and perhaps with loan repayments, for his assets were still considerable. Apart from the various vessels he owned, either in whole or in part, he had substantial holdings in real estate both in the city and at Carleton, and the latter property was valued in 1856 at £1,200 (Lancaster; H).

The confession of being "hard up" cannot have come easily for James after four years of trying to establish his independence of his father. When he returned from Cincinnati, he had not immediately been able to find himself another job. He may have been working in his father's office while looking for other work, for on one occasion he witnessed, and wrote up a formal memorandum of, the discussion between his father and a Mr. William Short about "the mill at Fredericton" (Memorandum; B4). Sometime in late 1856 or early 1857, however, De Mille came up with the idea of going into partnership with a gentleman by the name of Hazen Fillmore and starting a business as a bookseller and stationer. We must assume that the idea was his own, since it does not seem to be the sort of business that Nathan would suggest, although he probably helped his son with both capital and advice.

The result of De Mille's decision was the Colonial Book Store, which opened in premises at Foster's Corner, King Street, in Saint John, on 1 May 1857. It was advertised as being under the proprietorship of "De Mill & Fillmore," and since "Hazen S. Fillmore, Bookseller" was registered among "Freemen" for that year, it was probably Fillmore who made the arrangements for their business license (Saint John, Register; H). The initial advertisement in the *Morning News* announcing the opening of the store offered "Books! Books!! Books!!!" and invited customers to "call and examine" the stock (13 May 1857: 2). The advertisement in the *Christian Visitor*, however, which appeared the week before the one in the *Morning News*, gives evidence that the store was offering a wider range of goods and services than books alone:

> The subscribers have this day commenced doing business at the above well known stand, with a large and widely diversified stock. They purpose keeping on hand a constant and carefully selected supply of books, as follows:
> Religious. — Theological works, which are indispensable to every person. The standard religious reading of the day; assorted libraries, and books for the day schools and Sunday schools, collected from different publishing houses.
> Secular. — All the popular works in Science, History, and General Literature. Stationary [sic] of all kinds, always on hand. The newest and most popular Sheet Music. Arrangements have been made by means of which any book not on our list can be supplied within a week from the time of giving the order. Maps, Globes, and Philosophical apparatus for school purposes can be supplied in the same time and manner. For sale at the lowest American prices.
> Terms Cash. Books will be forwarded to any part of the country free of expence, on receipt of the money. DeMill & Fillmore. St. John, May 1st, 1857. (6 May 1857: 75)[11]

The emphasis here on religious books, stationery, and school supplies suggests that De Mille was making a bid to appeal to the wide religious and educational interests of the Baptists in the province. Later, judging from the advertisements, he extended the range of goods even further, offering

THE UNCERTAIN YEARS, 1855-65

"Boxes of Water Colours" as suitable Christmas gifts (*Morning News* 4 Dec. 1857: 3). At one point, he and his partner even offered dolls for sale, for a paragraph on the editorial page of the *Morning News* announces that

> Messrs De Mill and Fillmore have sent us specimens of a new style of dolls — the "May Queen and Shepherdess" published by Brown, Taggard & Chase, Boston. They are original in design, well calculated to please children, and likely to create a revolution in the doll department of the nursery. (30 Apr. 1858: 2)

These may, however, have been paper dolls for cutting out, rather than real ones — the word "published" would certainly support such an interpretation. Clearly, in a generally weak economy and in the face of at least three already established bookstores in the city, this enterprise was both ambitious and risky.[12] For a while, at least, everything seemed to go well. The advertisements for books and periodicals available at the store appeared regularly throughout the remainder of 1857 and 1858.

De Mille also had social interests in Saint John, in addition to his business. In 1857, he was involved with his father and Elisha in the establishment of the new Marsh Bridge Baptist Church (a daughter church of the Leinster Street Church with which it was subsequently amalgamated). The plan for this had been initiated in February, and at the second meeting of the organizing committee, although neither James nor Elisha was present, the record of the proceedings names both of them among the church members who had arranged to receive letters of dismissal from other Baptist churches (Elisha from Amherst and James from the Brussels Street Church in Saint John). Elisha was called to be pastor of the new church, and James was appointed clerk. Later, when Nathan De Mill and the other members of his family transferred their memberships to the Marsh Bridge Church, Nathan became one of its trustees and one of its first deacons. James continued to act as clerk until sometime during the fall of 1858 (Prebble 75-80; G).

During 1857 and 1858, the Colonial Book Store seems to have prospered. In fact, by the fall of 1858 business must have been very good, for De Mille chose this time to marry his longtime fiancée, Elizabeth Anne Pryor. Annie, as she was always known among the family, was the third child and second daughter of the Reverend Dr. John Pryor, who was at this time pastor of the First Baptist Church in Cambridge, Massachusetts. She was born on 8 April 1834, in Wolfville,[13] during her father's term as president of Acadia College, of which he was one of the founders and supporters (Boggs 81; G).

MacMechan, who met her in later life, just after her husband's death, describes her as "handsome .... a lady evidently, dark eyes and hair, aquiline nose & strong chin" (H), and the only picture of her (p. 254) confirms this comment. De Mille had evidently met her during his years at Horton and Acadia, where they may have reached some understanding, although Burpee's claim that "he had become engaged to her while a student at Horton, her father being then head of the school" is certainly exaggerated, since it is hardly likely that either Dr. Pryor or Nathan De Mill would have permitted the engagement when both parties were still so young ("Biographical" 11; H).[14] Burpee also suggests that De Mille, "while at Brown ... frequently ran up to Cambridge" to visit Annie, her father having by that time become pastor of a Baptist church there ("Biographical" 11; H).[15] Although "frequently" is probably an exaggeration also, in view of the absences listed in De Mille's student records at Brown, some visiting may been possible. The marriage took place in Cambridge, in the First Baptist Church, on 26 November 1858,[16] and the couple returned to Saint John to live.

On their return, the opening of a "second branch" of the bookstore at the "opposite corner" by "J. De Mill, Prop." was announced in December (*Morning News* 24 Dec. 1858: 3), and De Mille himself registered as "a Merchant" to get his business license for this branch (Saint John, Register; H). In a letter to an unidentified correspondent, whom he addresses simply as Ralph, De Mille gives a brief glimpse of his life during this time:

> I hope you arrived safely in Wolfville. Allow me to suggest the propriety of the most strict attention to your health and a supply of Porter. Tom Pryor is back here again. Dr and Mrs Pryor have gone and I am going to try to get off to the States in a week — 10 d[ay]s or so. If you hear of a cow let me know. If you see Jim Fitch tell him to send me the names of the places where these people live whose notes he left. [Illegible name] bought 5 acres of land just back of mine from Robinson for £500[;] on surveying it he found only 4 acres. Road will be put through on the 15th this month. I'm getting the back lot fenced in.
>
> Annie encloses a letter here which she wants you to be particular & deliver your self. Please do so.
>
> I'm fitting up the attic of the store for Daguerreau Saloons & an upper room for an office. (B3)[17]

The mention of the Daguerreau Saloons suggests that De Mille was attempting to expand the business even further beyond books, stationery, and school supplies, now that the business seemed to be well established and he had a little more space. At the same time, his mention of the road being put through and "getting the back lot fenced in" makes it clear that he and Annie were not living over the store, and were probably outside the city itself. This possibility is strengthened by the fact that their first child, William Budd (named for his father's older brothers, William John and Elisha Budd) was born at Carleton (Raymond 61; H).[8] From the domestic point of view, therefore, 1859 seems on the whole to have been a good year for De Mille and his wife.

From the business point of view, however, things were beginning to go less well for De Mille. The continuing decline in the New Brunswick economy would obviously be a contributory factor, but De Mille had also been having problems with his own aptitude for a life in commerce and problems with his partner, Hazen Fillmore. Burpee says that De Mille was "utterly unsuited to such an occupation. It exasperated him to be interrupted in something he was writing in the back office, to attend to the wants of a customer in the shop," and that his partner was "uncongenial and, perhaps, dishonest" ("Biographical" 11; H). Separately, these three problems might have been coped with; together they threatened to overwhelm him.

De Mille's solution to his problems with the business was to dissolve the partnership by buying Fillmore out and to try to carry on the business alone. The dissolution took place early in 1859, and the *Morning News* advertisement of the stock for both branches of the Colonial Book Store in January lists only J. De Mill as "Prop" (14 Jan. 1859: 3). It was an expensive solution, and, according to Burpee, was carried out "at a ruinous figure" that left De Mille with considerable debts ("Biographical" 11; H). It was effected, moreover, at the very time he was also facing the added expenses of a child in the house. De Mille's financial position continued to worsen, and in the previously quoted letter to Alfred at Horton, De Mille admits not only that he is hard up, but that he "had to squeeze from Father for money for my wretched business," and adds, bitterly but almost certainly not seriously, "I wish I was a farmer in New Zealand" (19 May 1860; B3).[19] His creditors were becoming insistent: on 7 June 1860, for example, a judgement was handed down against him in the Supreme Court of New Brunswick for nonpayment of a debt of £174.16.1 to a certain Oliver Wilson,

Acadia, First College Hall

"et al," although the satisfaction and discharge of the debt was not recorded until 3 October 1872 (Saint John County [Property], 1854–63; H).[20] Moreover, in addition to being expensive, dissolving the partnership was only a partial solution, since it did not help De Mille to deal with his dislike for bookselling. If anything, it must have made things worse, for it threw the whole burden of operating the two stores upon De Mille alone and increased the rate of interruptions to his writing.

The real solution eventually came, however, from an unexpected direction, and very soon after De Mille's explosion of feeling in his letter to Alfred. It came in the form of an offer of the chair of classics at Acadia College. To De Mille, whether or not he had ever considered an academic career, it must have seemed ideal.

Acadia's offer came as the result of the resignation of the previous incumbent of the post, Professor A.W. Sawyer, who had been appointed to the chair in 1855 and submitted his resignation in June of 1860. The board of governors immediately set up a committee to "make enquiries in reference to a new professor" (Acadia, Board, 18 June 1860; H). The committee reported at the meeting of 3 July 1860 that "they had been in communication with James De Mill Esq of Saint John, NB, a Master of Arts of Brown University, who had expressed himself as willing to come but whose engagements were such that he could not leave within a year" (Acadia, Board, 3 July 1860; H). The "engagements" referred to would be the Colonial Book Store, for which De Mille would have to find a buyer, a task that might take considerable time, in view of its debt-encumbered state and the general economic situation in Saint John. Neither the committee nor the board, however, raised any objections to the delay, and in the course of the same meeting they voted that

> the report be adopted and that this Board extend an invitation to James De Mill Esq. A.M. of Saint John NB to the professorship in the classical department of Acadia College (vacant by the resignation of Rev. A. W. Sawyer) at a salary of £200 per an[num], granting him at the same time such leave of absence not exceeding a year from the first of September next [1860] as he may require — the payment of the salary to commence from the time he assumes the duties of the professorship. (Acadia, Board, 3 July 1860; H)[21]

The offer of leave of absence was more than generous, and the salary compared favourably with the £250 per annum which had been Sawyer's

(Acadia, Board, 12 Oct. 1859; H), considering Sawyer's seniority and teaching experience. Both sides of the agreement clearly felt that it was a good one.

In Saint John, De Mille set about finding a purchaser for the bookstores. Apparently, the premises had been leased, so that if he could sell the stock, he did not also have to find a buyer for the premises, but needed only to arrange for the transfer of the lease to the buyer. Perhaps this explains why he was able to find a buyer well within the 12 months of his leave of absence. In a notice dated 1 February 1861, he was able to announce the transfer of the Colonial Book Store to a new owner:

> The Subscriber has disposed of the Stock and good will of the Colonial Book Store to Mr. Thomas H. Hall, who will henceforth conduct the Business of that Establishment. With thanks for past favors, he begs leave to recommend his successor to the patronage formerly bestowed upon himself. (*Morning News* 6 Feb. 1861: 3).[22]

It is possible that the inclusion in the terms of the sale of "good will," which was as important then as it is now, having a cash value in the sale of businesses, indicates that the Colonial Book Store was not quite the total financial disaster that Burpee and other writers on De Mille have implied.

Having disposed of his burden, De Mille then turned to the completion of another project with which he had just become involved, although never openly. The project was the *Christian Watchman*, a new Baptist weekly newspaper that had been founded in Saint John in protest against what had been happening in the *Christian Visitor*. The problem, as set out in the leader of the first issue of the *Christian Watchman*, was that the *Visitor* had become not the "organ of the denomination in this province" that it had been intended to be originally (*Christian Visitor* 20 Oct. 1847: 2), but "private property" that "supplied the wants and represented the feelings of an individual rather than those of the Baptists of New Brunswick" (*Christian Watchman* 2 Jan. 1861: 2).[23] The proprietor of record, so to speak, at the founding of the *Watchman* was George W. Day, who also owned the Saint John *Morning News*. It is probable, however, that there was an organizing committee behind him, similar to the one that had originally made the decision to publish the *Visitor* in competition with the *Messenger* (which was published in Halifax), for in April, the *Watchman* announced that the paper had been purchased from Day and had become "the property of a Committee," called in the paper, "The 'Watchman' Committee" (10 Apr. 1861: 2). Nathan De Mill was a member of this committee, as he had been a member of the original committee of the *Visitor*.

The editor of the *Christian Watchman* was announced as the Reverend E.B. De Mill. Since 1857, Elisha had been the pastor of the Marsh Bridge Church, enlarging its membership and encouraging the building of the new church on Leinster Street. In October 1860, he had become seriously ill, and was granted a year's leave of absence (Prebble 78; G). By the end of 1860, however, he had recovered enough to be able to take on the rather less demanding work involved in putting out the weekly paper, presumably with the assurance that he would have, for at least part of the following year, the assistance of his brother. Certainly, a careful examination of the newspaper shows that James, although his name appears only two or three times in the 52 issues and never in a context that might suggest editorial responsibility of any kind, was doing a great deal of the donkeywork of filling the pages.

The *Christian Watchman* is a very good example of the small, interest-group newspaper of the period. It was published weekly, on Wednesday, as a tabloid-size paper of four pages. Normally, the front page was taken up by various articles (James's "Recollections of Rome," for example, and "Letters to a Young Minister," probably by Elisha). Page two was the editorial page, but it also carried the news of the denomination in the Maritimes, with correspondence and reports from individual churches (for example, a letter with the pen name "Horton," actually one of the Crawley brothers, who was a missionary in Burma, appeared on this page). Page three consisted of local and general news (including shipping movements), and advertisements for local stores. Page four carried, in addition to more advertising, poetry and fiction. The articles, fiction, and usually the verse were anonymous in the sense that they appeared either without any form of identification at all, or with identification consisting of initials or obvious pseudonyms. The paper ran from the beginning of 1861 to the end, producing 52 issues, and ceasing publication when Elisha's health returned to a level that enabled him to resume the pastorate of the Marsh Bridge Church.

De Mille's contributions to the *Christian Watchman* are numerous and varied. The full list of them, however, may never be known because of the practice of printing contributions anonymously.[24] The extent of his contribution to an issue was always substantial: to one, for example, in the form

Elisha Budd De Mill

of "Recollections of Rome, [XXI]. 'The Basilica of St. Peter's,' " "Hebrew Poetry, No. III. 'Its Growth — Variety — Form, and Use,' " and "Acadia College," he contributed approximately 4,000 words (11 Dec. 1861: 1–2). Moreover, although he did not always reach such an impressive word count, there is, during the entire year, only one issue (23 Oct.) in which there is nothing that can be identified as his. His contributions continue right up to the last issue, and it is possible that at least some of them had been written in advance to avoid too much extra work during his first term at Acadia.

It is not possible at this late date, particularly for anyone not a member of the denomination, to decide how well the *Christian Watchman* fulfilled its expressed mandate of supplying the wants and representing the feelings of New Brunswick Baptists from a religious point of view. In his farewell editorial, Elisha explains that "Providence has seen fit to restore us to such a state of health as permits us again to work in our chosen sphere. Of course we could not fill at once the pulpit and the editorial chair, and hence must vacate the latter," and he expresses the opinion that the circumstances responsible for the starting up of the *Watchman* now no longer threaten the denomination (26 Dec. 1861; 2). Since the paper ceased publication in an orderly fashion with his return to the pastorate, and no attempt was made to continue it with another editor, presumably other members of the church concurred with him.

From a secular point of view, the paper can be seen as a production of two bright, well-educated minds, with a keen sense of responsibility for their church, focusing on travel, literature, education, and religious affairs. It may well have had considerable appeal to the more educated members of the denomination. But for the less well educated majority, the editorials (whether by James or Elisha) on Poland and Hungary might well look pallid beside Bill's rousing diatribes in the *Christian Visitor* — for example, the one in which he denounces the government's failure to close the grogshops during the cholera epidemic.[25] Moreover, the more general sections of the *Watchman*, although including reports on European politics and the American Civil War, and travel articles, exclude anything like those of the *Visitor*'s offerings (at least in its earlier years) which were calculated to appeal to rural and women's interests. The *Visitor*, unlike the *Watchman*, carried columns on crop and stock care, as well as recipes and hints on housekeeping and childcare. In mundane matters and simply as a newspaper, in fact, the *Watchman* was never a serious competitor to the *Visitor*.

In the summer of 1861, De Mille took up his post at Acadia. His inaugural address was delivered at the Acadia College Anniversary, on Friday, 7 June, according to the report on the proceedings carried by the *Christian Watchman* (4 Sept. 1861: 1).[26] With the address, he made an immediate and favourable impression on the students, as well as on his colleagues. Herbert Creed, in a letter of 12 February 1890 to Archibald MacMechan, describes it as "One of the best addresses I have ever heard; the language clear, forcible, smooth; the delivery faultless," and adds "we were all charmed with him" (MacMechan; H). It is probable that De Mille had already moved from Saint John to Wolfville at the time of the anniversary, for the board's report to the convention of the Eastern New Brunswick Baptist Association in August includes among the items of report the information that "Mr De Mill has removed to Wolfville, and will be prepared to enter upon his duties at the commencement of the ensuing term" (*Christian Watchman* 4 Sept. 1861: 1), as indeed he and the other new faculty member, D.F. Higgins (professor of mathematics) did on "the 2nd day of September last" (Acadia, Board, 29 Oct. 1861; H). De Mille himself attended the convention and addressed the members on the subject of education.[27]

The recollections of people who knew De Mille at Acadia provide a vivid portrait of him. A number of these people recorded their memories in letters to Archibald MacMechan, who added the letters to his research notes. These recollections portray a much more confident personality than do the letters to Alfred from James, the worried businessman, during the operation of the bookstore. Writing Archibald MacMechan, D.M. Steele recalls his first impression of De Mille:

> When I returned to College in the autumn of that year — I remember seeing the new professor for the first time, walking on the main street of Wolfville. "Notable man" I said to myself, as I noticed his air & bearing. Tall, keen-eyed, or that keenness that appears from glasses: He always wore them, indoors and out, when reading, and in conversation; and was more terrible looking to the freshman by reason of their glinting and flashing. (MacMechan; H)

Herbert Creed adds to this description "that peculiar sarcastic smile of his" (MacMechan; H). Steele's account, perhaps deliberately, gives the impression that the impact of De Mille's physical presence reinforced the impact of his intellectual presence, for he says that De Mille "had the appearance of a Greek. He talked like a Greek — and I used to think — thought like a Greek" (MacMechan; H). This impression is supported by William Elder, for whom De Mille "seemed rather like some noble Roman of the literary type in the age of Augustus than a practical modern" (MacMechan; H). These descriptions of him, however, although coloured by the classical associations of the subjects he was teaching, are in accord with the portrait that has survived and seems to have been taken shortly after his arrival at Dalhousie College.

Opinions of De Mille's teaching methods are mixed. In his letter, Creed also describes De Mille as "an excellent teacher," and this is confirmed by Elder, himself a instructor at Colby College in Maine:

> He possessed the two-fold excellence which, rightly proportioned, forms the method of the true educator, always and everywhere, — power to do, and skill to secure the right amount and the right kind of labor. He inspired his pupils with a willingness to work to the full of their ability, while by judicious criticism and well-timed suggestion, he made the study on which they were engaged an introduction to the broader field of literature of which it formed a part. (MacMechan; H)

Steele makes it clear in his letter, however, that the students found him a demanding teacher:

> Prof de Mille insisted on a certain amount of what seemed to the students of those days unmitigated drudgery. He used to place long strips of English on the blackboard to be turned into Latin, or into Greek. This was a new thing thirty years ago, and not having had the preliminary drill we found it very difficult. (MacMechan; H)

His innovations startled them: "the professor's theory was alarming, viz., to be able to turn an ordinary newspaper article into classical Greek or Latin." Steele also voices the reservation that "he seized the literary minds in a class, and gave them an impetus, which did not fail them; but the others, he did not spend so much energy upon, giving them their lesson, fairly enough; but not encouraging them much, not coaxing them" (MacMechan; H). On the other hand, Elder emphasizes his considerable helpfulness to those who wanted to study:

He would willingly devote an hour a day to meet even a single student who was prepared to undertake study outside the regular course. Many others besides myself will remember that this was done so generously that we almost seemed to be conferring a favor by laying this extra tax on him. (MacMechan; H)

Even Steele concedes that outside the classroom De Mille's generosity and approachability were remarkable. The students took to "dropping in" on De Mille for "informal 'teas' . . . a good cup of tea, hot rolls, jams, and those little dainties not provided in our regular commons," and De Mille "laughed, joked, and made fun generally so that we forgot the 'grind' and were relieved of the pressure; the monotone was broken, and we went back to our den with lighter faces" (MacMechan; H). Such informality had not characterized De Mille's student days at Brown, and it is possible that, remembering those days, he was making a conscious effort from his position of authority to see that his students were treated less stiffly.

But alongside this professional geniality is a hint of a private contempt. Steele recalls, perhaps out of personal experience, De Mille's sharp tongue: "His fine satire so delicate that, like a blade of keenest edge, it cut into a fellow so deftly, that he hardly knew it, until he felt the blood trickling down" (MacMechan; H). Creed is more penetrating in his observations:

> In private intercourse — and I frequently spent pleasant evenings at his home in Wolfville — he was always genial and agreeable. In his conversation there was usually a tinge of the satirical. While he was doubtless a sincere Christian, and occasionally occupied the pulpit very acceptably, he took delight in ridiculing everything like cant, and even the ordinary words and actions of the 'pious' sort of people often brought to his keen eye and thin curling lip that peculiar sarcastic smile of his. (MacMechan; H)

This comment is the first suggestion of an ambivalence in De Mille's personality that his dual life as writer and academic necessitated, although quite how much of his life was that of writer during this period is difficult to determine (this question will be discussed further in chapter 7). The use of the term "satiric" in these two accounts by his former students suggests an awareness on their part of the latent social critic in De Mille's personality.

But there was no ambivalence in his attitude to the classical studies he taught. His inaugural address had been on the continuing importance of a classical education in an increasingly scientific age. This attitude was also emphasized in discussions with students, according to Steele, and was supported by the introduction, although not necessarily on De Mille's initiative, of the system of honours classes in which "those who wished could read as much as they could master" (MacMechan; H). It was a curiously conservative position for someone whose teaching methods were so innovative and whose own education had included so much science. It was also curiously at odds with the recent introduction at Acadia, in 1859, of "a course without the Classics" for candidates for the ministry (Longley 76; G).

Domestically, during these years, his life seems with few exceptions to have run fairly smoothly. Two of the exceptions, however, must have caused him severe distress. The first of these was the death of his brother Elisha, on 1 August 1863 (Prebble 79; G), which deprived him of his closest friend. Coming so soon, too, after Elisha's apparent restoration to health at the end of 1861, and his remarriage, to Elizabeth Seely, in 1862 (Saint John, Marriage, vol. F. 288; H),[28] its impact must have been much harder to bear. The second cause of distress was the death of his father in 1864. According to Burpee, the relationship between Nathan and his children had not always been warm, but James had been "devoted" to his father and "was one of the very few who understood him, and knew the real kindliness that lay underneath that stern and dour exterior" ("Biographical" 2a; H). The terms of Nathan's will, dated 14 December 1864, two weeks before his death on 26 December, nevertheless, reveal nothing of this relationship. In it, Nathan seems to ignore his eldest surviving son completely, without even a token remembrance:

> I have not given my sons James and Alfred B. [sic] any share in my Estate as I consider that a sufficient sum has been expended by me in their education and otherwise to be equal to the shares of my other children in my estate but it is my wish and desire that until such distribution my son Alfred B. [sic] may if he thinks proper reside in my dwelling house with the rest of the family contributing his share with the others of the necessary expenses of provisions and attendance. (Saint John County, Probate, vol. K. 337–41; H)

From a purely practical point of view this decision makes perfect sense: the younger, still dependent, children had to be provided for until they could

Frederick, Eliza, Emily, and Alice in the grounds of the house on the Bay Shore

provide for themselves, whereas James was by this time completely independent. Nathan was by temperament unsentimental, and he clearly felt he had done his duty by James in educating him to that level of independence. There is nothing to suggest that James did not understand his father's action. If Burpee is correct about the relationship between the two, then James would have been very grieved at the loss of his father. He did, however, have the consolation of his own family: Willie, as William Budd was always known in the family, was growing rapidly, and by the beginning of 1864, Annie was expecting a second child.²⁹

Professionally, De Mille's life at Acadia was going very well. His work was apparently satisfying to him, as far as his students could tell from the enjoyment he displayed in his classes. Moreover, it was apparently also satisfactory to the Acadia Board of Governors, for in 1863 he was voted a raise in salary to "$1000 per ann[um]" (Acadia, Board, 24 Aug. 1863). Liked by his students, and approved by his employers, he seemed set for a long stay in Wolfville and a lifetime of teaching classical languages and literature.

This scenario changed abruptly in August of 1865. At the meeting of the board of governors on 19 August 1865, "The Secretary presented the resignation of James de Mill Esq of his position as classical professor in Acadia College. Voted that it be accepted" (H).³⁰ It was, as it almost had to be, accepted at once by the board. Immediately, long before the effective date of his new appointment, De Mille had packed up and moved to begin his work as professor of rhetoric and history at Dalhousie College in Halifax.

NOTES

1 "Faith, Hope, and Love" was annotated "for the *Christian Visitor*," which is an indication that it was an original contribution to the paper in which it appeared, not reprinted from somewhere else, and it was signed "Aleph." In the pages of the *Christian Watchman*, the pen name "Aleph" was attached to "The Powers of Conscience Illustrated," a short piece on *Macbeth* (*Christian Watchman* 18 Dec. 1861: 4). For a list of possible contributions by De Mille to the *Christian Visitor*, see appendix B; for a list of possible contributions to the *Christian Watchman*, see appendix A.

2 "Encourage Your Minister" ran for 13 instalments, beginning in the issue for 3 January 1855 and ending in the issue for 18 April 1855, and was usually signed "Amicus" (see appendix B).

3 The Reverend John Francis, who was appointed by the Eastern Baptist Association to visit pastors around the region and to solicit funds on behalf of the church, reported regularly to church members in letters to the *Visitor*.

4 Francis continues:

> She left for Parsboro' on Monday last, accompanied by her mother and sister and Dr. Tupper. Bro. Demill remained a few hours to arrange his affairs, and then left also, overtaking the family [that] same evening. Mrs D. sustained the journey to Parsboro' better than could be expected, since which we have not heard from them. (*Christian Visitor* 20 June 1855: 99)

5 The information is actually given in a copy of a published statement by the board, dated 19 July 1855, that has been clipped from the *Christian Visitor* (where it appeared on pages 1 and 2 on 25 July 1855), and pasted into the minute book.

6 In spite of its title, the information in *William's Cincinnati Directory, City Guide and Business Mirror: Or, Cincinnati in 1856* is for 1855, since De Mille was back in Saint John at the beginning of 1856.

7 In another letter, written on 21 March 1856 to Dr. Pryor, Crawley writes, "We all continue quite well. Eliz[abeth] sends her love to you & 'Aunt Elizabeth': as well as to Annie & Jam[es] but is as lazy about writing as ever," and in the same letter he is still talking of setting up the ladies seminary, "Mt Auburn Young Ladies Institute," and asking for "prospectusses [sic] of female schools" to be sent to him, so that it is clearly not yet established (Crawley; H). Moreover, as late as June of that year, the *Christian Visitor* reports that

> the following notice of Dr. Crawley appears in the New York *Examiner*: — "A New Female Seminary is about to be established on Mt. Auburn, Cincinnati. Twenty thousand dollars have been pledged for the purpose by eight members of the new church in that locality. Dr. Crawley, recently from Nova Scotia, is to be Principal of the Seminary and pastor of the Church." (11 June 1856: 94).

8 "Another new ship, called the *Favourite*, measuring 787 tons, N.M., and 846 tons, O.M., was recently towed into this port from Hopewell, where she was built by Mr Nathan Bennett for Mr N. S. Demill of this city. / Another new ship, called the *Melicite*, measuring 1147 tons, N.M., was recently towed to this port from Hopewell, she was also built by Mr Bennett, for Mr Demill" (*Morning News* 29 Nov. 1854: 3).

9 Having a note dishonoured was the equivalent of having a cheque returned for lack of funds to cover it, or failing to make the payments on a loan. De Mille is very casual about punctuation in his correspondence, and I have inserted apostrophes and full stops, here and elsewhere, and have expanded some less obvious abbreviations.

10 Elizabeth De Mill's letter to Alfred is dated 15 September, but the year is lacking (although it is probably 1859).

11 Later, "person" is corrected to "Pastor" (*Christian Visitor* 20 May 1857: 83).

12 According to other advertisements in the pages of the *Morning News*, De Mille and Fillmore's Colonial Book Store was competing against Henry S. Beek's "New Book and Stationery Store" at 83 King Street (1 May 1857: 4), against W.K. Crawford at 38 King Street (5 May 1857: 2), and against the Phoenix Book Store of J. and A. McMillan (5 May 1857: 2).

13 Annie's birthdate is shown as 1834 on the death certificate that was issued by the California State Board of Health Bureau of Vital Statistics. At the time of her death in 1910, she had been living for some years with her son, Alban Bertram De Mille, and his family, during the years Alban was teaching at Belmont College. Annie's birthplace is given as Wolfville by Raymond (61; H).

14 Burpee is confusing Horton Academy with Acadia College in this remark, possibly because both were located in Horton (the town was only later renamed Wolfville), and in earlier days Horton seems to have been used indifferently to refer to the town, the college, and the academy.

15 Burpee says "a Baptist church in Lexington," but he is confusing this first pastorate in Massachusetts with Pryor's later one (in the 1870s).

16 "At Old Cambridge, Boston, on the 26th ult., by the Rev. J. Pryor, D.D., James DeMill, Esq., of St. John, N.B., Elizabeth A.A. Pryor, daughter of the officiating clergyman" (*Christian Messenger* 15 Dec. 1858: 395).

17 The letter is undated, but was most probably written between De Mille's marriage to Annie and the birth of the couple's first child, who is not mentioned. Tom Pryor was one of Annie's brothers.

18 Raymond gives the date as 25 December 1860. This is contradicted by the baptismal record at St. Luke's Church, Halifax (H), which gives 24 December 1859, and was presumably supplied to the officiating clergyman by De Mille and Annie. A birthdate in 1860, however, agrees better with his age as supplied on the census records for 1871 and 1881 (census H), than one in 1859.

19 A "New Zealand Emigration Company" was being widely advertised in the Saint John papers during the late 1850s (see, for example, *Morning News* 5 May 1857: 4).

20 This record contradicts Annie's statement to MacMechan that De Mille "had paid off all his debt before they moved to Halifax in 1865" (MacMechan; H).

21 At this meeting, the same committee was instructed "in the meantime to secure the services of a Tutor at a Salary not exceeding £100 per an[num]," and Brenton Eaton was engaged at that maximum figure. Several years later, Eaton was to become involved in Dr. Pryor's confrontation with the Granville Street Baptist Church in Halifax. Currency became metric in 1860, on the advice of a committee of the legislature, which recommended that "a pound shall represent 4 dollars" (Tilley; H). De Mille's starting salary was, therefore, $800.

22 The accompanying notice by the new owner is phrased in a way that suggests that he was satisfied with what he was getting:

The Subscriber having purchased the Business of the Colonial Book Store, begs leave to give notice that he will conduct that Establishment henceforth, where he will keep constantly on hand every variety of Books and Stationary, both English and American. It is his intention to spare no efforts to satisfy the wants of the public in his department. He hopes that he will receive a continuance of the patronage so liberally bestowed on his predecessor. (*Morning News* 6 Feb. 1861: 3)

23 The individual concerned must have been the Reverend I. E. Bill himself. Subsequently, either Elisha or James also incautiously implied, in a piece in the fifth issue of the *Christian Watchman*, that Bill had not lived up to the terms of his agreement with the Baptist Association in New Brunswick when he took over the *Christian Visitor*, and the dispute that arose from this comment had to be resolved by the annual convention through a committee of enquiry.

24 For a list of De Mille's contributions, so far as they can be determined, see appendix A.

25 Bill never resorted to understatement:

Did his Excellency tell the Board of Health in his "practical advice respecting precautionary measures" that *Intoxicating Liquor Shops* were all just so many hot beds of Cholera, and that as such the Public health demanded that they should be closed and closed forever? . . . What awful disclosures have been made of the power of the intoxicating bowl to produce Cholera, since the breaking out of disease in this City. — Poor inebriates have gone into the dram shops of the City, yes, and licensed Portland also, drank to excess — came out staggering drunk — in a short time seized with Cholera — and in a few short hours hurried to the bar of God, overwhelmed with the guilt of drunkenness. This we regret to say is as true of women as well as men, and another startling fact has come out as with the brightness of a sunbeam, and that is this: The road to death and to perdition is just as short from a *licensed* as an unlicensed dram shop. Let it be written in large capitals of living light on the door posts of everyone of these licensed and unlicensed shops of ruin: CHOLERA PRODUCED HERE, — DEATH AND DAMNATION SOLD HERE. . . . Temperance men, the Providence of God tells you in tones of thunder to sustain the principle of prohibition, and if you fail to do it you are recreant to the cause that bears upon it the stamp of divine approval. Go and wash all the streets of this City — go and remove every particle of filth — go and sprinkle every back place with the Chloride of lime — go and build your hospitals for the dead and for the dying, and leave these rum nuisances untouched, and what have you done? You have left a source of Cholera in our midst that is a hundred fold more prolific of this terrible scourge than all other causes combined. So long as these exist there is a worm at the root of all physical, commercial, social, intellectual, moral and religious health and prosperity. We say, in the name of bleeding, trampled down humanity, close them up — in the name of starving orphans and weeping widows, close them up — and in the prospect of the fearful retributions of the last day, close them now, and forever. (*Christian Visitor* 4 Aug 1854: 652)

The rhetoric of such polemical pieces may well have contributed to the distaste for religious enthusiasm that at least one student, Herbert Creed, recognized in De Mille as early as his first term as a faculty member at Acadia (MacMechan; H).

26 The address itself had already been published in the issue following the anniversary (12 June 1861: 1–2).

27 Some of what he said (it is not clear whether or not he made a formal address) was reported in the *Christian Messenger*:

When we entered the meeting, Professor De Mill was speaking on the importance of teachers being pious men. Heaven was the highest object of all education. The teacher should be able to look through the future into eternity, for the completion of his work. . . . He spoke of the present being but the beginning of operations and hoped before many years had expired to see a large increase in the staff of teachers and the number of students. (4 Sept 1861: 282)

28 The marriage certificate is dated 10 December 1862, but the place is not given, although presumably it would be in Saint John, since it is recorded in the Saint John registers, and almost certainly in the church of which Elisha was the pastor.

29 Louise's baptismal record gives 1864 for her birthdate, but Raymond's date of 1865 is the one that agrees with Louise's age as given in the census records of 1871 and 1881 (census H), and on her burial certificate (Camp Hill, Register 1844–78; H).

30 The suddenness of the resignation is underlined in the *Christian Messenger*'s coverage of the report of the board of governors to the convention of the Baptist Association:

In addition to these ordinary contents of the Report, it stated that three days previous to the Convention, Professor De Mill had sent in his resignation. The notice had been so sudden and unexpected, that the Governors could only at present assure the Convention that every effort would immediately be made to secure the services of an adequate successor, so as to keep the College up to its present standard of efficiency. (30 Aug. 1865: 274)

CHAPTER 5

At Dalhousie College, 1865-80

With his move to Halifax, De Mille entered the final phase of his life. He was now established in a professional career: he was an academic, moving from one college to another. Nevertheless, the precise reasons that prompted the decision to exchange Wolfville for Halifax, Acadia for Dalhousie, are impossible to determine. Certainly, he may have felt that he would be more at home in a large coastal city comparable in many ways to the one he grew up in than in a small inland town, but he can hardly have believed, in 1865, that Dalhousie College, with its sorry history up to that point, was a substantial improvement over Acadia.

It is not surprising that De Mille should have been attracted to the idea of living in Halifax, for in the late nineteenth century the city had much to recommend it in many ways. In her portrait of the city, *Glimpses of Halifax, 1867–1900*, Phyllis Blakeley, citing the *Acadian Recorder*, points out that "Haligonians were proud of the appearance of their city 'as one of the cleanest, best-drained, and most handsomely-situated dominions in the Queen's British North American possessions' " (6; G). Halifax then was considerably smaller than it is today, bounded by the waterfront and Citadel Hill to east and west, and by North Street and South Street in the other directions, with only country lanes and isolated houses across the rest of the peninsula. In addition to its importance as a commercial centre for imports of all sorts (molasses, coffee, rum, salt, and fruit from the West Indies, fish and agricultural produce from Cape Breton, and manufactured goods from England), it was an industrial centre for the production of many other items (small local factories produced "furniture, pianos, clothing, boots and shoes, hats and caps, rope, gunpowder, paper, skates, railway scabbards and ties, spikes, nails, tools, paint, steam engines and machinery, tobacco, biscuits, wooden ware, brooms, brushes, soap and candles" ([Blakeley 30; G]). Local produce and fish were offered for sale at the Green Market and the Fish Market respectively. Economic prosperity allowed the city to provide many amenities for its citizens, such as the City and Provincial Hospital, the Poor Asylum, and, in due course, railway and telephone services, gaslighting for the streets, and regular and efficient policing. But its bustle and liveliness were not due to trade alone: Halifax was the foremost military garrison and naval dockyard of the British presence in North America, and the officers and men of the services stationed there contributed in many ways to the liveliness of the social life of the city. Halifax felt itself to be a centre of culture, too, for it could point to cultural events in the form of regular visits of lecturers such as William Jennings Bryan, Henry Ward Beecher, and General William Booth of the Salvation Army, of frequent theatrical productions by professional touring companies in its two theatres, and of the public library, opened in 1873. There were handsome buildings, such as Government House, Province House, and the Courthouse, and parks, such as the Public Gardens and Point Pleasant. There were churches, too, in abundance, and many schools, the Halifax Grammar School among them, besides Dalhousie College. If the citizens of Halifax were proud, it was because they had much to be proud of in their city.

Dalhousie College itself had originally been founded in 1818 by the Lieutenant-Governor of Nova Scotia, Lord Dalhousie. According to David Allison's *History of Nova Scotia*, Lord Dalhousie decided that a "seminary for the higher branches of education was much wanted in Halifax" and determined to fill the vacancy with a "non-sectarian" foundation, from which "no one should be excluded . . . by reason of his religious tenets or affiliations" (Allison 2: 839; G). The plan was straightforward, and was in keeping with his Scottish respect for education, but perhaps Lord Dalhousie should have remembered, in the words of his national poet Robert Burns,

Dalhousie College, the original building, from a watercolour by John F. Woolford

AT DALHOUSIE COLLEGE, 1865-80

that "The best-laid schemes o' mice an' men / Gang aft a-gley" (62; G). For as D.C. Harvey, echoing Joseph Howe's 1843 condemnation of the situation as "a monument of folly,"[1] pointed out in his *Introduction to the History of Dalhousie University*,

> Dalhousie College was an idea prematurely born into an alien and unfriendly world, deserted by its parents, betrayed by its guardians, and throughout its minority abused by its friends and enemies alike. Its history cannot be dissociated from the struggle of democracy against monopoly and privilege in church and state. (Harvey 9; G)

For, after a brisk and promising start — the cornerstone for the college building was laid by Lord Dalhousie and the structure quickly completed (Allison 2: 842; G) — the college was bedevilled by apathy on the part of the provincial authorities and by bitter wrangling among members of the various religious denominations.[2] In 1863, after 40 years of such treatment, the college was in danger of going out of existence. In April of that year, however, it was rescued and reorganized by the passing of "An Act Respecting Dalhousie College" in the provincial legislature. The act gave the college a new lease on life:

> Under the provisions of this Act the College was re-opened in the autumn of 1863 with a staff of six professors. Of these, the governors had selected Dr. William Lyall of the University of Glasgow, for the chair of Logic and Metaphysics; Dr. George Lawson of Toronto, for that of Chemistry; and John Johnson, M.A., for that of Classics; the Presbyterian church of the Lower Provinces nominated Rev. James Ross, D.D., for the chair of Ethics; and Thomas McCulloch, a son of the former president, for that of Natural Philosophy; while the Church of Scotland nominated Charles Macdonald, M.A. of the University of Aberdeen, for that of Mathematics. . . . To Dr. Ross . . . was assigned the presidency and this position he held for a period of twenty-two years, until in 1885 failing health compelled him to retire." (Allison 2; 839–40; G)

The distribution of the right to appoint professors to the college had been worked out very carefully in order to satisfy all interested parties, and it seemed to be working very well. In particular, the appointment of Professor

Ross as president was an outstandingly fortunate one,[3] for not all Dalhousie's problems were solved by the reorganization, and under Ross's leadership, many of the remaining ones were skilfully handled.

The reorganized college functioned smoothly with this same faculty for almost two years, until early in 1865 the sudden and untimely death of Professor McCulloch created a vacancy. In February of 1865, the board of governors of the college met to consider the problem. After discussion, it was "Resolved that Messrs McKinley[,] Grant & Robson be a committee to arrange with United Presbyterians relative to appointment of a new Professor thereto" (Dalhousie, Board Minutes, 28 Feb. 1865; H). The discussion with the Presbyterians was required because under the terms of the 1863 act, since McCulloch had been nominated by the Presbyterians, they were entitled to nominate his successor. Four months later, thanks to the tact of the board's committee and the generosity and courtesy of the Presbyterian synod, the result was an arrangement under which "the patronage of [McCulloch's] chair [of natural philosophy] be commuted for the Chair of Mental Philosophy and Metaphysics now filled by the Revd. Professor Lyall," which in turn would "enable the Governors to offer the vacant chair for competition" (Dalhousie, Board Minutes, 1 July 1865; H). In essence, this meant that the synod now had the right of appointment to the chair of mental philosophy (which encompassed logic, aesthetics, and psychology), rather than to that of natural philosophy (which covered mathematical and experimental physics), but that it agreed in these special circumstances to continue with the present holder, Professor William Lyall, who was originally the board's nominee. Lyall, therefore, continued teach what he had previously taught.[4] The new arrangement left the chair of natural philosophy vacant and in the appointment of the governors, who immediately advertised a vacant position on the faculty, but did not, for some unfathomable reason, specify in the advertisement that they required someone to teach natural philosophy.

De Mille at once applied for this position. He must have been in an advantageous position to do so, for the four months of negotiations following McCulloch's death cannot have been kept confidential in a busy and close-knit community such as Halifax. Moreover, De Mille's father-in-law, John Pryor, was the pastor of the Granville Street Baptist Church at the time, and was well placed to have information about the appointment since he had himself been offered the chair of classics during the reorganization in 1863, on the condition that he "give up his pastoral charge" of the

Granville Street Church (Dalhousie, Board Minutes, 17 Oct. 1863; H). He had not been able to agree to this condition, however, and the chair had been given to John Johnson (Dalhousie, Board Minutes, 19 Oct. 1863; H).[5] If Raymond is correct in saying that Louise's date of birth was July 1865, and that it took place in Halifax, presumably in Mrs. De Mille's parents home, De Mille may even have been in Halifax for at least part of the summer, since it is unlikely that Annie would have travelled from Wolfville without her husband in the later stages of her pregnancy (Raymond 61; H). De Mille's letter of application was, in fact, dated 2 July 1865 (the day following the board's decision to offer the vacancy for competition) and was sent from Chester. In it, De Mille said simply, "I hereby beg leave to make application for the Professorship now vacant in Dalhousie College," signing his name "James De Mill" without the final "e" (Dalhousie, Board Correspondence, 2 July 1865; H). The letter was read to the governors at their next meeting, and a committee of three, chaired by President Ross himself, was immediately set up "to enquire what new arrangement of the curriculum & of the branches taught by the present professors would be necessary in order to enable the Board to appoint Mr De Mill to a chair of Rhetoric & History" (Dalhousie Board Minutes, 14 July 1865; H). Professor Charles Macdonald, who taught mathematics and acted as Ross's assistant in the running of the college, was the second member of the committee,[6] and the third was Professor Lawson.[7] By the middle of August, the outcome of the enquiry was already sufficiently positive to allow (presumably) an informal offer to De Mille, who was then able to submit his resignation to the Acadia Board of Governors. On 11 September, the Dalhousie Board of Governors "unanimously Resolved that James De Mill be appointed to the Chair of Rhetoric and History — such appointment to take place from the 18th day of October next" (Dalhousie, Board Minutes, 11 Sept. 1865). No salary was mentioned, but in the absence of any record of change since the Board's initial determination of salaries for the chairs of classics and mathematics during the reorganization in 1863, it would hardly be less than what was offered then: £300 (or $1,200) a year.[8]

The effects of rearranging the curriculum to accommodate De Mille's position had to be considered carefully because of the tight structure of the degree programme. During the college reorganization, the curriculum for the four-year B.A. programme was also redesigned and set out in the *Statutes and Bye-Laws for the Regulation and Management of Dalhousie College*, published in 1864. In this revised version, the curriculum became demanding and inflexible. Each academic year was then, as now, divided into two terms, or sessions: the winter session ran from October to the first week of April (with a break of 10 days over Christmas), and the summer session ran from the second week of April to the end of June. The course of studies for the winter session of each year of a student's programme, except the fourth, was unvarying. In their first year, students were required to take classics (Latin and Greek), mathematics, and logic. In their second year, they continued with classics and mathematics, and took metaphysics and belles lettres in place of logic. In their third year, they continued with classics (Latin only) and mathematics, took natural philosophy and modern languages in place of metaphysics and belles lettres, and added psychology and elementary chemistry "on different days" (Dalhousie, *Statutes* 3; H). In their fourth year, they were required to take chemistry, modern languages, ethics and political economy and to choose between classics and mathematics. Since "attendance at the summer Session shall be optional," the programme for the summer session was a little more flexible:

> In the summer term classes will be opened for instruction in Classics, Mathematics, and the Modern Languages, and lectures will be given in such branches of science as may from time to time be thought most expedient, such as Classical and English Literature, Rhetoric, History, Botany, Geology, Mineralogy, &c. (Dalhousie, *Statutes* 3–4; H)

Even so, some constraints were necessary on what was offered because "undergraduates attending the summer Sessions [in addition to the winter sessions] shall be considered as having completed their course" (Dalhousie, *Statutes* 3; H). After De Mille's arrival, the students were expected to take rhetoric in their first year and history in their fourth year, in the winter session. Although the extremely strict arrangement of the curriculum, which Allison calls "Draconian" (Allison 2: 840; G) was unusual, the overall content was fairly standard for the period, closely resembling what De Mille had experienced previously — as a student at Brown and as a teacher at Acadia.

There was much in student life outside the classrooms, too, to remind De Mille of his days at Brown. Duncan Fraser of the class of '72, and hence one of De Mille's students (although he does not mention De Mille), describes student life during his years at Dalhousie in his "Reminiscences of 1872" in the *Dalhousie Gazette*. There was no student residence at the time, and the students boarded in Halifax homes:

> For the poorer lads, "lodging" was the usual method employed. A student paid so much a week for cooking, room and bed. He purchased the coal, light and food. In this way he could live as high, or he did live as cheaply as possible. Generally a number lodged together, each in turn for a week acting as purveyor. We had no "table d'hote," but exclusively partook of our meals alone. The several tastes of all were studied, though we all were agreed on such fundamentals as porridge, salt fish, corned beef, potatoes and "Scriven's" bread. . . though I remember on one or two occasions we indulged in a goose and a barrel of apples. (112–13; G)[9]

Fraser's account continues by touching on the way students worked and spent their free time. Away from the college building, they worked as well as ate in their own rooms: "After our meals our study was our own, and there we worked, disputed, assisted, and exercised our physical powers to our hearts' content." They helped each other with work, and loaned one another "a new necktie" or a "warm pair of gloves" for visits to a "best girl." These visits were one of the very few social occasions open to students, which were otherwise limited to "church twice each Sunday and Bible class in the [Sunday] afternoon," and, on weekdays, to "Y.M.C.A. lectures each month, and occasional visits to the strangers' gallery of the House of Assembly." Unlike De Mille and his contemporaries at Brown, Dalhousie students enjoyed the pleasure of sport on Saturday afternoons: "Football on the Common . . . we considered almost as binding as class attendance." Like the students at Brown, they also enjoyed the pleasure of debate: "Friday evening was always sacredly devoted to debate. Latterly we had a Senior and Junior Debating Society. The speaking was general; every student was expected to take part" (Fraser 114; G). Moreover, as well as sport, Dalhousie students had a student newspaper, which students at Brown had been without. The *Dalhousie Gazette*, which De Mille encouraged, was started independently by a small group of students in 1868–1869, and "in the following session . . . taken under the control of the students [as a whole], and . . . published by them as the college organ." In the "cap and gown," which had to be worn in the street, the small and slowly growing number of Dalhousie students was becoming a familiar sight in Halifax by the beginning of De Mille's time at the college (Fraser 115, 116; G).[10]

De Mille himself might well have been a familiar figure in Halifax during his career at Dalhousie, for the family always lived a considerable distance from the college building, and De Mille always had to walk as far as, if not further than, any of his students from his home to get there. He was not able, apparently, on his arrival in Halifax, to afford immediately to buy a house, and for the first 10 years the family lived in rented accommodation. Before the first publication of the the *Halifax City Directory* in 1869, the location of this rented accommodation is not officially recorded. But for at least a part of the time between 1865 and 1869, they were living on Le Marchant Street quite close to the modern campus of Dalhousie University, then one of the outlying areas of the city and almost rural in the sparseness of its occupancy. One of their neighbours there recalls: "When I was a child I lived in Le Marchant street in Halifax. There were only four houses on the street then. . . . and next door to us lived Prof. DeMille" (Hamilton; H).[11] By 1869, however, they had already moved to a house on South Park Street (*Halifax*; G). They continued to live there until 1874,[12] by which time De Mille and Annie had added two servants, Bella and Margaret Henderson, to their household (Census 1871; H),[13] and the three younger children had been born: Ethel Maud in 1872 (St. Luke's; H),[14] Alban Bertram in 1873 (Raymond 61; H),[15] and Frank Wilfred in 1874 (Raymond 61; H).[16] The family moved yet again, in 1874, this time to 41 Inglis Street (*Halifax*; G). In April of 1876, however, De Mille was in a position to buy a house. With the aid of a privately financed mortgage, he purchased at public auction the house at number 72 "on the west side of South Park Street" for the sum of $3,900 (Halifax County, Deeds; H). It was a large and handsome house (judging by its present appearance), and De Mille must have been pleased by its location in the south end of the city, the pleasures of which he wrote about in a letter to his brother Alfred: "I find it quite pleasant here now — we are not far from the Tower Woods [now Point Pleasant Park] and the Arm, go in swimming everyday, and go out boating" (B3).[17] The family was still living here at the time of De Mille's death in 1880.

De Mille was made warmly welcome on his arrival at Dalhousie. The effective date of his appointment, Monday, 18 October 1865, was the day of the official college opening. In those days, the opening was evidently a public occasion of some importance, for De Mille's arrival was mentioned in a report of the proceedings in the *Novascotian*, under the heading "Dalhousie College":

The Winter Session of this College was opened Wednesday at 11 o'clock a.m., in presence of a large number of visitors. . . . Professor De Mill, late of Acadia College, but recently appointed to a Chair in Dalhousie, was introduced by the Provincial Secretary. (*Novascotian* 23 Oct. 1865: 6)

The board of governors had earlier in the day been officially notified of De Mille's presence, when the principal formally reported to them that

> in consequence of the death of the late Professor McCulloch a change had been made in the classes & Professor DeMill elected to the Chair of Rhetoric and History. That the change thus made had added to the efficiency of the institution by enlarging the range of subjects its course embraced. (Dalhousie, Board Minutes, 18 Oct. 1865; H)

Most importantly, however, De Mille also attended the first senate meeting of his career, at which he was formally installed in his chair:

> This day the Senate of Dalhousie College met in the College Buildings, to open the Winter Session 1865–1866. . . . The Principal having opened the Meeting with prayer, the Inaugural address was delivered by Professor Macdonald; after which the Secretary to the Governors read the Minute of the appointment of James De Mill M.A. to the Chair of Rhetoric and History in this College. Professor De Mill was then welcomed as a Colleague by the Members of the Senate. (Dalhousie, Senate, 18 Oct. 1865; H).

Once formally introduced, De Mille began a closer acquaintance with the colleagues who had welcomed him, and with whom he was to work for the rest of his life. Together, De Mille and his colleagues, Ross, Macdonald, Lyall, Johnson, Lawson, and the newly appointed tutor in modern languages, James Liechti,[18] formed an extraordinarily talented group, which must have seemed to those concerned to offer some promise that Dalhousie's worst days of struggle were over.

De Mille fitted into Dalhousie very comfortably, both personally and professionally. His colleagues and students remembered him very well during the years immediately after his death, when Archibald MacMechan began to solicit their contributions to his proposed biography, and they contributed freely to the information gathering. In the notes MacMechan made from his interviews and the letters he received, there is a very vivid picture of De Mille, although it is not necessarily as clear as it is vivid, since the various comments offered to MacMechan are sometimes contradictory. Even his appearance was called into question: John Johnson, the professor of classics at the time, mentions his "pale face" and calls him "the dark, handsome show man of the staff" (MacMechan; H), but in his *Dalhousie Gazette* article, H.P. Scott calls him "the common-place looking Dalhousie Professor," and goes on to give some detail:

> During these years he took good care of his health. In person he was a tall, dark, thin man, with black hair, and short, black beard and moustache. His knees bent rather awkwardly in walking, but he strode along with a swinging step. He wore spectacles. (135; E)

The brevity of MacMechan's notes does not help to reconcile the differences.

In general, De Mille seems to have been well liked by students. George Patterson, who was among them in the last year De Mille taught at Dalhousie, comments on this very revealingly in his memoir:

> Looking back now, I find it difficult to explain the extraordinary place DeMille held in our affection. I can understand our admiration, but we gave him much more than that. Tho' always courteous — no student had ever to complain of a sarcastic or cutting remark from him — he was dignified and aloof in manner, cold apparently, and certainly inviting no familiarity — no one ever thought of calling him Jamie or Jimmie; short-sighted, he could not recognize us on the street; yet, in some indefinable way we knew he loved his boys and we unstintedly gave him ours in return. (Patterson 146; G)[19]

Mrs. Lawson remembered him as "not deep" but "a cheerful, genial humorous man," who was "fond of his children, spent time making them toys . . . [and] could do anything with his hands" (MacMechan; H).[20] Edwin Crowell, one of De Mille's honours students, supports the picture of De Mille as a man fond of his children by mentioning that "His son was a frequent companion in his walks for exercise" (MacMechan; H).[21] Several of MacMechan's informants and correspondents describe De Mille as physically active. Lawson is recorded as saying that he was a "great walker, killed himself with bathing, lived in the water," and remarks attributed to Johnson include not only the comment that De Mille was "fond of long walks" and "did not play good whist," but also the extraordinary statement that when swimming, he "used to drop into water with his clothes on." A Mr. King (not further identified) is credited with the information that De Mille used to go skating, and that on one occasion, De Mille and another member of the party "went through [the ice]" and King "pulled them out" (MacMechan; H). These descriptions accord well with De Mille's statement about himself in a letter of 21 January 1875 to John Goforth: "I . . . pass my time in writing with an equal amount of fishing, shooting, and roughing it in the bush. This with an occasional [mission] to Boston or New York makes up my life" (B3).[22] De Mille also offered a similar description of his life in Halifax to his brother, Alfred (in the undated letter previously quoted): "we are not far from the Tower Woods & the Arm, go in swimming everyday, & go out boating" (B3). He would have found the water there clean, but quite cool for most of the summer, although not unbearably cold for swimming.

Another characteristic that MacMechan gathered from several people was De Mille's conversational ability. Daniel Gordon wrote to MacMechan on 3 December 1889:

> My chief recollection is of his charming conversational power. I have been told that in the presence of a room full he was usually silent, but that with a small circle he allowed more play to his power of pleasing talk. It was only in the latter condition that I ever met him, and I have seldom been more delighted with any man's conversation than I was with his. His wide range of reading, his genial kindly humour, his fluent command of language made him an admirable talker. Some speak of conversation as one of the lost arts, but it had not yet disappeared when De Mill was with us. (MacMechan; H)

Dr. George Grant also acknowledged this point about De Mille's conversational powers in his letter to MacMechan of 10 December 1889, saying that "He was a charming talker, partly because of his wealth of historical & literary allusion & partly because of his perfect frankness of manner & spirit."[23] A Mr. McDonald confirms that De Mille was "not much of a talker in general company, best with one or two."[24] Mrs. Lawson thought he had "good repartee," but added that he "liked to talk about himself" (MacMechan; H).

Professionally, he was by no means at a disadvantage among his distinguished peers, although opinions of his professional ability were varied. Dr. Grant replies only coolly and briefly to this point when answering MacMechan's letter of enquiry, but says that the Dalhousie governors were "very glad to be able to get [De Mille]." MecMechan also records that Professor Macdonald spoke of De Mille's "vast scholarship" and "thinks he must have used translations [but] once when out fishing began to talk Latin and nothing but Latin, kept it up for five or six hours." McDonald, however, apparently had "not much opinion of [De Mille's] Greek, disputed with him about accents, & found him deficient in accuracy, [De Mille] had a novel plan of reading Greek, mostly translations and when he came to a specially fine passage, read the original." McDonald's remarks are supported to some extent by those of Mr. Bell (also not further unidentified), who told MacMechan that De Mille "read his classics with pony, small blame to him" (MacMechan; H).

Some reservations about De Mille's teaching also surface in the notes. McDonald informed MacMechan that De Mille "worked hard for himself *not* for the college." Crowell, however, offers a more generous contribution on this point:

> the mechanical element was so evident in his lectures and class work generally that I could readily believe he was mainly interested in some other work but lay "anchored["] to the College duties and might appear to the public to be absorbed in them. The mechanical and sometimes [perfunctory] preoccupied air may have grown upon his method of teaching. (MacMechan; H)

Since De Mille's "preoccupied air" does not match very well his recorded liveliness in conversation, it may be necessary to reconcile the discrepancy by assuming that his classroom behaviour was affected both by the reserve he always displayed in "general company," and by the fatigue felt by any teacher forced to teach the same material over and over again on an inflexible schedule.[25]

Yet in spite of these criticisms, De Mille's former students and others who knew his classroom style seem, on the whole, to approve of him and his teaching, although there are some sharp discrepancies on specific points. On the one hand, for example, from his interview with H. W. Johnston, J.W. Longley, and H. Murray, MacMechan records that De Mille had a "calm manner in lecturing[, was] never flurried[,] spoke slowly distinctly, [had a] pleasant voice, [and] read his lectures." On the other hand, Crowell says in his letter that De Mille "read so rapidly for forty minutes from his MS that it needed considerable decision and judgment, to say nothing of speed in writing, to preserve the salient points of his lectures . . . for the recitation of the next day" (MacMechan; H). Crowell is corroborated, moreover, by an anonymous comment in the *Dalhousie Gazette* of 1873:

> Some of the Notebooks in the History Class are literary curiosities. One word frequently stands for a whole sentence: subject, verb, object, and dependent clauses to boot. Not unfrequently [sic] students cannot read their own notes. (13 Dec. 1873: 23)

Since, however, Johnston had been De Mille's classmate at Brown but not one of his students, and Longley and Murray do not appear on the list of Dalhousie graduates, the comments from that interview must be regarded cautiously. They could have been referring to De Mille's public lectures, which were probably somewhat different from his classroom ones in style of delivery. But on the whole, Crowell seems to be more credible.

The accounts of his teaching of different subjects reveal much about De Mille's approach. The previously mentioned Mr. Bell is reported to have "approved of Rhetoric, though there was too much system" (thus echoing Crowell, perhaps). But he also adds (very interestingly, from a modern point of view), that De Mille "gave weekly essays in composition [and] spent a good deal of time correcting them too." Crowell also says that De Mille's teaching of rhetoric was "copiously illustrated, with little or no practice on the part of the Class" (MacMechan; H), and this complaint is supplemented in an anonymous editorial in the *Dalhousie Gazette* just after De Mille's death: "Even during the professorship of our late instructor in Rhetoric we were of opinion that too little time was spared from the ordinary classwork to devote to the work of elocution" (14 Feb. 1880: 78; H). Crowell also comments briefly on De Mille's history classes ("the History was good reading with occasional flashes of life and humor") and more extensively on the elocution class:

> If I remember aright, his teaching[s] on Elocution were extempore and illustrative. He approved an arbitrary gesticulation in which the intensity of the sentiment was accentuated by proportionate arm

movement. Both hands in descent at once with open palms forward was a sort of maximum. Its advantage as a mode seems to be in its simplicity to teach and acquire. (MacMechan; H)

Unfortunately, no description survives of the few classes De Mille taught in political economy, which can have been very little to his taste. In spite of Bell's complaint that De Mille's classes were "No fun. They were the hardest classes," it is clear that De Mille made himself felt in the classroom. Crowell says flatly that "In the most unimpassioned way, however, he had the power of compelling attention and securing respect for his theme. He seemed to see us with his spectacles and be looking into the world of literature or history with his real eyes" (MacMechan; H). From all the accounts, therefore, De Mille, if not a wholly dedicated teacher, was at least a hardworking, conscientious, and impressive one.

After the formalities of the opening were over, the students and faculty of the college settled down to the regular work of the new academic year. De Mille had been appointed to teach rhetoric and history, and the work outline of the two courses had been announced in the university calendar for 1865–66. For his first-year class in rhetoric, he chose to use Campbell's *Philosophy of Rhetoric* and Whately's *Elements of Rhetoric*, both of which had been his textbooks as a student at Brown. For the fourth-year history class, he chose Taylor's *Modern History*, Guizot's *History of Civilization*, and Chamber's *Cyclopoedia [sic] of English Literature* (Dalhousie, *Calendar* 12; H). His choice of books for this first year of classes had perhaps been determined in some haste, for it did not remain long unchanged. In the following year, 1866–67, for example, he added a third text, in addition to Whately and Campbell, for the rhetoric class, Latham's *Handbook of the English Language*, and a note specifies that there will be "Essays once a fortnight" (Dalhousie, *Calendar* 1866–67: 23; H) He also made much more substantial changes in his book list for the history class, which read as follows:

> Text Books: Gibbon's *Decline and Fall of the Roman Empire*, Hume's *History of England*, Martin's *History of France*, Hallam's *Middle Ages*, Sismondi's *Italian Republics*, Taylor's *Manual of Modern History*. Books Recommended: Guizot's *History of Civilization*, Michelet's *History of France*, Hallam's *Constitutional History*. (Dalhousie, *Calendar* 23; H)

In 1867–68 he added yet another book to the list for the rhetoric class, Angus's *English Language*, but he did not change the history texts at all. For his summer session class in English literature he used Chamber's *Cyclopedia of English Literature* and Craik's *English Literature* (Dalhousie, *Calendar* 22; H). The arrangement he had reached by this point seemed to satisfy him, and he continued to use the same texts with minor variations for the next three years.

In the following year, 1871–72, as a result of the introduction of the honours courses, not only De Mille's texts but also the organization of his classes changed. The ordinary course in history and rhetoric consisted of first-year rhetoric (the textbooks used were those of Whately and Campbell), first-year English language (Angus), and first-year elocution (Porter's *Analysis of the Principles of Rhetorical Delivery* and Russell's *Elocution*), and fourth-year history, for which the books remained unchanged from 1867–68. The honours course introduced third-year English language (Shute's *Anglo-Saxon Manual*; Corson's *Selections from Saxon and English Literature*; George P. Marsh's *Lectures on the English Language*; F.A. Marsh's *Study of the English Language*; Latham's *English Language*; and Trench's *English Past and Present, Glossary, and Study of Words*) and fourth-year history (Bede's *Ecclesiastical History of England*, William of Malmesbury's *Chronicle*, Freeman's *History of [the] Norman Conquest of England*, Hallam's *Constitutional History*, Bryce's *Holy Roman Empire*, Stephen's *Lectures on the History of France*, Mallet's *Northern Antiquities*, Smythe's *Lectures on Modern History*, and Buckle's *History of Civilization*) (Dalhousie, *Calendar* 16; H). From this point, with one exception (the introduction in 1878–79 of his own textbook, *The Elements of Rhetoric*, following its publication in 1878),[26] De Mille contented himself with a few minor changes in the selection of textbooks for these classes. An omnivorous and voracious reader himself, De Mille clearly expected similar dedication from his students. How the students coped with the amount of assigned reading as it grew heavier, particularly in the absence of any indication, in the calendar, of where the texts could be obtained or consulted, is not recorded. After the library was established in 1868, textbooks were sometimes, as they had been at Brown, placed there on reserve, but otherwise, students seem to have been expected to provide for themselves. With a couple of exceptions (once when De Mille taught political economy in addition to his usual classes, and once when he helped to fill in for Professor Johnson after the latter's skating accident), his classes also remained unchanged until 1878.

In 1878, however, De Mille made a radical introduction into the curriculum. He offered a "special course" in the "History of Canada," at the fourth-year level. It is not clear from the description whether the class was also open to students taking the honours course in history and rhetoric, for which English history was normally studied. De Mille's required textbooks for his special course were "Garneau's *History of Canada* (Bell's translation), Murdoch's *History of Nova Scotia*, and Archer's *History of Canada*" (Dalhousie, *Calendar* 19; H).[27] The course was radical, not merely in terms of Dalhousie's curriculum, but of the history curricula in other Canadian universities, and James De Mille may well have been the first person to offer a course in Canadian history in a Canadian university,[28] although his early death prevented its continuation.

Before 1878, however, De Mille's major contribution to Dalhousie's progress, in addition to his classroom teaching and academic administration, was his part in the setting up of the library. This work, however, did not begin until April of 1867, in spite of the fact that the formation of a library had been agreed upon at a meeting of the board of governors as early as April 1864, when it was "resolved that the Matriculation fee be devoted to the formation of a Library" (Dalhousie, Board Minutes, 27 Apr. 1864; H). At the senate meeting of 24 April 1867, the idea of the libary was raised and some offers of "subscriptions" reported. At the following meeting, the matter was discussed further and it was agreed to advertise in the local papers (Dalhousie, Senate, 24 Apr., 30 Apr. 1867; H). The secretary to the governors, Mr. Thomson, was appointed "Treasurer of the Library Fund," and De Mille and Lawson were appointed as a "Committee on the Library Scheme." By June, the senate was discussing space for the library and being frustrated in its attempt to evict the "Mechanics' Museum" from the college building so that the room it occupied could be converted to a library, and considering what could be done about increasing the library fund (Dalhousie, Senate, 3 June, 17 June 1867; H). At the meeting of 24 June, they began to consider how to go about the process of selecting books, and Professor Macdonald was asked to request Dr. Grant's assistance in obtaining catalogues for the selection of books. This request produced no apparent results, and in December, the senate agreed to go ahead with preparing their lists of needed books (Dalhousie, Senate, 24 June, 2 Dec. 1867; H). The lists were produced at the following meeting, when it was agreed that they should be sent to a bookseller "with an injunction to furnish these

Books to the Library, provided he can do so at a discount of one Sixth on the published prices," and De Mille was appointed to attend to "the Catalogues of Books for the Library, American Editions, &c." (Dalhousie, Senate, 17 Dec. 1867; H). The stipulation for a discount was clearly necessary because the college had little money to spend, in spite of the fund that had been set up. It is clear from the minutes of the same meeting, however, that the project for the library was attracting attention outside the college and consequently assistance, notably in the form of gifts, which were reported and gratefully acknowledged in, for example, the senate minutes of 17 December 1867, and 6 January 1868, and 2 March.

The gifts, although gratefully received, did not, nevertheless, constitute a systematic collection of the sort necessary for the support of the subjects being taught. The building of such a collection required a bookseller's professional services. In February of 1868, the secretary reported to the meeting of the senate that a Mr. G. Walker of Aberdeen had undertaken "to furnish Books to the Library on the terms proposed by the Senate," and the senate immediately turned its attention to trying to "obtain control of the East Room [of the college], occupied at present with the Museum; with the view of placing in that room the Library Books which are expected soon to arrive" (Dalhousie, Senate, 3 Feb. 1868; H). In anticipation of being successful in gaining control of the room, De Mille and Macdonald were "appointed [as] a Committee to draw up rules for the Management of the Library" (Dalhousie, Senate, 3 Feb. 1868; H). But the space problem was not yet settled, and it was not until May that the senate took control of the East Room. They then requested that Lawson "see to the clearing out of the 'Museum' and fitting it up with shelves, so as to utilize the Books as soon as possible," and, since the academic year was now almost at an end, appointed De Mille "to take charge of the Library Books during the summer Session" (Dalhousie, Senate, 6 May 1868; H). At the last meeting of the year, the senate, once again thinking about the question of funding, agreed "to recommend to the Governors to appoint that Students attending more Classes than one in this College shall pay an annual Fee of One Dollar for the Library" (Dalhousie, Senate, 17 June 1868; H). The report of the "Committee on Rules for the Library" (De Mille and Macdonald) was considered at the senate meetings of 16 and 19 November 1868, and approved "after discussion of particulars" at the latter.

The library obviously came into use immediately, for at the following meeting it was agreed "that Students who wish to borrow books from the

Library for the remainder of this Session shall have to pay one half Dollar: which sum will be received by Professor De Mill on a day to be fixed hereafter" (Dalhousie, Senate, 7 Dec. 1868; H). De Mille's service on the Library Rules Committee and this appointment to receive the library fees somehow evolved into his *de facto* appointment as librarian, which he held until December of 1872, when he tendered his resignation and was succeeded by Lyall (Dalhousie, Senate, 3 Dec. 1872; H). Funding continued, however, to be uncertain and not entirely within the control of the senate. The secretary to the board of governors paid the bills on request from the senate,[29] and before any order for books could be placed, it was necessary to find out from him how much money was available,[30] which must have been irritating and have caused many delays. Nevertheless, the growth of the library was steady, from "about 700 volumes" in 1869 (*Novascotian* 3 May 1869: 5; G) to "upwards of 1300 volumes" in 1874, and by the fall of 1875 to "upwards of 1600 volumes" (Dalhousie *Calendar*, 1874–75: 15; *Calendar* 1875–76: 14; H). It continued to grow steadily throughout De Mille's career, in spite of intermittent difficulty with obtaining funds for new acquisitions.

De Mille was, of course, involved in other academic chores from the beginning. Even before he began to be involved with the setting up of the library, he was drafted to a committee on the annual register book in his first month at the college, and, at the beginning of January 1866, to a committee on "the public forms of graduation" (Dalhousie, Senate, 31 Oct. 1865, 13 Feb. 1866; H). The senate minutes from then on show him participating in the various activities necessary for keeping the college running smoothly. Since the teaching staff of the college was so small (the staff in the Faculty of Arts during De Mille's time consisted of six professors and one tutor, until the opening of the science department, when one professor was added to the Faculty of Arts and two to the science department) and the administrative staff nonexistent, none of this was mere busy work, and all the professors had to do their fair share. In March of 1866, for example, De Mille undertook to "make enquiries respecting the printing of the B.A. Diploma" and, when he had reported on the possibilities, he "undertook to have two copies printed against Tuesday, 3 April" (Dalhousie, Senate, 22 Mar., 30 Mar. 1866; H). The diplomas were in preparation for the senate meeting of 4 April, which was also the convocation for the year, when two students (I.H. Chase and R. Shaw) were going to graduate (Dalhousie, Senate, 4 Apr. 1866; H).[31] In between obtaining the diplomas and attending the formal graduation ceremony, De Mille took part in the difficult and unpleasant discussion which occupied most of the meeting of 3 April, which ran from 10 o'clock in the morning until late evening with only short breaks for lunch and tea, and was taken up with the problem of widespread cheating in the third-year examinations (Dalhousie, Senate, 3 Apr. 1866; H). Later in the summer, he acted as "Secretary pro: tem" to the meetings (Dalhousie, Senate, 12 June 1866; H), continuing to sign the minutes as secretary until the end of the academic year later that month. In the winter terms of both 1867 and 1868, he was on the committee to examine essays for the Grant and Roy prizes (Dalhousie, Senate, 4 Feb. 1867, 6 Jan. 1868, 24 Mar. 1868; H). In 1867, too, he was a member, with Johnson and Macdonald, of a committee on the calendar (Dalhousie, Senate, 13 May 1867; H), and in 1868, he prepared and delivered the inaugural address for the ceremonial opening of the new academic year (Dalhousie, Senate, 28 Oct. 1868; H). As indicated by the record, therefore, De Mille was kept quietly but steadily busy in these first years at the college.

The tranquil record of De Mille's professional life in 1867 and 1868, however, concealed a disturbance of more than minor proportions in his personal life. In April of 1867, his father-in-law, Dr. John Pryor, became involved in a scandal that resulted in his suspension from his charge of the Granville Street Baptist Church, where he had been minister since 1862, and that led eventually to his removal from Halifax to the United States. De Mille was involved from the beginning on his father-in-law's behalf.

The scandal broke very suddenly. On the evening of Tuesday, 23 April 1867, Dr. and Mrs. Pryor visited De Mille and Annie at their home (the house on Le Marchant Street), and Mrs. Pryor decided to stay the night with the De Milles because one of her grandchildren was ill. Dr. Pryor left at about 9 o'clock to return home alone across the South Common. Dr. Pryor's own account of what followed has not survived, except as reported by other people.[32] According to published accounts, at 2 o'clock on Wednesday morning, 24 April 1867, Dr. Pryor was "caught coming from a house in Pleasant Street [now part of Barrington Street] where he had been staying in the depth of night, for about two hours, with a young woman not of good repute, whose husband was abroad" (Brenton H. Eaton 7; G). The man who apprehended him, James Baxter, reported him to the church elders. On the Thursday evening, by which time, Eaton adds, "a whirlwind of damaging reports was going through all the streets of the city," Pryor was called to a meeting with the elders of the church (Parker, Selden, and

The Rev. Dr. John Pryor

Beckwith) at Dr. Parker's house. At this meeting, he admitted to having called on Mrs. McMillan (the woman in question) after a late supper with a neighbour, but he was unable to satisfy the elders with his explanation of the incident (Brenton H. Eaton 38–39; G).[33] At a second meeting the next day, this time of all the "male members" of the church, was held on Friday, it was decided to deprive Pryor of his pulpit. One of the church members delivered a letter to Pryor, informing him of this decision (Brenton H. Eaton, 39; G), to which Pryor replied, "Whatever the brethren decide upon, I, of course, assent to. It seems, however, not exactly in accordance with the usual custom. Will it not look as if my brethren thought me guilty?" (Johnston, *Memorial* 6; G).[34] On the Saturday morning, De Mille called on his father-in-law, and was shown the letter Pryor had received. In his own letter to J.W. Johnston, De Mille explains briefly what he did:

> I at once went to Mr. Selden's office, and denounced the action of the Church as hasty and injurious on various grounds. Mr. Selden defended the action of the Church on various grounds. I then called on Dr. Parker between 2 and 3 p.m., and reiterated to him my denunciation of this act of the Church. He defended it with earnestness. (Johnston, *Memorial* 6; G)[35]

De Mille did not, however, succeed in having the decision rescinded, and a substitute minister, Mr. Welton, was called upon, and he preached in the Granville Street Church on Sunday (Brenton H. Eaton 8; G). The immediate incident was over at this point.

The consequences, however, escalated. Dr. Pryor requested, as was his right, a council to hear the matter. This council, a panel of 12 disinterested church members drawn from the Maritime provinces and agreed on by both parties, met in Halifax on Tuesday, 3 September 1867, to examine the evidence and to hear the witnesses, among whom was De Mille himself (Brenton H. Eaton 75; G). The council reached the "unanimous decision that Dr. Pryor was not guilty of the immorality alleged against him" although he had been wanting in discretion and prudence (Johnston, *Memorial* 35; G). The Granville Street Church chose to ignore the council's recommendation and to continue to exclude Dr. Pryor from the pulpit, appointing the Reverend Edward Manning Saunders to be their pastor as of 15 September 1867. As Philip Griffin-Allwood has pointed out, the Granville Street Church's decision to ignore the council's verdict shifted the issue from the question of Dr. Pryor's guilt or innocence to the question of the right to self-government of individual churches within the Central Association of Baptist Churches. Although, at the association's meeting held in June of 1867, Dr. Pryor's right to a council had been upheld, at the meeting in June of 1868, "the authority of the local church to ignore council decisions was affirmed" (Griffin-Allwood 86; G). In 1869, therefore, Pryor, having lost his final battle for vindication in the Halifax Baptist community, left Halifax and returned to the United States to take up the ministry of the First Baptist Church of Lexington in Massachusetts, leaving the whole affair behind him.

De Mille, however, was unable to leave, and the aftershocks of the scandal continued to affect him. He was, to begin with, both well known and closely associated with Pryor in a city "ablaze with the matter" within 24 hours of its occurrence (Brenton H. Eaton, 7; G). Moreover, as his letter to Johnston reveals, he had taken an active part in dealing with the church on his father-in-law's behalf at the time of the original scandal, and people (possibly with the best of intentions) had not refrained from discussing it with him. After describing the sequence of events leading to his conversations with Dr. Parker and Deacon Selden, De Mille continues:

> At these interviews I asserted that this act of suspension would be regarded in the community as a virtual condemnation of Dr. Pryor. My opinion was confirmed by the event. From various quarters I learned that the public believed the action of the Church a sure proof of guilt. In the language of an influential gentleman of this city, — "By this act the Church gave their endorsement to the public scandal." (Johnston, *Memorial* 7; G)

Moreover, at the September council, De Mille had read for Pryor an explanatory statement concerning a second charge of financial mismanagement in the affairs of a Miss Vass: "The Council convened for its evening session at 7 1/2 o'clock. . . . Professor DeMill read to the Council a document explaining the discrepancies in Dr. Pryor's accounts with Miss Vass" (Brenton H. Eaton, 75; G).[36] It also appears that some of the hostility on the part of Dr. Pryor's accusers was directed towards De Mille himself, for Johnston records that "Mr. Selden told Dr. Pryor that his son-in-law was his worst enemy"; and whichever way one reads the second "his" (as referring to Pryor or Selden), it does not eliminate the evident animosity of the remark (Johnston *Letter* 7; G). In all the high-minded mudslinging that went on in the affair, De Mille could hardly have avoided getting splashed. Moreover, the affair continued to be remembered, so much so that it was one of the matters that De Mille's colleague, Johnson, mentioned to Archibald MacMechan when the latter was researching De Mille's life for his proposed biography,[37] and Lawson, another colleague, also mentioned it when MacMechan interviewed him (MacMechan; H).[38] Living in a relatively small (by modern standards) community with constant reminders of something as embarrassing and painful as this incident must have made De Mille's life very difficult.

The most obvious outward effect on him was a change in his religious affiliation. Up to this point, the family had been attending the Granville Street Baptist Church, and in January 1867, Annie De Mille had taken the trouble for the first time since her marriage, to request, in a letter dated 14 January 1867, that her church membership be transferred from Old Cambridge Baptist Church, where she had been a member before her marriage, to the Granville Street Church (Paul; H).[39] At some point between Dr. Pryor's departure from Halifax and the beginning of 1871, however, De Mille abandoned the Baptist church and became an Anglican, for the 1871 census describes the family members of the household as belonging to the "Church of England" (Census 1871; H). On 2 May 1872, moreover, the new baby, Ethel Maud, and the two older De Mille children were all baptized together in St. Luke's Church in Halifax (St. Luke's; H). Caroline Lawson (Dr. Lawson's wife), in her comment to MacMechan that De Mille was "not taken up by the E[piscopalian] C[hurch] people," seems to imply that, at least in her opinion, there was some element of social climbing involved in the change (MacMechan; H).[40] The Reverend I.E. Bill, however, with whom De Mille had had some differences in the days of the *Christian Watchman*, gives no hint in his memorial notice of De Mille's death in 1880 of any ulterior motive on De Mille's part, commenting simply that "Owing to unpleasant circumstances, he cast in his lot in late years with the Episcopalians" (*Christian Visitor* 4 Feb. 1880: 4), and as a member of the council that investigated the charges against Dr. Pryor (Johnston, *Letter* 40; G), Bill was well aware of the precise nature of those "unpleasant circumstances."[41] De Mille, in fact, subsequently delivered to the Church of England Institute a paper entitled *The Early English Church*, which he was serious enough about to have published privately in 1877.[42] In spite of his change of denomination, there is no evidence at all that he was not entirely sincere in his religious beliefs.

A second effect of the aftermath of the Pryor scandal on De Mille was apparently to make him turn more and more to his writing, as though to use it as a method to escape, either psychologically or physically, from the pressures of Halifax. That he became a little less sociable at this time is at least hinted at by the fact that he discontinued his membership in the Nova Scotian Institute of Natural Science, which he had joined in 1866.[43] Depression as well as withdrawal is also suggested in another interview by MacMechan, who approached not only De Mille's former colleagues and students, but also others who knew him, including the Reverend Dr. Edward Manning Saunders (Pryor's successor as pastor of the Granville Street Church). MacMechan's note of this conversation contains a clear and disinterested view of De Mille during the critical year of 1867: "Called on Dr. E.M. Saunders. Educed the fact that in 1867 De Mille was discouraged, wanted to get away to N.Y. Talk to a man one evening and you knew all he knew and he knew all you knew. Lacked intellectual companionship" (MacMechan; H). De Mille might well be "discouraged" at this particular time. But if he lacked "intellectual companionship" it must be assumed that it was specifically literary "intellectual companionship" he was referring to, since his colleagues at Dalhousie were certainly intellectually respectable (to say the least) in their own fields.

That he may have proposed to "get away" by means of his writing is supported by the sudden increase in his publications at this time. There had been two previous periods of intensive writing in his life: the years at Brown and the year of the *Christian Watchman* (1861) in Saint John. But apart from the *Watchman* material (which included the serial version of two novels "Andy O'Hara" and "The Missionary's Son"), little of the remaining work known or suspected to be by De Mille appears to have been written between 1854 and 1866 — probably only *John Wheeler's Two Uncles* (1860?), *The Soldier and the Spy* (1865?), the *The Arkansas Ranger* (1865?), *Helena's Household* (1858?), and *The Martyr of the Catacombs* (1858?). For all five, however, either the existence, the attribution, or the date is extremely doubtful.[44] Moreover, even if all five could be shown to be unquestionably his and to be written in this period, five novels in 12 years is an extremely low rate of production compared to what follows.

After the Pryor scandal erupted, this trickle of writing began suddenly to increase in volume. This increase springs to the eye in an examination of the dates of first publication — usually in serial form for the adult novels and book form for the juvenile material — of his remaining works.[45] In

1867, *The Dodge Club* and *Cord and Creese* appeared in serial form; both were quickly issued in book form (1869). In 1869, he published "The Minnehaha Mines" (serial), "The Earl's Daughter" (four episodes of a parody of popular society novels, written for the *Dalhousie Gazette*), and *The B.O.W.C.* (which stands for "Brethren of the White Cross," first in the B.O.W.C. Series for juveniles). In 1870, four novels appeared: *The American Baron*, *The Lady of the Ice*, *The Boys of Grand Pré School*, and *Lost in the Fog* (the last two both in the B.O.W.C. Series). In 1871, he brought out *Fire in the Woods* (B.O.W.C. Series) and *Among the Brigands* (the first in the Young Dodge Club Series). In 1872, *A Comedy of Terrors* (serial and book), *An Open Question* (serial), and *Picked Up Adrift* (B.O.W.C. Series) were published. In 1873, he added *The Living Link* (serial), *The Treasure of the Seas* (last of the B.O.W.C. Series), and *The Seven Hills* (Young Dodge Club Series). This extraordinary flood of writing — almost three novels a year over a period of six years — is all the more extraordinary for having been produced concurrently with De Mille's normal academic duties and apparently normal family life.

After six years, however, the flood of popular fiction slows to a trickle once again. In 1874, he published only *The Lily and the Cross* (serial and book), and after 1874, he published only three books of fiction: *The Babes in the Wood* (1875), *The Winged Lion* (1877 — last of the Young Dodge Club Series), and *A Castle in Spain* (1878). Nothing at all was published in 1876. Moreover, apparently only two or three manuscripts (the lost "Isles of Greece," the unfinished "Ashdod Webster and His Starring Tour," and the more-or-less-finished, but posthumously published, *A Strange Manuscript Found in a Copper Cylinder*) were found among his papers after his death (Arthur De Mille; H).[46] It seems, therefore, as though De Mille was beginning to turn his attention away from writing as a career and as an attempt to get away from Halifax. Instead, in 1877 he published the scholarly pamphlet referred to earlier, *The Early English Church*, and in 1878, the solid and carefully constructed textbook, *The Elements of Rhetoric*.

The appearance of the latter, taken together with the purchase of the house at 72 South Park Street early in 1876, indicates clearly that the turbulence that the Pryor scandal had stirred up in De Mille was beginning to settle down by 1876. The anxiety to get away was subsiding, and, if the fact that according to the records of the Institute of Science he was reelected to membership in December of 1879 is significant (Nova Scotian Institute 5.2: 2; G), he was even regaining something of his earlier sociability. In spite of De Mille's apparent disturbance and depression in the immediate aftermath of the scandal, the scandal itself does not figure very largely in the recollections of his life at Dalhousie, and it is clear that within his own circle he was by no means a recluse. Moreover, his profession was, if not exactly strengthening its appeal, at least seeming to offer more opportunities. The college was growing, and there were new faces as well as older friends among his colleagues and the regular influx of new students in his classes.

De Mille's other academic duties besides teaching continued, of course, during the period of his prolific writing, and they gradually increased as the number of students in the college approached almost one hundred in 1876.[47] By 1875, the work of the senate occupied much of the time of all the members of the faculty when they were not actually in the classroom. Most of De Mille's activities were matters of everyday routine, so that, for example, on 6 April 1875, he took the chair of the senate, and he was appointed, with professors Ross and Lyall, to be an examiner for the Young Elocution Prize, and was also appointed, with Professor Ross, to the committee on M.A. theses (Dalhousie, Senate, 6 Apr. 1875; H). Some activities recurred regularly, but less frequently. At the beginning of 1878, for example, he was on the committee set up to discuss and report on the improvement of the curriculum (Dalhousie, Senate, 21 Jan. 1878; H), and, at roughly the same time, he was also (with Professor Lawson) a member of the committee appointed to report on the proposal for a science course (Dalhousie, Senate, 3 May 1878; H).

Occasionally his academic activities were less routine. In 1878, for example, he was involved in an issue of censorship within the college. The fourth-year graduating class was objecting to the new college regulation requiring that the valedictorian's address be read by the principal before it was delivered. To support their objection, the students were refusing to appoint a valedictorian at all. At the senate meeting of 4 March 1878, the matter was discussed and

> it was agreed by the Senate, Dr Lyall dissenting, that the Principal and Professor Lawson should be appointed to meet with the Students of the Fourth year and explain to them the reasons for the resolution passed unanimously by the Senate at last Meeting, with the view of obviating the objections expressed by them to appointing a Valedictorian. (Dalhousie, Senate, 4 Mar. 1878; H)

It is not clear why Lyall chose to dissent only at this stage if the resolution had been passed unanimously at the previous meeting (22 February), for which he was present. The explanation did not satisfy the students, and when the matter came up at the next meeting, it was recorded again that "the Students [of the fourth year] had not appointed a Valedictorian." Although only Lyall had expressed dissent at the meeting of 4 March, he was now joined in his dissent by De Mille, for "It was moved by Dr Lyall and seconded by Professor De Mill that that part of the resolution of Senate requiring the Valedictory to be submitted for approval of the Principal be rescinded: which motion was not carried" (Dalhousie, Senate, 8 Mar. 1878; H). De Mille had certainly been present at the meeting when the regulation had been unanimously passed, so that his support of Lyall may well have resulted from some persuasion on Lyall's part. The word "approval" seems to have been what the students, as well as Lyall and De Mille, were objecting to, since it would give the principal a power of censorship over something that had been, by tradition entirely a student matter. There was also the side issue of whether or not Lyall had the right to make his dissent public. The students, however, refused to give in, and the convocation proceeded without a valedictory being delivered. The *Dalhousie Gazette* reports that a "Valedictory" was read by J.H. Cameron of the graduating class (who would presumably have been the chosen valedictorian) to the final students' meeting of the year, which was held in the college earlier on the day of the convocation ceremony (1 May 1878: 141; H). As printed in the same issue of the *Gazette*, the valedictory is very mildly critical of Dalhousie ("even in Dalhousie there is room for improvement" [135]), but it is not clear whether suspicion of this caused the demand that it should be read in advance by the principal. The matter was not raised again in senate within De Mille's lifetime.

De Mille's increased involvement in his academic work at this time included not only this protest on behalf of the students, but also proposals put forward by him about the evaluation of students. His attitude to essays and examinations, for example, is described by former student Edwin Crowell to MacMechan:

> His sympathis [sic] were with more frequent exams, and a distribution of tests through the term. When just before his death, the time of my honour exams was discussed, he consented to give me some of the exams previous to the Sessionals at intervals of a few days.

De Mille's grave in Camp Hill Cemetery

Historical essays were also marked to the Credit of the writers, and subjects were chosen, I now suppose as much to compel extensive reading as to develope [sic] a facility in style of writing. (Mac-Mechan; H)

De Mille's opinion, although not necessarily the only one tending in the same direction, undoubtedly influenced the senate's decision in 1877 that "Essays and periodical Examinations, written as well as oral, be hereafter combined with the results of the final Sessional Examinations, for determining the standing of Students" (Dalhousie, Senate. 30 Apr. 1877; H). He seems, also, to have favoured increasing the flexibility of the curriculum in general, and in June of 1879, he not only moved to have Latin and Greek considered as one subject at the sessional examinations in first-year and second-year classes, but also supported a move (by Lyall) to allow supplemental examinations for third-year students in certain circumstances, although neither motion passed (Dalhousie, Senate, 26 June 1879; H). De Mille's friendship with Lawson and Macdonald and his support of Lyall, together with his own interest in science, also suggest that his inclination was to reform the traditional curriculum to a wider one that had more room for the sciences. He seems to have been developing, in these last years, into a much more active and not particularly conservative participant in academic affairs.

At the beginning of the academic year 1879–80, therefore, De Mille appeared to be well settled in his profession and in his home life, without having abandoned writing completely. The fall term passed in the normal routine of teaching and administration, and at the beginning of January, he was occupied by a new committee formed to report on the science curriculum. He was also more active in the community than he had been for a long time, and he began to accept speaking engagements for public lectures.

Towards the end of January, he went to Saint John for one of these engagements to lecture on satire at the Mechanics Institute. On his return, he was taken ill with what was thought to be a cold. In spite of this illness, he managed to continue teaching for several days. By the following Monday, 25 January, however, he was seriously ill, and by the following day his condition had become a "congestion of the lungs" (probably a form of pneumonia) and was considered "critical." At 2 a.m. on Wednesday, 28 January 1880, he died. The funeral was held at St. Luke's Church, and he was buried in Camp Hill Cemetery.[48]

NOTES

1 In 1843, Howe had written bitterly in the pages of the *Novascotian*:

It appears to have been the fate of this institution to have had foisted into its management those who were hostile to its interests; whose names were in its trust, but whose hearts were on other institutions. These, if they did nothing against, took care to do nothing for it; their object was to smother it with indifference. Surrounded by such men, and clothed with a sectarian character, for twenty-three years it stood a monument of folly. (Allison 2: 836; G)

2 The college also had to contend with less dangerous but more bizarre threats from other sources:

In 1853 . . . a committee of the City Council wished to use the southern portion of the Parade as a temporary market while a new market building was being erected. This request was at first refused, but later granted under pressure. In 1854, Mr E.G. Fuller asked permission to use the College grounds for a *circus*. This petition was rejected without hesitation. (Harvey 69; G)

3 According to E.D. Millar's biographical sketch, the Reverend Dr. James Ross was a Nova Scotian, born in West River (Pictou County) in 1811. A staunch Presbyterian, and, like De Mille's father, a staunch temperance supporter, he was educated at Pictou Academy, where he subsequently taught for many years, for some of which he also had a ministerial charge (Millar, passim; G). Ephraim Scott, one of the first group of students to attend Dalhousie after the reorganization, recalls Ross's teaching style as "leisurely" (153; G). J. MacDonald Oxley, also recalling this period, describes the man and his lectures more vividly but less gently: "[his] lectures . . . were delivered from exquisitely neat notes with . . . a marked absence of enthusiasm. . . . However, he made some compensation for this by the exceeding lenience he showed in dealing with the examination papers, it being almost an unknown thing for any one to be plucked in his subject" (160; E). Ross's amiable personality was not hinted at in his appearance, and his fierce, deeply set eyes and handsome but hawkish features, set off by flowing grey muttonchops, must have given the students some qualms until they came to know him better.

4 William Lyall was born at Paisley, near Glasgow, in 1811, and educated at Paisley Academy, and at the universities of both Glasgow and Edinburgh; he served for several years as a minister, before being appointed, in 1848, as a tutor at Knox College, Toronto. In 1850, he became professor of classics and mental philosophy in the Free Church College in Halifax, and, in 1860, moved to the Presbyterian College at Truro. He was appointed to Dalhousie during the reorganization of 1863, by which time he was beginning to be recognized as a distinguished figure in his field: in 1864, he was given an honorary LL.D. by McGill, and, in 1882, he became one of the original members of the Royal Society of Canada. His major publication was *Intellect, the Emotions and*

the Moral Nature (1855), but he also published "numerous contributions to current literature." His abilities, however, do not seem to have impressed his students. Ephraim Scott calls him vaguely "the sensitive Lyall" (153; E), and Oxley comments patronizingly that

> Professor Lyall presided over the domain of pure thought, and did it with a manifestly sincere belief in the practical value of Metaphysics and Esthetics that was very touching even if it was not altogether convincing. . . . His whole system of philosophy is perhaps hopelessly out-of-date now, for there has been progress in pure thought as in more matter-of-fact provinces of human activity, but no one who studied under him could forget his genial, gentle, almost appealing way of presenting the airy speculations that were to him of such positive moment. (161–62; E)

He married late in life, in 1870, several years after he came to Halifax; his wife was Charlotte Tremaine, a daughter of Scott Tremaine of Halifax. He died in 1890. (This information is taken, except where otherwise noted, from "A Professorial Who's Who" [E].)

5 John Johnson, whom the Dalhousie Board of Governors had appointed professor of classics in 1863, was the only Irishman and the only Anglican in the original group of professors. He was born in Dublin in 1835, where he entered Trinity College in 1853, and received his B.A. in 1860. In 1861, he emigrated to Montreal where he spent two years as a classics master in high school, before his appointment to Dalhousie. President Mackenzie, recording Johnson's death in the Dalhousie annual report in 1915, describes him as being "of a reserved disposition and but little known in the community, and even by his students, [but] . . . possessed of a personality of rare charm . . . though outwardly cold and even austere, and taking little part in College activities beyond the academic ones" (Dalhousie, *President's Report 1914–15*: 1–2; H). Johnson's students seem to have agreed with this assessment of his personality. Oxley remembers that "he had a cool precise manner which effectually checked all impulses towards sociability, and . . . a keeness [sic] of irony which hardly conduced to popularity" (161; E). Oxley also recalls, however, that,

> while skating on the Dartmouth Lakes [Johnson] fell so violently as to break one of his legs just above the ankle. This happened at the far end of the Second Lake, and he had no companion. I chanced to be within hail, and he called upon me for aid. The problem was how to get him to the foot of the First Lake where a sleigh could be procured. It was solved by making a rude conveyance out of a young spruce tree whereon he was dragged the whole distance over the ice. His sufferings may be imagined. Yet not a groan or a sigh passed his lips. He seemed indeed the most composed and cheerful of the party. No Spartan could have shown more superb self-control. (161; E)

Johnson, too, married shortly after coming to Dalhousie, having apparently met his future wife, Harriet Heriot, while living in Quebec, for she came from Drummondville. He retired in 1894, and in 1900 was given an LL.D. by Dalhousie in recognition of his services. He died in Drummondville in 1914. (This information is taken, except where otherwise noted, from "A Professorial Who's Who" [E].)

6 Professor Charles Macdonald occupied the chair of mathematics. Born in Aberdeen in 1830 and educated at King's College, Aberdeen, from which he received his M.A. in 1850, together with the College's Hutton Prize "as the most distinguished scholar at the termination of the Arts Curriculum," he subsequently studied divinity at the Church of Scotland Divinity Hall, and received his licence to preach in 1856. Until his appointment to Dalhousie in 1863 during the reorganization, he was college chaplain and a teacher at Aberdeen Grammar School. A tough, thickset man, Macdonald was both liked and feared by the students. Oxley calls him "a splendid teacher," who "threw himself into his work, investing the otherwise dry subject of mathematics with an interest that even the dullest student could not fail to appreciate," although he also did his share of the "improving treatment" of "taking the conceit out of" the students (160; E). J.W. Logan, a student of Macdonald's who later joined the Dalhousie faculty, offers examples (adding his own emphasis) of tart professorial comments recorded in his mathematics notebook: " 'your arguments lack cogency; it's a *spley* method of speech ye have. It's not gude' . . . 'Use the first equation *as a sort of sledge-hammer* to break up the others' " (56; G). In 1882, Macdonald married Mary, a daughter of the Hon. W.J. Stairs of Halifax. He died in 1901, still apparently a member of the college faculty. (This information is taken, except where otherwise noted, from "A Professorial Who's Who" [E].)

7 George Lawson, who occupied the chair of chemistry, was by far the most distinguished of this early group of faculty members, obtaining national and international recognition for his work. He was born at Newport in Fifeshire, Scotland, in 1827, and educated at Edinburgh University, where he subsequently lectured in natural science, before obtaining his doctorate at Giessen, Germany, in 1857. In 1858, he was appointed professor of chemistry and natural history at Queen's University in Kingston, and, in 1863, to the chair of chemistry at Dalhousie. Like his colleague, Lyall, he was given an LL.D. by McGill, and became one of the original members of the Royal Society of Canada. In 1891, he became "Founder and President of Botanical Society, Canada," and was

> at different times made Fellow of Botanical and Royal Physical Societies, Edinburgh, Institute of Chemistry, Great Britain; member of Edinburgh Geological and Scottish Aboricultural Societies; Royal Horticultural Society, London; Society [for the] Natural Sciences, Cherbourg, British and American Associations for Advancement of Science, Royal Scottish Society of Arts, Nova Scotia Institute of Science, and associate of Canadian Society of Civil Engineers.

AT DALHOUSIE COLLEGE, 1865-80

Although appointed to teach chemistry, in which he was hampered by "the meagre equipment of apparatus at his disposal" (Oxley 162; E), Lawson was by inclination, apparently, less a chemist than a botanist:

> In addition to the work of his chair he also for many years conducted a class in botany, entirely without remuneration from the Board of Governors. In former years this class was held in summer; and many of his old students will remember the enthusiasm with which he led them to the haunts of his well-loved plants. As in chemistry so also in botany he would have liked to make his teaching largely observational and experimental; but lack of appliances stood in his way. (Obituary 76; G)

The writer adds that as teacher of botany, Lawson had

> a rare power of rousing enthusiasm in his pupils, and stimulating them to exercise and develop their own powers of observation. The writer was assured some few years ago by one of the leading botanists of Canada that at that date all the leading Canadian botanists, who had been trained in Canada, were pupils of Dr. Lawson; and this fact speaks volumes for the ability of their teacher. (78; G)

Ephraim Scott describes him "the imperturbable Lawson, calmly demonstrating Chemistry whether the students listened or loafed" (153; E), and perhaps it is fortunate that he was imperturbable, in view of the emergencies that could arise in the laboratory, one of which is vividly remembered by Oxley:

> I learned one lesson in his class-room, however, that there was small fear of my forgetting, to wit the destructive power of sulphuric acid. Some of us were engaged in the production of a silicate. The retort exploded spattering the hot acid in all directions. A shower of it struck my face and head, and but for the promptness of Professor Lawson in plunging my head into a bath of lime-water happily at hand I would have been badly injured. As it was I looked like an incipient case of small-pox. Thenceforward I took care not to be on such intimate terms with the apparatus. (162; E)

In addition to his teaching, Lawson published prolifically, his more important works including a textbook, *On First Principles of Chemistry* (1887), and a botanical monograph, *The Fern Flora of Canada* (1889). His first wife, Lucy Stapley, whom he married before coming to Canada, died in 1871, and, in 1876, he remarried, his second wife being Caroline Knox. Lawson died in Halifax in 1895. (This information is taken, except where otherwise noted, from "A Professorial Who's Who" [E].)

8 As part of the process of reorganization, the Board had decided that an "Advertizement be inserted in the Newspapers requesting applicants for the Professorial Chairs of the Classics and Chemistry. . . . Such Advertizement to state that the Salaries of the Chairs will be £300 per annum with fees" (Dalhousie, Board Minutes, 6 Aug. 1863; H).

9 Duncan Cameron Fraser was one of the early Dalhousie students who made a mark on the province, for he was lieutenant governor of Nova Scotia from 30 March 1906 to 21 October 1910, and his contribution to the *Dalhousie Gazette* was sent from "Government House, Halifax."

10 Dalhousie students were, however, much fewer in number than Brown students in De Mille's time, according to Allison, who comments that

> the Macdonald-Johnsonian system had a decidedly repressive effect upon the number of students in attendance at [Dalhousie] University. In the session of 1873–74, ten years after the opening, the number of undergraduates in arts had only grown from 40 to fifty-one; another ten years saw this increased to 61; in the following year it had receded to 58. Thus at the end of twenty-one years, the rate of growth had been less than one undergraduate student per year. (Allison 2: 841; G)

11 P. St. C. Hamilton, literary editor of *Montreal Star*, mentions this in his letter of 28 May 1910 to Miss Freida Creighton, of Halifax. The original of this letter is in the possession of Miss Edith Creighton, Freida's older sister, who copied it on 24 March 1982. The copy of the letter is to be found in the Public Archives of Nova Scotia, Halifax.

12 The city directory for 1872–73 shows De Mille living at 24, rather than 26, South Park, but this may simply be a mistake (Halifax; G).

13 The entry for the De Mille household in the 1871 national census record shows that it consisted of James, Elizabeth ("Annie"), William ("Willie"), and Louise, with Bella and Margaret Henderson listed as "servants". William, aged 11, and Louise, aged 6, are described as "going to school" (Census 1871; H).

14 Ethel Maud was born on 21 February 1872, according to her baptismal record, and died the same year on 24 October, aged 8 months, of whooping cough (Halifax County, Death; H).

15 The date is confirmed by his baptismal record. Alban was always called Bertie by the family. He later became an academic like his father, and taught both in Canada (at the University of King's College) and in the United States.

16 This youngest son is always referred to as Frank, but may have been baptised Frederick after De Mille's younger brother. No baptism certificate has been found. The date of his birth, however, has been confirmed as correct in conversation with Frank's son, Noel James De Mille, of Thorpeness, Suffolk, England.

17 The letter is unfortunately undated, although one of the references in it suggests that it was written not long after the Saint John fire of 1877.

18 James Liechti was appointed at the same time as De Mille: "It was unanimously Resolved that Mons. J. Liechti be appointed Tutor of Modern Languages with a salary of $400 per annum such appointment to take place from the 18th day of October next" (Dalhousie, Board Minutes, 11 Sept. 1865; H). Other than the fact that he was a "Swiss

Lutheran, who had reached Nova Scotia *via* New York six years previously and had considerable local experience in teaching" (Harvey 89; G) very little is recorded about Liechti (he is not, for example, included in the "Professorial Who's Who" in the *Dalhousie Gazette*). Oxley, however, knew and liked him, and writes that "With Professor Liechti my College experience was a renewal of the pleasant associations established at the Halifax Grammar School," describing him as "a very painstaking instructor, stronger perhaps in his German than in his French, and to those who showed genuine interest he was always genial and eager to help. In person he was exquisitely neat, and I remember admiring his dainty neck-ties and immaculate linen" (162–63; E). Ephraim Scott says that Liechti was "so impartial to Teuton and Frank alike that even the morning invocation was paid under tribute, and Unser Vater of yesterday was today Notre Pere" (153; E). He retired in 1906, receiving an honorary LL.D. for his long and devoted service, and died in retirement in Lunenburg in 1925, the last, as President Mackenzie said, of the "Old Guard" of Dalhousie faculty (Dalhousie, *President's Report*, 1924-25: 2; H).

19 Patterson contributed the second part, "As Teacher," to the essay "Concerning James De Mille," which is included in the collection of historical essays that Patterson edited under the title *More Studies in Nova Scotian History*; the first part, "As Writer," was contributed by A.J. Crockett. Patterson also records the friendship between De Mille and Charles Macdonald: "Charlie admitted few into the intimacies of friendship and DeMille was one of the few. They used to go fishing together, talking in Latin all the time . . . . Fishing was a cult with Charlie, and he would not profane its mysteries by speaking of them in English" ("As Teacher" 144; G). The strength of the friendship is indicated in Patterson's description of the occasion on which news of De Mille's death reached the students:

> I was in my second year at Dalhousie . . . . We were in Charlie's class in Mathematics when he was called out of the room. His back was hardly turned when we began high jinks, throwing note books about, and generally making a small sized disturbance. One of our number sitting near the door overheard some of the conversation outside. Making himself heard above the din, he shouted — "Be quiet boys — there's bad news about DeMille". The still that followed was intense. When Charlie returned, he, in a voice broken with emotion, dismissed the class — "I cannot go on, gentlemen; my beloved colleague Professor DeMille is dead." ("As Teacher" 144–45; G)

20 According to a report in the *Dalhousie Gazette*, the death of Dr. Lawson's first wife happened sometime in December 1870 (5 Jan. 1871: 30; H), so that MacMechan is referring to Caroline, Dr. Lawson's second wife, who would probably have known De Mille only from about 1872 on.

21 The Reverend Edwin Crowell's letter of 30 January 1890 in response to MacMechan's request for information about De Mille is a careful and thoughtful

description by a student who clearly knew De Mille better than most. Crowell graduated in 1880, winning *"The Marquis of Lorne's Gold Medal* — To the best student of the Graduating Class in Arts" (*Dalhousie Gazette* 29 Apr. 1880: 134).

22 De Mille is describing what seems like an ideal existence in this letter of 21 January 1875 to John Goforth (B3). (The letter is in the possession of the Historical Society of Pennsylvania, in their Dreer Collection, and is used by permission.) De Mille had become friends with Goforth at Brown University. His remark in the same letter about "last summer when I was in the woods for several months," however, sounds somewhat exaggerated, and if he was really as shortsighted as Patterson suggests ("he could not recognize us on the street" ["As Teacher" 146; G]), then his claim to go shooting strains credibility.

23 The Reverend Dr. George M. Grant was a member of the board of governors during most of De Mille's career at Dalhousie, and later became a forceful and popular principal of Queen's University at Kingston.

24 Mr. McDonald is not further identified, except to be distinguished from Professor Macdonald, although he is most probably Charles D. McDonald of Picton (class of '73).

25 The timetable in the calendar for 1870–71, for example, shows that first-year rhetoric was taught "Daily" from 10 a.m. to 11 a.m., and fourth-year history "Daily" from 11 a.m. to noon (Dalhousie, *Calendar* 17; H). Similar, although not identical, schedules are shown for De Mille's classes throughout his 15 years at Dalhousie.

26 The *Elements of Rhetoric* sold very poorly after De Mille's death, as Annie complained to MacMechan, probably because De Mille was not able to promote it himself (MacMechan, H). It differed considerably in style from the textbooks De Mille had used as a student and as a teacher. Its most interesting feature, from the point of view of its author's biography, is the lavish use of quotations from an extraordinarily wide range of literature and history.

27 Presumably De Mille chose the "free and faulty translation of the expurgated edition of 1859" of Francois-Xavier Garneau's *Histoire du Canada depuis sa découverte jusqu'à nos jours* "made by Andrew Bell in 1860" ("Garneau"; G), and Beamish Murdoch's *History of Nova Scotia, or Acadie* (1865). His third selection, Andrew Archer's *A History of Canada for the Use of Schools* (1875), although intended for school use and "prescribed by the Board of Education for New Brunswick," may well have been quite sufficient for De Mille's purposes at Dalhousie, since it ran to 476 pages and included maps. (Archer's more popular textbook on Canadian history, *Canada: A Short History of the Dominion of Canada* did not appear until 1884.)

28 Queen's, which, according to the president of the Canadian Historical Association in 1962, was entitled to claim the honour of being the first Canadian university to teach Canadian history (Preston 9; G), does not seem in fact to have begun doing so until 10 years after De Mille's course was offered. According to Hilda Neatby:

[Adam Shortt] had already laid the foundations of this still novel study in the university. Queen's was apparently the first English-speaking university to teach Canadian history. From 1890 history students were examined in set books on Canadian history; in 1895 lectures were instituted on the British and Canadian constitutions, and the same year Adam Shortt began his course on Canadian economic history. (Neatby 283; G)

29 "The Secretary reported that the late addition of Books to the Library had cost $264.30: which sum had been paid by the Secretary to the Board of Governors" (Dalhousie, Senate, 13 Nov. 1874; H).

30 "It was agreed that the Principal be requested to ascertain, from the Secretary to the Governors, the balance in hand of the sum voted to the library Fund last year, after payment of the recent Order of Books &c" (Dalhousie, Senate, 1 Dec. 1874; H).

31 According to an article in the *Dalhousie Gazette*'s historical number, "Dalhousie received power to confer degrees in 1841, but did not exercise it until 1866, when the degree of B.A. was conferred on R. Shaw, of P.E.I., and J.H. Chase (who is also the first M.A.)." The first M.A. was granted in 1869, the first M.D. in 1872, and the first B.Sc. in 1880 ("Statistician" 172–73; G).

32 The information about the scandal was made public in a series of documents, which were published and exchanged among various groups and individuals concerned. The most important of these are J.W. Johnston's *Letter to the Granville Street Church* and his *Memorial to the Central Baptist Association of Nova Scotia*, and Brenton H. Eaton's *Reply of the Granville St. Baptist Church* (G). The matter was also the subject of debate in the pages of the *Christian Messenger* in the fall of 1867 and the early months of 1868.

33 The information about the meeting between Pryor and the elders of the church is from the "Statement of Deacons S. Sheldon, Dr. Parker, and R.N. Beckwith," included as the appendix to Brenton H. Eaton's *Reply of the Granville Street Baptist Church* (38–39; G).

34 Pryor's letter to the Granville Street Baptist Church is reproduced in Johnston's *Memorial to the Central Baptist Association of Nova Scotia* (G), but the original has not survived.

35 De Mille's undated letter to J.W. Johnston is reproduced in Johnston's *Memorial* (G), but the original has not survived.

36 It is not altogether clear how this second charge managed to become attached to the charge of immorality; Dr. Pryor was exonerated of fraud, although he was reproved by the council for carelessness in handling Miss Vass's affairs (Johnston, *Memorial* 35; G).

37 In a note dated 30 November 1889, MacMechan records Johnson as saying that De Mille had a "loose way of quoting scripture at first, earnest Christian at last, after the scandal" (H). Interpreting MacMechan's rather telegraphic style, the note seems to mean that Johnson thought De Mille quoted Scripture in conversation either inappro-

priately or humorously before the scandal, but that afterwards he became much more sincere and respectful in his attitude to religion.

38 Lawson's comment was recorded in a note dated 2 December 1889: "Lawson . . . [a] fine fellow, told me scandal about Pryor . . . never heard anything discreditable to him" (MacMechan; H). Interpreting MacMechan again, the second half of the remark appears to mean that Lawson said that nothing discreditable was heard about De Mille himself.

39 The information about Annie's change of church membership was supplied by Robert Paul, the church archivist for the Old Cambridge Baptist Church, in his letter of 22 February 1983 to the author, and comes from the church records (Paul; H). The original of Annie's letter has not survived.

40 Caroline was almost certainly a Presbyterian, as was her husband. Her comment here, like the one quoted earlier, must be treated cautiously, since she probably knew De Mille for only about four years.

41 Whether Bill was, in fact, correct in attributing De Mille's change of affiliation *solely* to these unpleasant circumstances is perhaps open to question. Herbert Creed comments in his letter to MacMechan of 12 February 1890 that, as early De Mille's first years at Acadia,

> While he was doubtless a sincere Christian, and occasionally occupied the pulpit very acceptably, he took delight in ridiculing everything like cant, and even the ordinary words and actions of the "pious" sort of people often brought to his keen eye and thin curling lip that peculiar sarcastic smile of his. (MacMechan; H)

This suggestion of a certain disdain on De Mille's part for the behaviour of his coreligionists might be considered the perception sharpened by hindsight, if it were the only one. But a roughly contemporary comment, which tends to support it, is also to be found in the report of the proceedings of the Maritime Baptists Convention of 1865. De Mille's resignation and removal to Dalhousie are there discussed:

> Rev. Isa. Wallace . . . referred to the circumstance mentioned in the Governors' report of Professor De Mill's removal. He thought that the parties who engaged him had wished to get a Baptist in that Institution. On expressing a supposition that the Baptists would thus be represented there, an emphatic "No" was given from all parts of the Convention. (*Christian Messenger* 30 Aug. 1865: 274)

This reported exchange could well be interpreted to suggest that some doubt already existed in 1865 about the strength of De Mille's attachment to the denomination. In the aftermath of the scandal, however, evidence of the attitude Creed describes can be found in De Mille's work. There are, for example, some sharply satirical comments about "the Tabernacle people" made by a Church of England clergyman who is one of the major characters in *Cord and Creese* (1869).

42 There is a persistent rumour that De Mille wrote and published a second pamphlet in which he set out his reasons for leaving the Baptists and joining the Episcopalians, but if the pamphlet ever existed (and I have not found any solid documentary evidence that it did), it has apparently not survived. MacLeod, however, thinks that it is in *The Early English Church* (1877) that De Mille "gives his reasons for joining the Church of his ancestors" (MacLeod 40; F).

43 The Nova Scotian Institute of Natural Science (later the Nova Scotia Institute of Science) was founded in 1863. De Mille is shown in the list of members as having joined in 1866 (Nova Scotian Institute 2.1: 6; G). His name is on the list of members for the following year (Nova Scotian Institute 2.2: 5; G), but does not reappear on any list after that. His colleague at Dalhousie, Dr. Lawson, was an active and continuing member for many years: for example, he "read a paper 'On the Trichina' and exhibited specimens of internal parasites" at the meeting of 4 February 1867 (Nova Scotian Institute 2.1: 2; G), and it was probably Lawson who introduced De Mille to the institute.

44 Bibliographic problems will be discussed in part 2, in the chapters on De Mille's fiction.

45 The dates given here are those of first publication only, whether in serial or volume form. In subsequent discussions of the work in part 2, I have included both first serial and first volume publication dates, where the distinction seemed appropriate.

46 Three letters from Arthur C. De Mille (9 April, 18 May, and 29 July 1880) to Harper and Brothers of New York, refer to the manuscript of "The Isles of Greece," but it has not been identified; the manuscript of "Ashod Webster" is still in the Killam Library Archives at Dalhousie University; and the manuscript of *A Strange Manuscript Found in a Copper Cylinder* was found and published belatedly in 1888.

47 "The Class-Lists were revised and it was found that there were 94 Students in attendance at College, 47 Undergraduates and 47 General Students" (Dalhousie, Senate, 21 Nov. 1876; H).

48 The information in this paragraph is taken from the selection of newspaper obituaries clipped and included in Frederick De Mill's Notebook (H). The cause of death quoted in the various accounts is also given on the 1880 death record for James De Mille (Halifax County, Death; H).

PART II

CHAPTER 6

De Mille's Occasional and Light Verse

The posthumous publication in 1893 of De Mille's long poem, *Behind the Veil*, drew attention to an aspect of his literary activity that was not as generally known as his fiction. For although he was an accomplished writer of occasional and light verse, only a very small sample was ever made public. In addition to *Behind the Veil*, his verse consists of two other major pieces, the "Class Poem 1854" and the "Phi Beta Kappa Poem" (1879), and a number of shorter ones: some appearing in magazines and student publications during his student days, some contributed to the *Christian Watchman*, and some (mostly fragments) found only in manuscript or in transcripts made by Archibald MacMechan. It is not at all clear what proportion of the whole has survived, for MacMechan records seeing a manuscript notebook containing verse among those of De Mille's papers that were in the possession of Annie De Mille in the years following De Mille's death, but he did not transcribe all he saw, and indeed he may not have seen it all (since, for example, he makes no reference to the "Class Poem" manuscript). Although De Mille's verse is of minor literary value, it does warrant some consideration in the context of his life, since it is clear that he took at least some of it seriously.

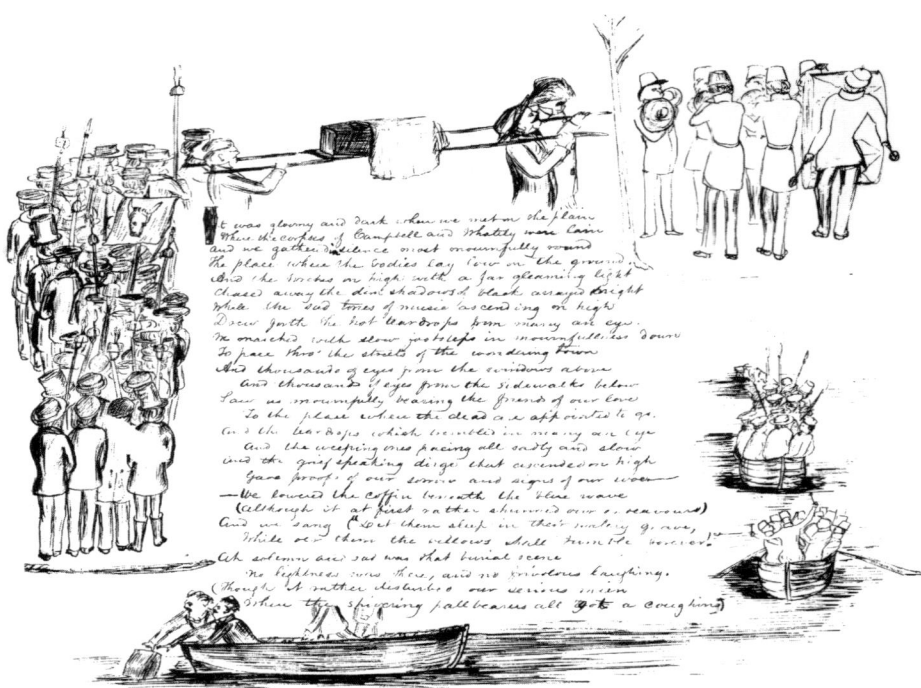

*Illustrated manuscript page of "Class Poem — 1854,"
describing the Junior Burial*

De Mille's earliest major poem is his "Class Poem 1854." It was first delivered as the traditional "class ode" at the class dinner, which formed part of the commencement ceremonies, when De Mille graduated from Brown University in September 1854, and was probably written after the conclusion of his examinations in July and the September ceremonies. The poem cannot ever have been intended for publication, for although it is finished in the sense that it is complete, it has clearly not received any kind of careful polishing. It was intended for oral delivery on a single occasion to an audience who had shared De Mille's experiences at Brown: it is a cheerful verse history (with illustrations by De Mille himself) of the class of 1854's collective progress through their four years at Brown. It begins with a reference to the "dinner of college" (line 11; A3),[1] referring not only to the intellectual sustenance they might be supposed to have received but also to the occasion of the poem's delivery, for one of the illustrations on the opening page shows a long banquet table with seated figures and waiters carrying dishes. In closing, De Mille declares the students' feelings for their "old Alma Mater":

> And the being who cheered us in earlier days
> For the rest of our lives we will zealously praise.
> Oh, let for one moment misfortune alight,
> Let the tempest contend, or the hurricane rack her —
> How quickly would all of us rush to the fight —
> How all — like old smokers — would love — toback her!
>
> (lines 411–16; A3)

Even at the last, it should be noted, De Mille was unable to resist a pun (on "to back her" and "tobacco"), thus upsetting the supposed gravity of the fierce affirmation of support for Brown. In between, the poem proceeds briskly in a well-organized narrative, falling naturally into seven distinct sections: a short introduction (1–20), a section on the freshman year (21–76), one on the sophomore year (77–154), one on the junior year (155–238), one on the senior year (239–319), one on the various careers in prospect for the members of the class (320–96), and a short conclusion (397–416).

The lines on the Junior Burial form a quite respectable specimen of descriptive verse. In its economy, rhythm, pace, and vividness, this section conveys very clearly a sense of the occasion that was then and later a high point of the college year not only for Brown students but for the people of Providence as well. The "Torch-Light Procession," which according to the elaborate printed programme consisted of the "Chief Marshall and aids," "Haskell's Sax-Horn Band," "escort from the Sophomore Class," "Pall Bearers," "Orators and Poet," "the Junior Class," and a "Deputation from the Senior Class," was evidently designed to include as many students as possible (Brown, Junior, 1853; H).[2] The procession formed in the early evening "at the corner of Hope and Waterman streets," with copies of the textbooks (Campbell's *Philosophy of Rhetoric* and Whately's *Elements of Rhetoric*) in the "coffin" (a weighted wooden box), marched along a circuitous route through the city, and finally rowed out into the harbour, to the deep water off Fox Point at the tip of Narragansett Bay. Here the funeral service itself took place, with the appropriate music, orations, burial service, committal (when the "coffin" was dropped overboard), and eulogy. De Mille's own description is vivid and humorous:

> It was gloomy and dark when we met on the plain
> Where the corpses of Campbell and Whately were lain,
> And we gathered in silence most mournfully round
> The place where the bodies lay low on the ground.
> And the torches on high with a far-gleaming light
> Chased away the dim shadows of black-arrayed night,
> While the sad tones of music ascending on high
> Drew forth the hot teardrops from many an eye.
> We marched with slow footsteps in mournfullness down
> To pace thro' the streets of the wondering town,
> And thousands of eyes from the windows above
> And thousands of eyes from the sidewalks below
> Saw us mournfully bearing the friends of our love
> To the place where the dead are appointed to go.
> And the teardrops which trembled in many an eye
> And the weeping ones pacing all sadly and slow
> And the grief-speaking dirge that ascended on high
> Gave proofs of our sorrow and signs of our woe —
> — We lowered the coffin beneath the blue wave
> (Although it at first rather shunned our endeavour),
> And we sang "Let them sleep in their watery grave,
> While o'er them the billows shall tumble forever!"
> Ah, solemn and sad was that burial scene —
> No lightness was there, and no frivolous laughing

(Though it rather disturbed our serious mien
When the shivering pallbearers all got a coughing). (lines 213–38)

After the service was finished, the participants rowed back to Ferry Wharf, disembarked, and marched back through the town by the direct route to the university, where the procession disbanded.

The satirical approach of the "Class Poem 1854" is perhaps not unexpected in the festive circumstances of the poem's occasion, but the ironic eye of the satirist is not always opened quite so early in life, particularly in a devoutly religious home of the sort from which De Mille had come to Brown only two years before, in the early months of 1852. The commentary, developed in lines 325–95, on the careers in prospect for himself and his classmates, makes obvious points, but it makes them with some pretence to wit and some plain good humour. Ironically, for example, in view of De Mille's own subsequent life, he writes in his advice about careers: "Don't be an Author. They always are debtors, / And in general perish by means of starvation" (327–28). Through cut the poem, in fact, the makings of the shrewd observer of the "Phi Beta Kappa Poem" and of *A Strange Manuscript Found in a Copper Cylinder* are already present, but the finished observer still has to be developed by wider experience of human folly and increased technical skill.

Taking the limitation of occasion and audience into account, we should be careful not to expect too much of the poem technically. Even after making such allowances, the poem can only be called clever, but rough. When De Mille speaks of addressing his audience in "doggerel rhyme," for example, he is being not modest, but accurate: he uses a line that is basically an anapaestic tetrameter, characterized by a great deal of variation, including frequent hypermetric syllables at the beginning or end, frequent use of initial trochaic feet, and an occasional shift into dactylic rhythm, and this looseness of rhythm contrasts sharply with the smooth, elegantly varied, and neatly managed rhythms of the "Phi Beta Kappa Poem." Nevertheless, the result is an engagingly rollicking rhythm, the tendency of which to accelerate in being read aloud would presumably be controlled by the poet as he read. The rhyme scheme is equally loose, again in sharp contrast to the regular couplets of the "Phi Beta Kappa Poem" (which are varied only occasionally, and then merely by the standard form of variation, the triplet). The "Class Poem" shifts frequently and unpredictably between couplets and alternating rhyme. The irregularity of the rhyme scheme, however, is undoubtedly a suitable match, like the irregular rhythm, for the considerable exuberance exhibited in the content of the poem.

This exuberance also affects the type of rhyme word chosen. In rhyming "rehearse it he" and "university" (4, 6), De Mille is clearly being deliberately playful; elsewhere, he uses similarly surprising rhymes in order to get himself out of a difficulty: "soon yours" and "Juniors" (155–56), or even to enable him to perpetrate a pun: "sky men" and "Hymen" (124–25). In a curious way, some of these surprising rhymes suggest those of Byron, whose work was certainly known to De Mille, and even anticipate those of W.S. Gilbert.

The punning rhymes are a further manifestation of the same exuberance, but they are by no means the only puns in the poem. The text, in fact, is full of them — for De Mille seems to make the pun his chief instrument of humour — beginning with that on "desert" and "dessert" (14) and ending with that on "toback her" and "tobacco" (416). Occasionally, the meaning is clear only after an examination of the drawings surrounding the text.[3] Although the pun is no longer fashionable, some of De Mille's puns must nevertheless be acknowledged as remarkably ingenious and quite funny.

There is, however, more to the poem than evidence of a simple talent for ingenious puns and wild rhymes. It offers for, example, the only extended commentary by De Mille on part of his own experience. It provides a very lively sketch (both in words and pictures) of life at Brown University in the early 1850s, and one that is the more interesting for being contemporaneous with what it describes.

The poem came to light only recently and, with the exception of the prose manuscript of "Ashdod Webster and His Starring Tour," is the longest complete holograph manuscript of De Mille's known to exist,[4] and by far the earliest, since both "Ashdod Webster" and the incomplete manuscript of "Behind the Veil," although not yet precisely dated, are clearly late productions. Consequently, the "Class Poem" offers a substantial sample of writing from the very beginning of De Mille's career, just as the "Phi Beta Kappa Poem" offers a sample from the very end of it.

De Mille's surviving shorter poems also include specimens written during his student years. In his junior year he wrote, as a contribution to a student collection, a piece of seminonsense verse called "The Brunensian Hippodrome," which appears, among other things, to commemorate the time-honoured student custom of taking the president's horse up to the top of a college building, although there is no evidence that De Mille himself ever took part in such an incident (B2).[5] In the same year he wrote one of two so-called "songs," or lyrics set to existing tunes. One of them, beginning with the words, "Ye whimpering coves assembled here," and designed to be sung to the tune of "Auld Lang Syne," was, as previously mentioned, written for the Junior Burial of 1853. The second, which begins with the words "Hearken to the Loud Resounding," and seems to have been intended to be sung to an unidentified contemporary hymn tune, was written for De Mille's fraternity, Psi Upsilon ("Song"; A3).

During his student days, De Mille also published a few of these shorter pieces. One of them, "Lord Hilbert. A Ballad," describes a medieval elopement in rather uncertain quatrains, which do not even approximate the traditional ballad stanza. "The Oaken Tree" is a pointless description of a tree's growth to maturity and descent to death. "The Maranon" presents a florid description of a river, apparently the Marañon River in northern Peru, which De Mille could have found references to in his reading about Central and South America during this period at Brown. Like the short stories he published during this period, the poems are similar in approach and competence to those of other contributors to the same magazines, but they do not really add anything to De Mille's status as a writer.

Some years later, in 1861 when he was helping Elisha publish the *Christian Watchman*, De Mille appears to have collaborated with his brothers Elisha and Alfred to put out a spoof supplement (the *Double XXtra*) to one of the Saint John newspapers, the *Morning News*, to which he contributed a group of poems satirizing the current political situation. The attribution to De Mille comes from another younger brother, Frederick, who, in his scrapbook (a large manuscript book full of pasted-in clippings from newspapers, on a variety of subjects) annotated his clippings of various poems with the letter "J" (Frederick De Mill, Scrapbook; H). The poems so marked are "A Bray from a Dunkie," "A Fenian Song," "The Mic-Mac Chief," "Moses Et Ingens Dux," and a group attributed to "Goliah O'Gahagan": "A Oad! To an Angle. Hon Angelus sed Anglin est," "A Oad On the Late Struggle," "A Oad. Porthrayin the Tory Party." Another poem attributed to him, "A Oad Detaylin a Resint Visit Till the Club's Domain," identified as being among the poems in the *Double XXtra*, does not appear among Frederick's clippings from it, but is nevertheless almost certainly De Mille's. The poems attributed to "Goliah O'Gahaghan" (or "Goliath O'Gahachan," or "Goliah O'Gahagan" — the variation in spelling is unlikely to be significant of anything other than haste) are written in a thick, pseudo-Irish brogue, and their author is described as a "Bombardier in the Royal Artillery," although he is alleged to be "The Spicial Reporter Till the 'Fraymen' " on the occasion of the "Oad. Porthrayin the Tory Party."[6] As a group, the poems from the *Double XXtra* are of some minor interest, for they show that De Mille took a quite partisan interest in local politics while living in Saint John. But any humour in the verse has long evaporated, and the dialect of the "O'Gahaghan" poems is both disagreeable and difficult to read. Individually none of the group assists De Mille's reputation as a satirist.

De Mille's assistance to Elisha in the publication of the *Christian Watchman* throughout 1861 included writing verse as well as prose. The first issue of the paper included the poem "Dies Irae. A New Translation," which Frederick acknowledges in an annotated clipping to be De Mille's work. Frederick also attributes, "The Death of Havelock," by "Lamed" to De Mille, although rather curiously he does not clip out an earlier poem on the same topic, "Havelock's March," which it is probably safe to consider as De Mille's also, although it appears with a different initial. A clipping of a poem entitled "Jesus — After the Manner of 'Stabat Mater' " is also annotated with the initial "J" in the scrapbook, but the newspaper in question has not been identified (Frederick De Mill, Scrapbook; H).

Other verse in the *Christian Watchman* presents a problem. The problematic verse is that which is included in his travel articles, "Recollections of Rome," for although, in describing De Mille's contribution to the *Christian Watchman*, Frederick includes "Recollections of Rome (much in verse)" (De Mill, Notebook; H), there is no reason to assume that it is all De Mille's own. Some of it is clearly not: the extensive quotations from Byron's *Childe Harold* can quickly be sorted out, although they are not acknowledged.[7]

Some of it, however, may be original work by De Mille, and the most obvious candidate is a long and apparently complete, but untitled, poem on the history of Rome. Unless De Mille plagiarized the whole poem from some as-yet-unidentified source, this is an original piece. It runs to 540 lines, and is written in fifteener (trochaic octometer curtailed) couplets, the metre of Tennyson's *Locksley Hall*, with a great deal of variation. It falls into nine sections, interpolated into some of the instalments of the "Recollections of Rome," although there is no indication that the division into sections is anything more than a consequence of being published serially. It begins with a description of what appears to be De Mille's first impressions of the city and his feelings of being at home there:

> Throned beside the yellow Tiber, Lo! the sevenhilled city stands,
> And she sways a double sceptre in her everlasting hands.
>
> For a spiritual honor, she has changed her old renown,
> And the diadem of Caesar for the triple Papal crown.
> . . . .
> Now at last my eyes behold thee, Oh, my country! Oh, my home!
> And my inmost heart rejoices in the very dust of Rome.
> Through the streets I walk familiar. I am not a stranger here.
> Every stone to me is precious. Every spot to me is dear.
> . . . .
> Here my spirit first awakened. Thought was gloriously born,
> Here I first arose from darkness, to an intellectual morn.
>
> And with years the knowledge deepened, for with each advancing year
> Hope, and wish, and thought, and feeling ever fondly centered here.
>
> Now at last my eyes behold thee, and I claim thee as my home,
> One among the world of scholars, I'm a citizen of Rome.[8]

In section 2, he continues by reflecting briefly that "Here Antiquity surrounds me . . . Potent in its fascination" (lines 37–54; appendix A), and in section 3, on the difference between the "depth of ruin" he sees and the "eternal city at the moment of her pride" in the days of the emperors (55–82). In section 4, he looks outward to the surroundings of the city — to the *campagna*, with the "Alban mountains" beyond, and to the Pontine marshes — and then reflects on the "solemn catacombs" under the city (83–100). In section 5, he goes back in imagination to the founding of the city, and follows its history down to the expulsion of the "bloody house of Tarquin" (101–46). In section 6, which is much the longest (166 lines), he traces the history of the Roman Republic down to the aftermath of the war with Carthage (147–312). Section 7 describes the rise of the Roman Empire with the coming of Julius Caesar (313–410), and section 8 narrates how the "dynasty of madmen" brings Rome itself into a state of decadence, ending with "a strain of music far away in Bethlehem / Sounding promise for the future" (411–76). Section 9 evokes Rome's return to glory as the centre of a new, Christian empire (477–540). If the length of the section on the Republic is any guide, it is there that De Mille's fascination with Rome is most strongly focused. Although the quality of this verse is not high it is certainly above average when one considers that it was written at the age of 18, if, as seems most probable, it was composed at the time of the European tour. The fifteener couplets are both unusual and ambitious. Moreover, taken with the prose it accompanies, the verse does much to fill in De Mille's emotional response to a key experience in his early life, for it reveals a deep feeling about what he saw and heard.

De Mille's most famous poem during his lifetime and immediately following his death seems never to have achieved a firm title, although it is now more often than not called "The Maiden of Passamaquoddy." Two different versions of it seem to exist. It was first published in the *Boston Commercial Bulletin* on 26 March 1870, as part of chapter 34 of De Mille's serial "The Minnehaha Mines"; the serial was reprinted in the Saint John *New Dominion and True Humorist*, and the poem appeared there on 16 April 1870. In this version, the original, it consists of 12 quatrains, and the title is "Lines. To Florence Huntingdon, Passamaquoddy, Maine" (A3). Frederick De Mill's clippings include a different version, the variant, which consists of five eight-line stanzas; it has been clipped from an unidentified newspaper, under an illegible date, with the published title ("Sweet Maiden of Quoddy") amended, in Frederick's handwriting, to "The Maiden of Quoddy" (Frederick de Mill, Scrapbook; H). The original version was reprinted in the *Journal of Education* in December 1932, accompanying an article on Indian place-names; it was supplied by Archibald MacMechan. He kept a clipping of the article when it appeared, and attached to it a typed copy of the variant version, which he annotated "An earlier version" (A3). It is the variant version that is reproduced (with a modern parody) in the *Atlantic Advocate*, where it is given the title "In New Brunswick You'll Find It" (A3).[9]

Other short pieces of light verse were discovered among De Mille's papers, and have survived. In De Mille's own hand, there are "Sympathy," a humorous piece about a knight and lady who meet while each is trying to commit suicide and end by consoling each other instead, and the well-known illustrated nonsense poem, "Eggs Eggs Eggs," which had been published, in a slightly different version, as "A Nightmare" in chapter 9 of *The Dodge Club*. Both of these manuscripts are complete (B2). Five other short, but apparently complete, pieces were transcribed by Archibald MacMechan. According to him, the transcript is taken from a notebook full of verse found among De Mille's papers ("The Cook He Flung His Dipper Down," "In Barbary," "Oh Its Ferra Wet in Ta Highlands," "Oh the Fashions Are Queer," and "Oh What Is That Glides Softly"). A number of fragments are also included ("And Dost Thou Hope My Favour," "The Fisher," "A Gallant Highwayman,"[10] "In That High Hall," "Oh Meet Me by Moonlight," "Oh the Chieftain is Gone," "There Was a Captive in a Prison," "Thy Friend He is False"). All of them can be taken to be De Mille's on MacMechan's authority.

In addition, several pieces of verse are attributed to De Mille on very doubtful grounds, and their status is uncertain. "A Raggedy Gang" is included by Eliza Ritchie in her anthology *Songs of the Maritimes*, and is identified by her as being by James De Mille (Ritchie 206; G), but unlike "The Gallant Highwayman" with which it appears in *Songs of the Maritimes*, "A Raggedy Gang" is not part of MacMechan's transcripts. Similarly, W.D. Lighthall attributes "The Indian Names of Acadia" to James De Mille on including it in his anthology *Songs of the Great Dominion*, but it is not among MacMechan's transcripts, and it is not mentioned in any other accounts of De Mille's writing (Lighthall 285–86; G).

De Mille's second major poem to survive is *Behind the Veil*, an experiment with religious mysticism, which was published posthumously, the manuscript having been found among his papers. MacMechan, who found it, probably while doing the research for his projected biography of De Mille soon after his arrival at Dalhousie, was extremely impressed by it. Even before preparing it for publication, he commended it enthusiastically to the readers of the *Week*, in a letter dated 26 November 1892, as "the most remarkable long poem ever written by a Canadian" (MacMechan, "Important" 37; F). With Mrs. De Mille's permission, it was prepared and published in 1893. Although it owes much to De Mille's reading, particularly of Richter, Tennyson, and the romantics, it also demonstrates considerable individuality of thought and feeling, and shows De Mille to be a thoughtful and complex personality.

In spite of MacMechan's efforts to promote it, the poem does not seem to have been widely or warmly reviewed. MacMechan's colleagues at Dalhousie praised it in reviews: W.C. Murray called it De Mille's "best piece of literary work" (78; F), and James Liechti characterized it as "a daring flight of the imagination . . . wonderfully clearly drawn" (81; F).

But Charles G.D. Roberts, who reviewed it for the *Week*, was guarded in his remarks, and described it tactfully as "interesting in design, elevated in conception, and measurably skilful in execution" (301; F). A more recent critic, Fred Cogswell, is more forthright in his condemnation of it as a "bad poetical exercise" (112; F). The anonymous reviewer for the *Dial* dismissed it as "a rhapsody upon a familiar plan, and of doubtful poetic value" (84; F). Most of De Mille's later critics choose to ignore the poem altogether.

No information about the poem is available. MacMechan attempted no investigation of its background, and no date for its composition has subsequently been established. In the absence of any evidence to the contrary, however, it is probably safe to assume that it was written after De Mille had moved to Halifax. Internal evidence, in the form of some similarities between the poem and the mystical experience of one of the characters in *Cord and Creese*, may help in narrowing down the date of composition to the late 1860s. Content, setting, and tone of this part of the novel match those of the poem very closely: the descriptions of the spirit world, although very brief and lacking in detail reflect what is described in *Behind the Veil*; the wilderness promontory, which is the setting for an encounter with the spirit world, coincides exactly with the setting of the opening of the poem; and the relationship of two of the novel's characters matches that of the Spirit and the Seer in the poem. Given these similarities, it is probable that the two pieces were written within a short time of each other. Since *Cord and Creese* began serial publication in *Harper's Bazaar* in November of 1867, and the first book edition appeared in 1869 (Edwards 13; D),[11] it seems most likely that the composition of *Behind the Veil* took place in the late 1860s.

In the poem, De Mille presents a vision of immortality described by a narrator, the Seer, who is permitted to journey into the world beyond the veil of mortality and is instructed in its nature by a Spirit. In the introduction (stanzas 1–8),[12] the Seer has been driven by grief at the death of his beloved to live in seclusion, and by prayer and fasting he achieves communication with the Spirit who grants his request to be allowed to see his beloved. At the Spirit's invitation, he leaves his body and starts his journey. In part 1, which is a vision of earth (stanzas 9–27), the Seer uses his new faculty of "Absolute Knowledge," and at first sees only scenes of the earth he has just left, but he discovers that he is not limited to viewing earthly scenes and may go wherever he chooses, simply by the power of his will. In part 2, the journey through the universe (stanzas 28–44), he travels rapidly through star systems perpetually increasing in magnitude, until he comes to a barrier that is the edge of a system so vast that everything he has seen so far is minute in comparison, and he learns that beyond this one are others that are proportionately even greater. He is terrified, but the Spirit encourages him by explaining that only God can comprehend the infinity of his creation. In part 3, the vision of the immortals (stanzas 45–60), the Seer turns from contemplation of the infinite universe to observation of its various ranks of spirits, some no different from himself, others so splendid that he can hardly comprehend them; again he is terrified, and again he has to be encouraged by the Spirit. In part 4, recollections of the loved and lost one (stanzas 78–91), the beloved appears to the Seer in the form of a great and radiant spirit, but he is unable to attract her attention, which is turned to God above her. Grief overwhelms him, and he falters and is about to fall headlong into despair. In part 5, the Spirit's discourse on divine love (stanzas 92–123), the Spirit intervenes to stop the Seer's fall, and explains to him the essence of the life of the invisible world: it is inhabited by the loving and the loved who move through an infinite progression of joyous unions towards the highest, which is union with the infinite, in an eternal upward movement towards God; God, in turn, reaches downward towards the least of these souls. At the end of this exposition, the Spirit accedes to the Seer's request and appears to him in his full majesty, causing the Seer to confuse him with God himself, for which he is rebuked because the Spirit, despite the majesty of his appearance, is only a created being like the Seer himself, and has put aside his greatness to assist those on Earth. In the concluding section (stanzas 124–25), the Spirit releases the Seer, who returns to his body, having in earthly terms been away only a few moments, for there is no time in the spirit world.

The subject and its development in *Behind the Veil*, even allowing for the abruptness of the conclusion, are undoubtedly on the grand scale, and they are treated very formally. De Mille prefaces the work with a quotation, in the original Greek, from Plato's *Apologia Socratis*, describing poets as "inspired, like the prophets and givers of oracles" (Plato 85; G). The quotation suggests that the poem is the result of divine inspiration. The poem consists of 125 stanzas of five (occasionally six) lines of unequal length (4–4–4–8–8 feet respectively, with the last foot of the second and the fourth lines incomplete), in a basically trochaic rhythm, rhyming ABABB. It is a difficult stanza form and perhaps not ideally suited to its purpose of narrative discourse, although the poem has clear overall dramatic shape —

the search for, and encounter with, the spirit of the woman the Seer has loved — and the reader is not only conscious of this narrative framework, but also aware that everything is artistically subordinated to it. In the margin of the text appear a number of glosses that summarize the action, somewhat in the manner of Coleridge's *Rime of the Ancient Mariner*, although De Mille's glosses are rather more plain and matter-of-fact than Coleridge's.

What results from his inspiration is a vision of the overwhelming vastness and otherness of the divine nature, from which De Mille's understanding of the nature of immortality can be characterized quite specifically. The mode of immortality in *Behind the Veil* is asymptotic: the soul ascends towards God "in infinite progression" (stanza 98). But although he refers to "infinite progression" and relies on the constant reiteration of words such as "forever," "evermore," "perpetual," and "unceasing," his marginal gloss says that the "highest joy is union with the Infinite" (God), which suggests that he sees eventual union with God as a possible end to the infinite progression.

The evidence for immortality depends not on God's justice but on his love. God, De Mille says, "comes down / And in love He ceaseth never / To assist each aspiration" (stanza 108). The infinite progression towards union with the divine is made in his vision by "soul with soul in union wrought" (stanza 98). The implication is that the earthly "sympathetic union" (stanza 64) that the Seer has enjoyed with his beloved is a foreshadowing of the ultimate union with God — a personal union in which the identity of the individual is retained.

The form in which the individual survives is that of the so-called "shadow man" (Flew 140; G). De Mille's narrator leaves his body and travels in its nonmaterial counterpart: "like a Thought, a thing of Light, / All my spirit darted up to an immeasurable height" (stanza 8). De Mille's spirits, although not described in detail, nevertheless at least resemble their physical counterparts, for the Seer unhesitatingly recognizes "the Loved and the Lost One" in her spirit form (although this recognition is presumably made through his temporarily borrowed faculty of absolute knowledge, not his ordinary mortal senses).

The universe of immortality appears to the Seer to be infinite. When he asks about this, the Spirit explains that the universe only seems to be infinite to the minds of its finite, created inhabitants. The gradations of created being are infinite, but the *set* (from the infinite Creator's point of view) is finite. It is, moreover, an inhabited universe. The Seer is not only constantly accompanied by his spirit guide, but also discovers that "All the worldless void was peopled by that spiritual host" (stanza 48), who are are instantly visible to him as a result of his new faculty of absolute knowledge.

The separation of the mortal from the immortal is produced by the veil of the title. The phrase "beyond the veil" is an orthodox figurative allusion to the next world that was already current at the time De Mille wrote, and was possibly both more familiar and less of a cliché then than now.[13] Beyond using it in his title, however, De Mille does not develop the allusion. His religious background would certainly, however, have made him familiar with the biblical reference, and he would also have known Tennyson's use of the phrase ("In Memoriam" 56.25-28; G).[14] The veil, for De Mille, is the veil of mortality and of the corporeal body: it cuts the mortal off from the immortal, those still in the body from the spirits. Much of De Mille's vision of the immortal world beyond the veil is influenced by his reading of the German romantic philosopher-novelist, Jean-Paul Friedrich Richter. Richter wrote two works involving a vision of immortality: the "Traum Über das All," and the *Campaner Tal*. Smeed points out that De Quincey's translation of the "Traum Über das All" (which appeared under the title "Dream upon the Universe" in *London Magazine* [1824]), was only one of a number of Richter's works to appear in English (Smeed 86 n10; G). De Mille certainly knew De Quincey's translation of the "Traum Über das All," since he quotes it in the *Elements of Rhetoric*.[15] There are, however, considerable differences between his vision and that of Richter, as well as some obvious similarities.

The most important similarity between De Mille and Richter is that both have glimpsed the "holy" — what Rudolf Otto, in *The Idea of the Holy*, defines as the "mysterium tremendum," which is at the same time fascinating ("fascinans"), and which evokes both fear and desire in the beholder (12, 30; G). But unlike Richter, whose speaker is overwhelmed with joyful desire, De Mille has focused almost exclusively on the "tremendum" — the element that evokes fear by virtue of its strangeness. The recognition of the centrality of the "mysterium tremendum" to De Mille's poem, however, provides a way of reconciling the several self-contradictions or paradoxes in the poem, which are otherwise hard to understand. For De Mille writes a poem distinguished by its formality of structure and rational discourse, yet prefaces it with a quotation that defines poetic inspiration as nonrational. He presents the apparently joyous and inspiring theme of immortality and spirit life in a narrative in which they appear to become a source rather of fear and dismay than of joy and wonder. And in a poem whose cosmology is clearly designed to represent, as a tribute to the Creator, an astronomically accurate picture of the size and magnificence of the universe, almost all De Mille's warmth of feeling is reserved for the vision of the earth itself and for the mortal bodies that inhabit it. Moreover, the grief that is made more unbearable for the Seer by the fact that life after death will not reunite the lovers does not appear (from the little that is known about him) to have any foundation in De Mille's own life. Left unreconciled, such a series of contradictions could add up merely to Cogswell's "bad poetical exercise." Reconciled, however, they fall into place as a series of attempts to recognize, comprehend, and accept the fear and the desire evoked in the creature by the vision of the creator.

The reconciliation is not total, but, nevertheless, it resolves most of the major difficulties with the poem. The formal precision of the verse, for example, emerges as an attempt to control an overwhelming experience, and is perhaps rather overdone, since what is intended to control the experience ends up by almost totally concealing it; the vision must be brought under some degree of control, however, as much to allow the visionary to cope with it, as to enable him to communicate it to others. Furthermore, the Seer's apparently naïve mistakings of lesser spirits for "the Infinite" also fall into place as repeated attempts to keep things down to manageable proportions; the Seer is already overwhelmed by the Spirit's appearance in all its majesty — the assumption that this is the Infinite protects him, as it were, from having to face the knowledge that something even greater and more overwhelmingly majestic exists. Moreover, since the Seer's understanding of the joy and wonder of immortality and divine love is evidently clouded by his much more immediate emotional encounter with the otherness of the divine nature, the divine love must be asserted consciously in the poem; yet such a conscious (and, I believe, genuine) affirmation of divine love is insufficient to balance out the visionary impact of divine otherness, and hence appears merely as a rather ponderous sermon on the subject. The warmth of feeling reserved for the earth also seems less strange in this context, for the earth is now seen as the part of the created universe which can be praised uninhibitedly because its relatively small size and its familiarity set it within the Seer's capacity to comprehend and love. On the other hand, a grief that has left no observable trace in De Mille's own life history (if indeed it actually had a biographical source), is, by force of its association with the spirit universe, itself magnified to cosmic proportions. These reconciliations, therefore, which bring apparent paradoxes into a comprehensible pattern, make *Behind the Veil* a surprising, even a startling poem, if it is looked at closely.

The last of De Mille's three major poems to survive is the "Phi Beta Kappa Poem," as it is now called. This poem on the state of humankind was delivered by the author himself at the anniversary reunion of the Phi Beta Kappa Society of Brown University on 16 June 1879. It exists in two versions: a manuscript in De Mille's younger brother Frederick's hand, preserved in the Killam Library Archives of Dalhousie University, and a published version included in the report of the reunion proceedings in the local paper, the *Providence Daily Journal*, for 18 June 1879. The manuscript has no title, and the heading in the published version is simply "Prof. De Mille's Poem." Except for occasional mentions and the publication of one excerpt (Koopman; E), the poem has been generally overlooked since De Mille's death.

The subject of the poem is organized with skill. The introductory section poses the general question, "How fares it with mankind?" and sets out the intention of the poem, which is "with equal eye to scan / The darker ills and brighter hopes of man" (lines 15–16; A3).[16] De Mille then characterizes the darker side of humanity in terms of the cult of self: he begins by condemning the greed that infects all levels of society. He starts with the schoolboy who copies texts linking virtue and wealth. The boy thus learns an attitude of mind that creates money-grubbing in the professions and culminates by producing the statesman who

> acts on Walpole's sage advice,
> Clothed in the maxim, "Each man has his price,"
> Holds most things false, but this, at least, as true,
> The paths of glory lead to fortune too. (lines 45–48)[17]

Having condemned those who seek wealth, he then goes on to condemn those who, having gained it, ostentatiously display it, including in this category not only those who show off money and property but also those who show off intellectual achievements — teachers who "seek, where'er they go, / Not sacred truths, but merely vulgar show" (61–62). He follows this with a stronger condemnation of those who distort truth in their ostentation: the preachers who sensationalize the gospel for the sake of fame (65–66), the "rampant Radicals who bawl 'Reform:' / Men who pervert all words, turn black to white" (68–69), and the "fashionable critic" who dismisses "the virtues prized through all the past" and ends up worshipping himself (83, 100–10).

After summarizing the evils of the day as "Self-seeking, self-indulgence, self-display" (111),[18] the poet goes on to point out that humankind should not be judged entirely by these examples, for "Behind the external show, they hold their place, / The better portion of the human race," which is "content to live obscure, / With this aim only, that their lives be pure" (123–30). The true leaders of humanity, he goes on to argue, are the "self-contained, the simple, the sincere" (132), and we should choose men of this sort, such as Socrates, Horace, Thoreau, and Wordsworth, as examples to follow, and in following them "the chief energies of life direct / Not to the income but the intellect" (147–48). But the poet warns that we should not, when we "single out the best" (153), judge by externals only; we should examine character, for in human nature "when its inner self is understood / Still is the evil balanced by the good" (155–56), and often a man (such as Shelley, Bacon, or Rousseau) who loves virtue is unable to practise it. Nevertheless, we must give such a one "credit for his good intent" in order to encourage him (192).

Generally, however, the poet continues, humanity is divided into those who seek "a present pleasure for the sense," and those who seek "a far off, future recompense" (197, 198). From the latter arise those "who follow virtue for herself alone" (206), and they form "the high and pure humanity / Whose judgment is the true *vox populi*" (209–10). Humanity is judged both by God and itself, so that "The heaven of God the just may hope to find, / And, joined to this, the memory of mankind" (221–22). Those heroes who give their lives in response to the call of duty are specially remembered (225–26). In America, such heroes are those of the Civil War on both sides, both in battle (Robert E. Lee and Thomas "Stonewall" Jackson) and in political action (John Brown and William Lloyd Garrison). What we learn from such heroes, De Mille contends, is that "Man may not live for his own self alone" (244): everyone has to choose between self-love and the love of God. In conclusion, he points out that, because we have a choice, good may still be found among humanity on earth in the form of the traditional virtues won for us by truth, which "For us the long laborious strife sustained, / Bearing these gifts of God through myriad years" (268–69), and the poem ends with a firm prediction of the eventual triumph of truth.

The view of the state of humanity presented in this poem is traditional in the values it affirms and in the criticisms it makes. The persona De Mille adopts is that of a moderate and reasonable man. In the opening lines, for example, he suggests that in judging humanity one should not adopt the position of either Leigh Hunt ("Write me as one who loves his fellow men" [10]) or Byron ("I have not loved the world, nor the world me" [12]), but instead should "walk awhile with each one hand-in-hand" (14), and look at humanity with an "equal eye" (15). Moreover, he presents himself as one of a consensus: "Be *ours* the task" (15; emphasis added).

The poem is equally traditional in form. De Mille's debt to the Age of Reason — to Pope, Johnson, and Goldsmith, in particular — is apparent in his choice of the heroic couplet. His own couplets, although perhaps not as expertly turned as those of his models, are, for the most part respectably, and occasionally even sharply executed. He writes, for example: "These things must be, the world shall never lack / The swindler and twaddler and the quack" (113-14). This couplet, without being obviously dependent on any particular rhetorical device, nevertheless fairly spits contempt. Yet, although De Mille handles his topic competently, his range of satirical techniques is fairly limited: he relies heavily on parallelism ("Some burst in laughter, some to weeping fall, / Banter with Horace, storm with Juvenal, / Find virtue all too weak, or vice too strong" [5-8]) and to a lesser extent on antithesis ("In love with virtue, yet by vice controlled" [170]). His sonic devices are restricted to alliteration, which he is inclined to overemphasize in phrases such as "Preaching polygamy and parricide," and "Ready alike to prattle or to pray" (77, 43). His figures are few and not particularly striking, except perhaps for his use, in discussing sin, of the metaphor of "the antidote of penitence" (180). He is also fond of personification, which he uses for Public Opinion, Good, and Truth (213, 255, 267). His diction is appropriate and smooth, in keeping with his low-key approach: he is not trying to shock people into change, for he knows that "These things must be."

De Mille's moderation is perhaps encouraged by the fact that he is very aware of his many predecessors in the criticism of human nature. Yet at the same time, he is far from adopting any single one of them as a model: he does not lean consistently towards the *saeva indignatio* of Swift, the persistent waspishness of Pope, the geniality of Dryden, or the melancholy of Johnson. Of all his eighteenth-century models, he is perhaps closest to Goldsmith in mood, for the point of the poem turns on a plea for mercy for errant humankind:

> Scan not too strictly how man's life is spent,
> But give him credit for his good intent;
> So may the path with good intentions paven
> Lead him, not down to hell, but up to Heaven. (191–94)

In the last line of this, the phrasing departs from Johnson's "Sir, hell is paved with good intentions" (Boswell 555; G), which De Mille would certainly have known and might well have in mind at the time of composition. But De Mille turns it to precisely the opposite effect, by rephrasing it to resemble the more usual modern wording attributed to Archbishop Trench (Benham 785). This manipulation of a literary maxim is one of the many allusions worked skilfully (and sometimes playfully) into the text of the poem, and, like all the others, it is more than a sign of a literary man addressing an audience of his peers. Allusion, whether it is played straight or given a satiric twist, is for De Mille a device for manipulating tone and for modulating it from the satiric opening, through the carefully reasoned middle section, into the almost passionate vision of the triumph of truth concludes the poem.

The satiric vision, however moderate, of the "Phi Beta Kappa Poem" makes very clear its links with De Mille's best-known work, *A Strange Manuscript Found in a Copper Cylinder.* Both the poem and the novel maintain a healthy scepticism about human society, recorded by a clear-eyed and keen-witted observer. The novel has an exuberance of fantastic imagination that in the poem is replaced by a more sober and tempered judgement, but the two works are nevertheless manifestly akin in their vision of the folly, and the potential for good, of human society.

Even when due allowance is made for the fact that personality is not always clearly visible in literary works, the personality of James De Mille that is reflected in his verse — both the major poems and the minor pieces taken as a whole — is somewhat bewildering. It is hard to reconcile the urbane but sharp-eyed and sharp-tongued social critic who wrote the "Phi Beta Kappa Poem," with the religious mystic whose vision is recorded in *Behind the Veil,* or with the lively undergraduate who wrote the "Class Poem 1854." Our understanding of De Mille, however, certainly becomes more three-dimensional as the various sides of his work are brought into a stronger relationship.

DE MILLE'S OCCASIONAL AND LIGHT VERSE

NOTES

1 These and all subsequent line references in parentheses in the text are to my published edition of the poem (A3).

2 The programme also includes a "Song by Messrs De Mille, Denny, & Holley/'Auld Lang Syne.' — Words by De Mille," (item 9), and a "Poem, By James De Mille" (item 4) (Brown, Junior, 1853; H). The words of the latter are not included, and if it has survived, it has not yet been identified.

3 The drawings have a vigour, clarity, and humour of their own, which makes them more than mere appendages to the verse, while at the same time, unlike the random doodlings of the notebook that has survived from De Mille's years at Brown and the rather overcrowded illustrations to the Virgil translation or to "Eggs Eggs Eggs," they form a vivid commentary on the text.

4 The manuscript, which is now in the archives of the John Hay Library of Brown University, is a small leather-covered book of unruled white paper, with the words "Class Poem 1854" stamped on its cover in gold capitals. The name "Annie Pryor" is written in Annie's own handwriting on the first blank leaf. On each page, the text, written in De Mille's small but legible hand, is surrounded by pen-and-ink illustrations.

5 The poem is, according to Brown University archivist Martha Mitchell,

included in a small volume with a title written in some years later in the hand of William Whitman Bailey, *Psi Upsilon Legends and Lyrics, by Marcus Waterman, James DeMille and John Fry Tobey — 1852 to 1855*. The writing is probably Waterman's, since it matches the rest of the book, and he did the illustrations (which, by the way, are in living colour) for De Mille's poem. (2 May 1983; H)

6 Four poems from the *Morning News* itself are also generally attributed to De Mille. The first of these, which appeared in early November of 1854, "A Solemn Dirge," with the initial "W," is included in Frederick's scrapbook, but is not annotated with the customary "J" (C). Frederick's omission may be an oversight, but is more likely a confirmation that the poem is not by De Mille. The second, "A Forlorn Stave," which appeared a week later with the same initial, is not included in the scrapbook at all, supporting the case that the previous one was not by De Mille (C). The third, "New Brunswick Land Jobbing" by "Shakespeare," which appeared in March of 1861, is an open question. De Mille was certainly in Saint John, and he was also certainly concerned, as is evident from the pages of the *Christian Watchman*, with the land-jobbing scandal, but the scrapbook does not include the poem (C). "A Ode to the Great Confederation" (December 1864) is doubtful. De Mille might have been in Saint John at this time, since his father was ill, but it is difficult to imagine him submitting satirical verse to a local newspaper in such circumstances.

7 In addition to the extensive borrowing from *Childe Harold*, there are numerous

fragments in several different forms, none of them acknowledged. Among these, for example, included in "Recollections of Naples 9, 'Sorrento,' " are several lines from Pope's translation of part of Book 7 of the *Odyssey*, "The Gardens of Alcinous" (*Christian Watchman* 19 June 1861).

8 These stanzas are from "Recollections of Rome III: 'The Modern City — Its Repulsions' " (*Christian Watchman* 31 July 1861). For other parts, see the *Christian Watchman* 32, 34, and 35–40 (appendix A).

9 "The Minnehaha Mines" included two other pieces of verse: an untitled piece beginning "3,000,000 bushels Coal!" and "Thoughts of Home. Dedicated to Florence Huntingdon," neither of which has attracted very much attention (A3).

10 This was published as "The Gallant Highwayman" in *Songs of the Maritimes: An Anthology of the Poetry of the Maritime Provinces*, edited by Eliza Ritchie, presumably on MacMechan's authority (Ritchie 7; G).

11 In *Cord and Creese*, Edith Brandon is left for dead with other victims during a cholera epidemic, and is almost buried alive. She is rescued by composer and violinist Paolo Langhetti, who, since her immediate family appear all to have died in the epidemic, takes her with him to Halifax and arranges for her to be cared for. There she reveals to her rescuer her belief that she had actually passed into the spirit world, and attempts a description of her experiences. Langhetti is anxious to share her vision of the spirit world more deeply, and achieves this experience by playing his violin to her. He is then inspired to write an opera, the music of which he plays to her for the first time at night in a wilderness setting.

12 Stanza numbers are introduced for the sake of convenient reference and do not appear in the original.

13 In the *Oxford English Dictionary*, under "veil," it is defined as a phrase used "figuratively or allusively . . . chiefly after Hebrews vi.19 . . . now commonly with reference to the next world." Both Hebrews 6.19 and 9.3 make reference to the veil of the temple in Jerusalem, which concealed the tabernacle from the worshippers.

14 Tennyson's last line is the *Oxford English Dictionary*'s earliest citation for the phrase (1850) in precisely these words.

15 I have discussed elsewhere the relationship between Richter's work and De Mille's poem (Monk; F).

16 These and all subsequent line references in parentheses in the text are to my published edition of the poem (A3).

17 The maxim about each man having his price is attributed to Sir Robert Walpole by many authorities, but is apparently a very much older proverbial expression. The line about the "paths of glory" offers an ironic twist to Thomas Gray's "The paths of glory lead but to the grave" (line 36; G).

18 Cf. Tennyson: "Self-reverence, self-knowledge, self-control, / These three alone lead life to sovereign power" ("Oenone" 142–43; G).

CHAPTER 7

De Mille's Early Fiction

In establishing the corpus of De Mille's fiction, his earliest work can conveniently be divided into two groups: the short stories, and the two religious novels. These groups, together with the children's books, will be discussed in this chapter. The satirical romances, as De Mille describes them, and the novels of sensation will be discussed in chapter 8, and the anomalous and posthumously published *Strange Manuscript Found in a Copper Cylinder* will be discussed in chapter 9. Problematic titles will be discussed in relation to the group in which they appear to fit.

Sixteen short stories appeared under De Mille's name during his final year at Brown University. Most of them appeared in a weekly magazine, *Flag of Our Union*: "Hugo von Ehrenfels" (February), "The Balloon Ascent" (March), "The Spanish Knight" (April), "The Contrabandist" (April), "The Captive's Flight" (May), "The Castle and Crucible" (May), "The Priestess of the Sun" (June), "The Were Wolf" (June), "The Corsair of Scio" (July), "The Australian Footman" (July), "The Artist of Florence" (August), and "The Rose of Acadie" (November). The others appeared in *Gleason's Pictorial Drawing-Room Companion*: "The Circassian's Revenge" (February), "The Traitor's Doom" (April), "Rudolph the Burgess" (June), and "The American Trooper" (June). Both magazines were published by Gleason's of Boston. Some years later, "The Loss of the

Hector" appeared in *Godey's Lady's Book* (May 1862).

Even De Mille's short stories, however, are not without problems. One story sometimes attributed to De Mille is "Bend or Break; A Story for Boys," which appeared in the *Christian Watchman* for 14 August 1861. It appeared, however, with the initials "J.D.C.," which De Mille does not use elsewhere in the *Watchman*, and unlike other contributions that can confidently be assigned to him, it is not tagged as specially written "for *The Christian Watchman*." It is, moreover, a rather simpleminded Sunday-school fable, quite unlike any of his other short stories. The same (except that there are no initials attached to it) is true of "The Highwayman," which appeared in the issue for 24 July, and which is also sometimes attributed to De Mille. It is possible that both attributions are correct, but it seems unlikely.

Beyond this problem, however, there is the assertion, in the list of De Mille's published work prepared by J.S. Knowles, that De Mille published "Many stories in N.Y. Ledger & other papers 1855 to 1860" (Knowles, List; H).[1] None of these have been identified. The assertion itself, moreover, may not be considered very reliable, since the list includes the titles for only two such stories, and both are elsewhere described as novels (*The Arkansas Ranger* and *The Soldier and the Spy*, both untraced). If De Mille did contribute stories anonymously to the *Ledger*, it is doubtful that any of them could be identified from internal evidence alone.

In style and content, the short stories in the magazines are all very similar. They are brief, anecdotal in structure, melodramatic in style, and set in exotic historical or contemporary locations, and they usually offer a romantic interest. "The Loss of the *Hector*: Or, the Transformation," is typical of them.

In this late tale, young George Pentonville meets and falls in love with Emma Randolph during a crossing of the Atlantic on board the *Hector*, which Emma believes to be the ship in which Pentonville has all his fortune invested. During a terrible storm at sea, the ship capsizes and sinks. Pentonville manages to get Emma (wearing an inflatable rubber life preserver that he provides for her) and her aunt safely to shore on Sable Island, where "the government of the neighboring province of Nova Scotia had built sheds and huts for the succor of the shipwrecked sailor" ("Loss" 256; A2). Competently, Pentonville lights a signal fire and raises a distress flag, and all three are rescued next day by a steamer travelling from Halifax to Boston, and taken to Boston. There Emma is reunited with her father, who immediately announces that he has arranged to marry her to Lord Eglinstone, whom she has not met before, in spite of her pleas, supported by those of her aunt, to be allowed to marry Pentonville even though (as she believes) he has lost his fortune in the wreck of the *Hector*. When Lord Eglinstone arrives, he reveals himself to be George Pentonville, who was only mistakenly identified as the owner of the ship by the captain, and had wooed her under another name in order not to be loved for his title alone. All, therefore, ends happily.

De Mille's limitations and capabilities as a writer of short stories are evident in this example. On the one hand, his plot is weak and hackneyed, and his characters are stiff and not sharply realized as individuals rather than types. On the other hand, Pentonville's prudence, an unusual characteristic in a romantic hero, in providing himself with a life preserver, is both refreshing and amusing, and suggests an attempt to break from the stereotype. Moreover, the description of the storm has considerable narrative vigour and vividness. All in all, as exemplified by "The Loss of the *Hector*," De Mille's short stories, although they cannot be considered to have great literary value, are nevertheless neatly suited to their purpose of entertainment, and are by no means negligible as examples of popular-magazine fiction of their period.

De Mille wrote two series of books for boys — the B.O.W.C. Series and the Young Dodge Club Series — and three singletons, unrelated to the series or to each other. A fourth unrelated and untraced work is attributed to De Mille. The former series consists of *"The B.O.W.C.": A Book for Boys* (1870), *The Boys of Grand Pré School* (1870), *Lost in the Fog* (1870), *Fire in the Woods* (1871), *Picked Up Adrift* (1872), and *The Treasure of the Seas* (1872). The latter series consists of *Among the Brigands* (1871), *The Seven Hills* (c.1872), and *The Winged Lion: Or, Stories of Venice* (1877). The three singletons are *Andy O'Hara: Or, The Child of Promise* (1861),[2] "The Missionary's Son" (1861),[3] and *The Lily and the Cross. A Tale of Acadia* (1874). Apart from the fact that no copy of the book version of *Andy O'Hara* can be located, there is no confusion or problem concerning publication date or attribution of any of the titles listed above.

The problematic book among De Mille's books for children is *John Wheeler's Two Uncles: Or, Launching into Life*. It was published in 1860 according to Watters's *Checklist of Canadian Literature* (273; D), in which Watters is following the *American Catalogue of Books* (D). Edwards, in her checklist, agrees with Watters (24; D). De Mille himself does not

177

mention the title in a list of his novels prepared for Messrs. Harnes (the publishers of *Literary World*) in 1878,[4] but since he omits all the juvenile titles, this may not be significant. It is mentioned in J.S. Knowles's list, where it is dated 1865 (List; H), and it is included in the list prepared by the family shortly after De Mille's death (a note on the back of the list says that it was done in "1890 or 1889" and adds, "Most out of print") for the librarian of the Legislative Library of Nova Scotia, which is probably quite trustworthy ("De Mille, Professor James"; H). It is not altogether clear, moreover, whether it is a book for children, since no copies have been located, and it has therefore not been possible to read it. The date of 1860, if Watters is correct, would place it immediately before *Andy O'Hara* and "The Missionary's Son," both of which are pietistic fictions of development written for the *Christian Watchman*, and each of which traces the development of a young boy from a Christian home who goes astray but returns to the fold in adult life. It would seem plausible that *John Wheeler's Two Uncles* would be of a similar nature, and the title, insofar as it may be trusted as a guide to the content, would also support the idea that it is a book for boys. It seems appropriate, therefore, that it should be placed, tentatively, until a copy turns up and can be definitively assessed, among De Mille's books for children.

De Mille's best-known books for children are the six volumes of the B.O.W.C. Series. The initials stand for "Brethren of the White Cross," a secret society organized by a group of five boys (Bart Damer, Bruce and Arthur Rawdon, Tom Crawford, and Phil Kennedy) at Grand Pré School. The five protagonists are introduced in *"The B.O.W.C."*:

> Two of these boys were big, brawny, broad-shouldered fellows, with Roman features, and dark, curling hair. They very closely resembled one another. These were the two Rawdons, to whom the rooms belonged. The elder was named Bruce, and the younger Arthur. Of the others, one was tall and slight, Tom Crawford by name; and the other was small and slight, and was called Phil Kennedy. (*"The B.O.W.C."* 17; A1)

The four are led by Bart Damer:

> In the midst of the uproar the door opened, and the Venerable Warden made his appearance. Throwing off his white robe, he disclosed the fair, round face of a fresh, handsome boy, with merry

mischievous eyes, and curling golden hair. That busy brain of his had been prolific in all sorts of plans dear to boys; while his generous nature and frank, pleasant manner made Bart Damer the favourite of Grand Pré School. ("*The B.O.W.C.*" 18; A1)

In this first book, the action concerns an ill-fated trip to Blomidon by members of the school during a vacation aboard the *Antelope* (formerly a potato schooner) under the command of Captain Corbet. Bart Damer is clearly both the ringleader and the focus of interest in the book, although the action is somewhat episodic. The book is dedicated to Willie, De Mille's eldest son, and it is possible that it originated, as have a number of classic children's books, as a series of bedtime stories told to the dedicatee by the author.

The later books in the series are less episodic and use other members of the group of five as protagonists. *The Boys of Grand Pré School* deals with the adventures of the members of the B.O.W.C. when they are lost in the woods on an expedition (during the same vacation) to look for Acadian antiquities, and the central character is not Bart Damer, but Bruce Rawdon, who in the end leads the others to safety. In *Lost in the Fog*, the focus is the adventures of Tom Crawford. Tom goes adrift in a small boat from the *Antelope*, on which the boys are taking a cruise, and is marooned for some time on Ile Haute in the Bay of Fundy. He survives by practising the appropriate survival techniques of building a fire and a shelter, and living off the land. In *Fire in the Woods*, Phil Kennedy and one of the other boys, after a narrow escape from drowning, are lost in the woods in the Miramichi area during a forest fire. In *Picked Up Adrift*, the whole group is marooned first aboard an abandoned schooner, and then on an island in the Gulf of the St. Lawrence. In *The Treasure of the Seas*, the group, with Bart Damer again the protagonist, are involved in a treasure hunt on Oak Island off the south shore of Nova Scotia, between Chester and Mahone Bay.

Each of the books carries out a double task, for De Mille is concerned both to entertain and to teach. The young reader is to be gripped and entertained by fast-moving action and lively characters. At the same time, a steady stream of practical information and moral teaching is introduced. The practical information comes sometimes in the descriptions of the characters' actions (for example, Tom's building of a fire in *Lost in the Fog*, mentioned previously) and sometimes directly, as when the boys, in a hurry to escape from one of the many dangers they face, employ the "Indian trot," which De Mille describes as follows: "the body bent forward, and the fore part of the foot touching the ground with its elastic tread, moving at that slow, steady, easy trot which is faster and lighter than a walk, and but little more fatiguing to those who have the knack of it" (*"The B.O.W.C."* 308; A1); here the description given offers almost direct instruction in how to carry out the action.

Moral instruction, however, is given only indirectly. Tom's behaviour while lost and alone on Ile Haute offers an example of what is expected of a boy in his society. Tom at one point gives way to tears, which he is probably entitled to do in the circumstances since he is only 12, but he immediately reproves himself: "Come now, Thomas, my son . . . this sort of thing will never do, you know. You're not a baby my boy. . . . Cheer up, then, like a man, and don't make me feel ashamed of you" (*Lost* 221; A1). The moral is clear: tears are a weakness, and boys do not cry or give way to weakness — they behave like men. Similarly, in *Fire in the Woods*, Pat Kennedy, another of the five boys, finds a way of visiting an island in the Saint John River, although Bart Damer, with whom he is staying, has told him that it is not allowed:

> he regarded Bart's objection as due to his father's command, and that command he did not consider as at all binding either upon himself or Phil. He did not suppose there was any actual danger, nor did he stop to think that Mr Damer's prohibition might be founded upon wise precautions and a knowledge of the perils of the place; for, as a matter of fact, though this fact was unknown to Pat, the Falls are sufficiently dangerous to cause the loss of one life per year on an average, besides many accidents which do not result in an actual loss of life; and it was this knowledge of the dangers attendant upon boating in these waters which had led to Mr. Damer's prohibition. (*Fire* 17; A1)

The lesson here is of obedience to adults: father knows best. Elsewhere, Bart Damer is shown, on different occasions, demonstrating concern for, and understanding of, the fears of other people, refraining from correcting or criticizing adults plainly in the wrong, and owning up to being wrong.

The code includes the notion of *mens sana in corpore sano*, for when Bruce Rawdon saves himself from falling from a cliff by clinging to a treeroot, De Mille observes, "Another boy might have fallen; but Bruce's muscles had been toughened by all kinds of manly exercise, and he had in him the germ and the promise of mighty strength and stature" (*"The B.O.W.C."* 75; A1). Throughout the series, in fact, it is clear from his examples of appropriate behaviour that what De Mille seeks to instil through them is a Victorian, middle-class, Protestant code, closely resembling the one in which he himself was brought up, and which is offered in many similar books of the period.

His teaching, however, is directed only to boys. Unlike many writers for children during this period, De Mille offers a world that is almost exclusively masculine. There are some women characters in very minor and peripheral roles (Mrs. Watson, for example, in *Lost in the Fog*), but they are stereotypical middle-aged mother figures, with few distinguishing characteristics. This emphasis is curious, especially since De Mille himself had grown up with three younger sisters, and at the time the books were being written, had a young daughter, Louise, who was only a few years younger than Willie, and who might well have expected some recognition in the stories her father wrote.

If considered in relation to other books of the period, De Mille's moral and practical didacticism is relatively restrained. He rarely exhorts his young readers directly to behave in a particular way, and when he does, it is is in an understated manner. In one of the few examples of this direct approach, he describes how the boys make up a song to keep themselves amused during one of their periods adrift in the *Antelope*:

> So passed the time. And when you take into consideration the solemn fact that all this time they were drifting, that the sea was smooth, that there wasn't a breath of wind, that there was no prospect of getting home, or anywhere else, for that matter, — you will come to the conclusion that these boys were jolly under creditable circumstances. And you will be right in that conclusion; for it was in the very face of calms, strong tides, empty larders, wanderings at sea, famine, and privations of all kinds, that these boys stood up and sang their song. (*"The B.O.W.C."* 299; A1)[5]

Throughout the series, the boys are presented as practising and sincere Christians, but their practice is not enlarged upon. In *Fire in the Woods*, for example, Phil Kennedy acknowledges that his escape from the forest fire is the work of God:

His heart was full of fervent gratitude for his astonishing escape, and as his memory brought back the terrible events that had happened since he left the island, a prayer of thankfulness was breathed forth from his inmost soul to the One who had preserved him. (*Fire* 65; A1)

But his actions are not dwelt on further, and the narrative continues immediately. As a form of counterbalance, moreover, Dr. Porter, the principal of Grand Pré School, although a kindly and Christian soul, is elsewhere gently mocked for impracticality when he manages to lose himself and the boys in the woods:

He . . . advised them, if they ever again went roaming through the forest, never to trust in the guidance of a doctor of divinity. He felt that he might be of some small service in guiding them through figurative forests, — in pointing out the true way through that "obscure wood" by which Dante once symbolized this world of man, — but as to ever again leading them, or having anything to do with them in any literal, material wood, he begged to be excused. (*Boys* 241; A1)

De Mille does not, however, resort to presenting the boys in the B.O.W.C. books behaving in the extravagantly pietistic manner of the characters in his early stories, *Andy O'Hara* and "The Missionary's Son."

It is clear that the series makes some general reference to De Mille's own school days. Grand Pré School resembles — its location, structure, staff, and students included — to a certain extent, the Horton Academy of De Mille's time. Some writers on De Mille, however, have treated the books as strongly autobiographical and realistic. Arthur W.H. Eaton, for example, not only describes them in these terms, but also offers a very detailed key to all the characters:

The portrayal in these books of student life in Wolfville about the middle of the nineteenth century has not only vivid local interest, but must appeal strongly to youth at large for generations to come. . . . the originals of the chief characters in these student-life books of DeMille's are as follows: *Dr. Porter* was the Rev. John Pryor, D.D.; *Mr. Long* was Rev. Edmund A. Crawley, D.D., D.C.L.; *Bart*

Damer was Rev. Elisha Budd De Mille; *Bruce Rawdon* was Henry T. Crawley; *Arthur Rawdon* was Rev. Arthur R.R. Crawley; *Thomas Crawford* was Rev. Thomas Crawley; *Phil Kennedy* was Rev. Stephen William DeBlois, D.D.; *Billy Mack* was Rev. William MacKenzie, D.D.; *Pat* was Rev. Patrick Shields; *David Digg* was Rev. David Freeman; *Jiggins* was Rev. Thomas A. Higgins, D.D. (363; G)

There is very little internal evidence in the novel to support these identifications, however, and Eaton offers no external support for them, so they must be regarded with some caution. Others, like Crockett, who offers a similar list, have supported the idea that Bart Damer is a romanticized self-portrait by De Mille, not a portrait of Elisha (Crockett, "As Writer" 132; E). There are some incidents in the novel that may be related, although distantly, to De Mille's own life: it is reasonable to recognize, for example, when the boys propose a burial of their textbooks to celebrate the end of the term in the opening chapter of *"The B.O.W.C.,"* a reference to De Mille's own experience of the Rhetorical Burial in his junior year at Brown University. The portrayal of life in school is very sketchy, particularly in the later books of the series. Moreover, the adventures of the boys aboard the *Antelope* during a summer vacation, as described in *Picked Up Adrift*, are far from realistic: there is no possibility that De Mille and his fellow students were allowed to go wandering round the Maritime provinces with only nominal supervision (the only adult with the boys is the irresponsible and incompetent Captain Corbet, for whom no real-life original has been identified). It is certainly true, as Crockett observes, that the books in this series are "full of the extravagance, boyishness and foolery of youth" ("As Writer" 131; E). But it is the youth De Mille may have wished that he had had, not the one he did have.

De Mille's other series, the Young Dodge Club stories, has similar links to his own experience. Frank and Clive Wilmot, and David and Robert (Bob) Clark, all in their early teens, are travelling in Europe, under the supervision of their uncle, Moses V. Sprole. Each of the three volumes of the series describes adventures in a different Italian city: Naples, Rome, and Venice, respectively. There are some striking parallels between the descriptions and responses of the boys to Italian art, architecture, and life, and De Mille's descriptions of Italy in his adult romantic comedies. The action in this series is much less lively than it is in the B.O.W.C. Series — the boys fall into more social scrapes than physical adventures, and there is less action overall. The three novels are not totally independent of each other: the narrative of the three forms a single continuous story of separations and reunions.

As it is in the B.O.W.C. books, adventure is here mixed with practical and moral instruction. The boys repeatedly regret, for example, their ignorance of the language, particularly when that ignorance gets them into difficulties. The moral instruction is even more subdued than in the other series, although it is not entirely absent. In *The Winged Lion*, Clive and David want to see Bologna, Ferrara, and Padua by themselves, and Uncle Moses unwillingly permits it on the condition that they will not go anywhere else. They break their promise, however, by going on to Pisa: "They knew that they were violating the strict letter of their promise to Uncle Moses, but they thought that they were keeping it in a general way" (*Winged Lion* 19; A1). Their violation of their promise, although it triggers adventures that form the action of the book, is nevertheless clearly indicated to be wrong, not only by the fact that they do not enjoy the city they have gone to see and become separated from Uncle Moses for longer than they want, but also by an explicit description of their repentance at the close of the book, just before they are reunited with him: "Formerly they had been accustomed to laugh at the anxiety of Uncle Moses; but now . . . they were shocked at the thought of the misery which must have been inflicted upon him by their own hasty and inconsiderate acts" (*Winged Lion* 268; A1).

Occasionally, as he never does in the B.O.W.C. Series, De Mille offers moral instruction that does not relate directly to the action. In *The Seven Hills*, there is, for example, a lecture on the evil of alcohol:

> It is an unfortunate fact that the Anglo-Saxon, or English-speaking race, if it be the greatest on earth, is also the most prone to drunkenness; while, on the other hand, the Italians, whatever their faults may be, are certainly a very abstemious and temperate people. . . . one may see many of these wild, lawless, and unlicensed Roman Carnivals, and yet never encounter a single drunken man. Such a season in England or America would be associated with unlimited drunkenness. . . . Here the Italian, even in the midst of his excitement, can restrain himself. And surely it is a sad thing that the English-speaking race, which has created the mightiest literature of modern times, and the noblest law, and the freest government, which has spread itself all over the world, and has carried the Book

of God with it wherever it has gone; which also promises to make its grand language universal among men of the future; — sad it is, and most miserable, that this great, this chosen race, should be thus distinguished beyond all others for that one vice which makes man most like the brutes. (237-38; A1)

Although this may reflect the fact that the boys concerned are older, and therefore more in need of a warning, the intrusion is symptomatic of a slightly less sure hand. Moreover, by the time he came to *The Winged Lion*, De Mille was running out of inspiration for action, and, as the subtitle (*Stories of Venice*) promises, the narrative of the boys' adventures is filled out with stories and legends from the history of Venice, narrated by one of the characters.

In *The Lily and the Cross. A Tale of Acadia*, De Mille returns to his own part of the world. In this historical tale set in New France, the hero is "a young fellow who called himself Claude Motier, of Randolph," whose "name as well as his face, had a foreign character; yet he spoke English with the accent of an Englishman, and had been brought up in Massachusetts, near Boston" (*Lily* 10; A1). Claude has discovered, on the death of his supposed father, that he is actually the son of Count Eugene de Montresor who, with his Huguenot wife, was driven into exile in Quebec and deprived of his estates by false charges brought against him by the efforts of the Comte de Cazeneau. The plot consists of Claude's adventures after he starts out to visit Louisbourg, on his way to France in an attempt to find out what happened to his real father, who disappeared soon after the death of his wife, Claude's mother.[6] The story resembles those of De Mille's novels of sensation, such as *The Cryptogram*, more closely than it does those of his other books for children. Although less convoluted in plot and less melodramatic in incident than the adult novels, it nevertheless remains sufficiently melodramatic, even given the difference in scale and the historical background, to set it apart even from the most dramatic story of the of the B.O.W.C. Series. It seems largely to have been eclipsed by both series, and although it was reprinted several times between 1874 and 1890 (Edwards 25-26; D), it does not appear to have ever achieved such widespread popularity.

It is, however, in some ways just as interesting and as readable. The opening chapters aboard ship, during which extensive explanations of earlier events leading up to the current situation take place, much of them in the form of dialogue, move rather slowly, but once started, the action moves rapidly to its conclusion. The narrative of Claude's flight from his arrest in Grand Pré, accompanied by the Indians whom Père Michel has induced to assist him, and of the duel that takes place during his encounter with Cazeneau, is lively and fast moving, and is given a setting that De Mille clearly cared about and knew well. Other parts of the narrative include equally affectionate descriptions of the area: as the party arrives in Grand Pré, on its way to Louisbourg, De Mille introduces a vivid picture of the scenery around the entrance to the Bay of Minas, which he describes as "wild and grand" and a "secluded corner of the universe" (*Lily* 93; A1). De Mille vividly and vigorously conveys the environment of his own childhood in all his books for children. Although the portrayal of the natural environment is never overdone in *The Lily and the Cross*, it is clearly one of the book's strongest points.

Another strong point of *The Lily and the Cross* is its theme. In theme, in fact, it is clearly much more ambitious than either of the series of books for children with their presentation of an orthodox, middle-class, Protestant code of behaviour. Here De Mille is concerned with more than the conflict between Claude and his father's persecutor, Cazeneau, and the reunion of the long-separated father and son. At the heart of the enmity between Claude and Cazeneau there is a conflict between the corruption of the Old World, exemplified by the French court, and the innocence of the New World, exemplified not only by Claude himself, but by such characters as Zac and the landlord of the inn at Grand Pré. This conflict is expressed explicitly at the close of the novel, as part of Claude's decision to stay in the New World:

> He did not feel himself entirely capable of playing the part of a noble in . . . that France which his father had described; of associating with such a society, or of courting the favor of such a king. Besides, his religion was the religion of his mother; and her fate was a sufficient warning. And so it was that Claude resolved to give up all thoughts of France, and return to the humble New England farm. (*Lily* 264; A1)

Into the New World, the best of the Old World (those who remain uncorrupted, such as Mimi and the Count de Montresor, and are persecuted for it), can be welcomed.

Perhaps this rather ambitious theme may have been a factor in the book's failure to gain as much popularity as his other books for children. It is not without its blemishes, but these are relatively minor. Certainly, they are not sufficient to account for the way *The Lily and the Cross* is generally overlooked in critical response to De Mille's work.

The general response to De Mille's books for children was approving. R.W. Douglas praises De Mille for the difference of approach and local colour of the B.O.W.C. Series:

> *The B.O.W.C* . . . is ostensibly a book written for boys, yet it is unlike boys' books in general. It shows no effort to write down to a boy's intellect. It relies upon action and incident for interest, and every page or so it gives glimpses of Nova Scotian scenery, admirable, accurate and beautiful . . . proving successful, it was followed a year later by "The Boys of Grand Pre [sic] School," . . . Then came "Fire in the Woods" a dramatic and lurid word painting — the only one in existence I believe — of the frightful Miramichi Forest fire, where hundreds of square miles of beautiful forest were devastated. (43; F)

Elsewhere, reviewers concentrated on more general qualities. *Literary World*, for example, said that *Lost in the Fog* "is even livelier than either of its predecessors. . . . it is just such a book as youngsters from ten upwards delight to read — exciting, but wholesome" (*Dalhousie Gazette* 2 Feb. 1870: 46; H). It is clear, however, that Arthur Eaton's claim that the books "must appeal strongly to youth at large for generations to come" was an exaggeration (363; G). Today there would be few, if any, younger readers who would want to struggle through them, and they could not be expected to do so without some guidance.

But if De Mille was not a great writer for children, and produced no enduring classic such as *Anne of Green Gables*, he was by no means an incompetent or a mere hack. His books for children are certainly a great deal better than, for example, the snobbish and stereotypical school stories of Frank Richards in England, and the unabashedly materialistic success stories of Horatio Alger in the United States. They were professional works published by a large and reputable firm specializing in books for children, they sold well, if not spectacularly, and they were enjoyed by his young readers. These were no mean feats, and the last, in particular, must have offered him considerable satisfaction.

De Mille wrote two religious historical novels, *The Martyr of the Catacombs* and *Helena's Household*, both of which were published anonymously. In spite of this, neither presents a serious problem of attribution, and both works can confidently be said to be his. Determining the date of publication, however, is problematic in both cases.

The Martyr of the Catacombs has survived, at least in part, by a curious accident, although no copies of the original edition can be located. It was possibly first published in 1858, according to Watters, who relies on the Kirk supplement to Allibone's *Critical Dictionary* to trace its publishing history (D), but no copies of this edition have been located, or of an 1865 edition, also suggested by Watters (273; D), possibly on the basis of J.S. Knowles's earlier suggestion (List; H). Crockett also gives the earlier date: "As early as 1858, he had published *The Martyr of the Catacombs*, a book of the Sunday School type" ("As Writer" 129; E). De Mille himself does not mention it in the list prepared for Messr. Harnes (B3). The foreword to a modern paperback edition, however, explains how that modern edition came about:

> An anonymous story entitled, *The Martyr of the Catacombs: A Tale of Ancient Rome*, was published many years ago. A copy of that book was salvaged from an American sailing vessel, commanded by Captain Richard Roberts, abandoned at sea, after a disastrous hurricane in January 1876. It is now in the possession of his son.
> This volume, bearing the same title, is a carefully edited reprint of that book. (Roberts 5; G)[7]

The story describes the dispatch of the Roman Praetorian Guard commander, Marcellus, to search out and destroy the community of early Christians living in hiding in the catacombs during the reign of Nero. He finds them, is converted by their leader, Alexander, and, after helping them to survive, sacrifices himself to save the others. Since the reprinted text is "carefully edited," however, little can be inferred from it about De Mille's writing. As it stands, for example, Marcellus's conversion is a textbook account, without any kind of psychological realism, and throughout the novel Marcellus himself, as well the other characters — such as Lucullus, Marcellus's sceptical friend, and the young boy, Pollio, who leads Marcellus into the catacombs — are simply lay figures. The dialogue is unrealistically stiff, with speakers addressing each other at length, undistinguished by speech variations. The religious lessons are pointed out rather heavy-handedly — for example, after the death of Marcellus,

> Lucullus went to his home, but he was a changed man. The gaiety of his nature seemed to have been driven out by the severe afflictions that he had endured.
> He had rightly said that he would not become a Christian. The death of his friend had filled him with sadness, *but there was no sorrow for sin, no repentance, no desire for a knowledge of the true and living God.* He had lost the power of taking pleasure in the world, but had gained no other source of happiness. (*Martyr* 157; A1)

The structure, too, as we have it, is a little odd. Chapter 5, for example, "The Cloud of Witnesses," consists almost entirely of inscriptions from the burial niches of various Christians who have died, and appears to be merely narrative padding, although it may have had some other purpose or effect in the original. The edited text does not deserve to be described, in the words used to describe the original by R.W. Douglas in 1922, as "a powerful little book" (39; F). But it is always possible that a copy of the original might have survived, and might emerge to be considered in its own right.

Helena's Household survived much better than *Martyr of the Catacombs*, and even gained a fair measure of popularity. The original year of publication is given as 1858 by Watters, who is again following Allibone's supplement, but no copies of this edition have been located. Nor have copies been found of an 1867 edition, which Watters provides as an alternative, using J.S. Knowles's list (H) as his source (Watters 273; D). De Mille does include *Helena's Household* in his own list prepared for the *Literary World*, but gives the date as 1866 (To Messrs G.H. Harnes: B3). Edwards follows Watters (Edwards 21; D). But although the question of the dates of composition and first publication are extremely vexed, 12 editions are recorded between 1867 and 1900, and at least one copy of each has been located (Edwards 21–22; D). In view of this solid record, De Mille's giving the date as 1866 instead of 1867 (the earliest recorded edition) might indicate only a slip of memory. Either of these two dates would agree with that given by H.P. Scott, writing in 1885, who describes the history of the novel's publication as follows:

> [De Mille] met with great difficulties in its publication. During his summer holidays of one year he went to New York and hawked it round among the publishers. They would not look at it. Returning to his home, now on the North-West Arm, Halifax, he wrote the book all over again, and having sent it to the States was this time successful. (135; F)[8]

Scott's description implies that the composition of *Helena's Household* took place in the early 1860s, during De Mille's years at Acadia College and his first two years at Dalhousie College. If Scott is correct, however, his evidence, together with De Mille's own remark, rules out the existence of the 1858 edition listed in the Allibone supplement. There is, moreover, a small piece of internal evidence suggesting that the composition may have begun within a year or so of De Mille's move to Acadia, for at one point in the novel, in his discussion of slavery in Rome, De Mille writes that "the position of the Roman slave was both better and worse than now. There was no bar of colour between him and his master" (*Helena* 66; A1).[9] The "bar of colour" clearly refers to the slavery of blacks in the United States, and "now" suggests that that kind of slavery was still in existence at the time of writing. The abolition of slavery in the United States, however, had been declared in 1863, and frequent mentions in the *Christian Watchman* of the progress of the Civil War show that news of it was readily available to De Mille, who, in his editorial capacity, may even have been responsible for the reports, using information from American papers. He would therefore certainly have known of the declaration when it took place. Since there would have been no point in introducing an allusion to American slavery subsequent to its abolition, the presence of the allusion suggests that at least some of the novel, if not all, had been written prior to 1863, and the allusion somehow escaped the various processes of revision described by Scott to remain in the final published text. Nevertheless, pushing the date of writing back in this way neither contradicts De Mille and Scott as to the date of first publication, nor supports the existence of the 1858 edition.

The novel is long, but not particularly complex. It follows the fortunes of the family of Lucius Sulpicius Labeo, his Greek wife Helena, their son Marcus, and Helena's brother Cineas, as well as a number of minor characters. The novel is set first in Rome during the persecutions of the Christians by Nero, and afterwards in Britain and Judaea.[10]

DE MILLE'S EARLY FICTION

Helena's Household received a mixed critical reaction. Some of De Mille's early critics, like the general public, approved of it. In his history of Dalhousie University, for example, D.C. Harvey cites a letter to De Mille from Sir William Young of the Dalhousie Board of Governors (the letter is undated, unfortunately, although the omission may be Young's rather than Harvey's) congratulating him on the novel:

> The characters of Nero, Isaac and Hegio are powerfully drawn — and the burning of Rome and the fall of Jerusalem and other scenes are depicted with the skill of a master. The only fault I find is that you have not put your name on the title page. It would have enhanced your own reputation and reflected credit on Dalhousie. (Harvey 91; G)

Douglas called it "a lurid, powerful, historical novel . . . perhaps more reserved than Whyte Melville's *Gladiator*, but . . . work of the same type" (41; F). Wylie Mahon, who considers it one of De Mille's best works and calls it "an admirable story in every way," also compares it to other popular novels of same type: "It is superior to *Darkness and Dawn*, — Farrar was not a story teller, De Mille was, — and while less powerfully dramatic than *Quo Vadis* it is free from the objectionable features of that somewhat voluptuous and realistic romance" (321; F). Vernon Rhodenizer goes so far as to suggest that De Mille's "novels of Rome in the time of the early Christians may have inspired *Ben Hur* and *Quo Vadis*" (139; F). Others, however, were less enthusiastic. Archibald MacMechan gives *Helena's Household* little attention, commenting merely that it is "a book which deserves to be better known" ("James De Mille" 413; F), and Lorne Pierce is very moderate in his appreciation: "The story is well written, the style being clear if not distinguished, and forceful if not felicitous" (165; F). H.P. Scott, too, after discussing the circumstances of its publication, and remarking that it was "widely and appreciatively read," dismisses it without further critical discussion as "written in a strongly-marked pietistic vein" (135; F).

Helena's Household exemplifies, in fact, both the strengths and weaknesses of its author. De Mille's strengths are those of a natural story-teller, for the central story line is strongly established and, although there are subplots (that concerning Lucius and Lydia, for example), they are few and carefully woven into the main plot, so that they support it, rather than distracting attention from it. Major characters are carefully identified on their first appearance, and are relatively few, so that there is little confusion among them. De Mille offers excellent vignettes of character in action, so that in the scene in which he introduces Nero, much is conveyed by the description of Nero's insistence on drawing Labeo instead of listening to his report on Britain (112–13; A1), and also of Labeo's discomfort at the un-Roman behaviour of his emperor and commander in chief.

De Mille can also expertly handle the description of action on a larger scale. The description of the burning of Rome is dramatic and vigorous: the narrative is divided between descriptions of general action (the spread of the flames and the movement of crowds) and specific incidents (such as the lioness's attempt to rescue her cub, and the successful rescue of Marcus by Galdus), and shifts smoothly between them. De Mille also adroitly interweaves such descriptions with accounts of the activities of the various characters in whom we are particularly interested (starting with Eubulus and Lydia, shifting to Labeo and Helena, and even including Nero). Similarly, the scenes of battle around Jotapata and Jerusalem towards the end of the novel are vividly and skilfully handled.

De Mille's weaknesses in the novel are those of an overenthusiastic researcher and an unpractised artist. He was, even at the time he wrote *Helena's Household*, extraordinarily well read in classical history, classical literature (including Hebrew), and religious history. The opening chapter is leisurely in tone, and De Mille makes no immediate attempt to capture his readers' interest in his story, offering instead a sweeping panorama of the state of the Roman Empire of the period, and sketching in the arrival of St. Paul and St. Luke in Italy. Much of the early part of the book is taken up by long, academic discussions between various characters, such as that between Cineas and Helena on the inadequacies of the Greek and Roman religions, and between Cineas and Isaac on the history, religion, and poetry of the Jews (this discussion being illustrated with numerous long quotations). The discussion is further deadened in many places by not being given as direct dialogue between the characters: for example, when Julius announces that he means to convert to Christianity, a long discussion of his reasons, and the arguments against doing so, follows, conveyed in the authorial voice as a synopsis preceded by the awkward introduction, "This brought on a long discussion" (233; A1). Elsewhere, De Mille's information is introduced as pure digression, as when Cineas, observing a Christian service, reflects on the hymns the Christians sing:

They began by singing a hymn, which to the educated and refined ears of Cineas seemed rude indeed, and barbarous in metre. The people present belonged to the lower orders, however, and the verses were adapted to their comprehension. These Christians knew little or nothing of the refinements of the great national poets. They understood nothing of their rules. They had their own vulgar songs, and their Christian hymns were formed in accordance with rules not known to ears polite. They had been accustomed to vulgar rhythms, where the quantitative metres of the literary classes were unknown, and the assonance of words was loved. Cineas listened to their songs, and thought of the verses of Nero. For Nero had only tried to elevate the popular forms, and make rhyme prevail among the acknowledged literary productions. These Christians sang the metres and the rhymes which they understood and appreciated, and in their hymns they expressed the divine sentiments of their religion, with all its hope, and purity, and devotion, and exaltation. (186–87; A1)

It is hardly possible to accuse De Mille of ironic commentary on the church hymns of his own life in comparison to other forms of literature and music, which would make more artistic sense than would pure digression, since the novel was dedicated to his father-in-law, Dr. Pryor. Nevertheless, some faint air of unconscious humour attaches to the passage, possibly because, although some brief comment on the music of the service would fit well, detailed critical analysis is hardly warranted by the demands of the story at this point.

The weaknesses of the novel are those of the unpractised literary artist, and are visible in such elements as characterization, dialogue, and setting. The physical appearance of the characters is described in very general terms: Helena is "a lady of exquisite beauty, who was yet in the bloom of her youth," and her son, Marcus, has a "heavenly mildness with features strikingly like those of his mother. He had her spiritual eyes, and sweet expressive mouth. He was not more than seven years old, and rather tall for his age" (21, 36; A1). Personality is similarly described in general terms, so that Labeo is said to have a "stern Roman nature, with all its restless energy and indomitable will" (139; A1). The overall impression we have of them all is that they are generic or stock characters — an impression reinforced by De Mille's failure to distinguish them by the use of speech idiosyncrasies. The most problematic aspect of *Helena's Household* is that the characters are described analytically and objectively from the outside, and are not realized subjectively from the inside. De Mille cannot get inside his characters' heads, and he makes no attempt to present the narrative from any point of view except that of the omniscient third-person narrator.

Nevertheless, the critics who recommended *Helena's Household* and the many members of the public who bought, read, and enjoyed it were not altogether wrong. The novel remains very readable, and it gains impetus as it goes along. That De Mille, after his difficulties and disappointments in finding a publisher for the novel, refused to try the genre again, is understandable. It is also the readers' loss.

NOTES

1 This is a handwritten list filed with the typescript of J.S. Knowles's essay "James De Mille" (H). The handwriting is not Knowles's, but might be Archibald MacMechan's.

2 "Andy O'Hara," attributed to "the author of *The Missionary's Son*" appeared in the *Christian Watchman* 16 April through 17 July 1861. The story is believed to have been published in book form in the same year by Carlton and Porter in New York, according to Watters in the *Checklist of Canadian Literature* (273; D), following the *American Catalogue of Books* (D). It is not in the *National Union Catalogue of Pre–1956 Imprints*, and no copy has been located.

3 "The Missionary's Son," attributed to "X," appeared in the *Christian Watchman* from 9 January through 10 April 1861.

4 De Mille's list forms part of his letter dated 31 May 1878 to Messrs. G.H. Harnes, publishers of *Literary World*, in which he appears to be responding to some sort of questionnaire. The letter is in the possession of Yale University's Beinecke Rare Book and Manuscript Library, in their collection of American literature.

5 De Mille is not averse to joking with his readers, however, about how the books are going to turn out: "And any boy who thinks there's going to be a ghost in the garret, or a phantom in the French orchard, had better, — well, he had better keep reading straight on. That's about the best advice I can give him" (*Boys* 92; A1).

6 In 1743, the schooner *Parson*, captained by a young New England seacaptain, Zion Awake Cox (known as Zac), is sailing from Boston to Louisbourg, with Claude Motier and Père Michel as passengers. They rescue the Comte de Laborde, his daughter Mimi, her maid Margot, and the Comte de Cazeneau, the new governor of Louisbourg, from a shipwreck. Claude reveals to Mimi that he is the son of the missing Count de Montresor on his way to France to find his father. The *Parson* is captured by another

French frigate, whose commander takes Claude as a prisoner of war, and the others as passengers. They reach Grand Pré, where Laborde dies, and Cazeneau proposes marriage to Mimi, before setting out with her and Père Michel towards Louisbourg, leaving Claude behind under guard. With help previously arranged by Père Michel, Claude escapes and follows Cazeneau to rescue Mimi. He meets Cazeneau alone and leaves him for dead in a duel. During Cazeneau's absence, Père Michel and Mimi have tried to escape towards Canso, where Zac, having freed the *Parson*, is waiting. On learning of Cazeneau's supposed death from Claude, however, Père Michel leads the party to Louisbourg. Here Cazeneau later arrives, having survived the duel, and takes command of the garrison. After a failed attempt to escape with Mimi, now his wife after a secret marriage, Claude is put on trial, during which Père Michel is revealed to be his father, the Count de Montresor. The story ends with the arrival of dispatches from France ordering the reinstatement of Cazeneau's predecessor, the arrest of Cazeneau, and the restoration of all rights to the Count de Montresor. Claude and Mimi are reunited, Margot marries Zac, and both couples, with the count, return to Boston.

7 Moody Press printed this edition on license from Loizeaux Brothers of Neptune, New Jersey, who inform me that they no longer have a copy of the book in their possession.

8 This quotation comes from a paper "*Read by H.P. Scott, M.A., before the Haliburton [Society]*," a society of the University of King's College, and was supplied to the *Gazette* by the Haliburton Society secretary. Scott's authority for his description of the composition is not clear, since he was not a Dalhousie graduate, and therefore not one of De Mille's own students, although he may have known the De Mille family. Nor is he is altogether reliable on detail — none of De Mille's homes in Halifax could have been described as being "on the North-West Arm," in the normal local use of the phrase.

9 The copy of *Helena's Household* to which the page references refer is in the Special Collections of Dalhousie University's Killam Library. This copy, one of the 1869 edition published by Thomas Nelson, was presented to the Dalhousie College Library by Professor J.G. MacGregor, who was briefly a colleague of De Mille's just before De Mille's death.

10 After an opening chapter picturing the Roman Empire in the reign of the Emperor Nero and mentioning the arrival of St. Paul and St. Luke at Puteoli, the narrative proper begins in a villa outside Rome, in the household of Helena, the Greek wife of a Roman commander, Lucius Sulpicius Labeo. Helena is awaiting the return of her husband from service in Britain. The family members are Helena, her brother Cineas, and her young son Marcus. There are also three household slaves who are major characters in the novel: Marcus's nurse Clymene, Labeo's Jewish librarian Isaac, and the dishonest steward Hegio. Helena discovers that Clymene has converted Marcus to Christianity, and soon, with the assistance of a neighbouring Roman widow, Pomponia

Eliza, Emily, Frederick, Mrs. De Mill, Alice

Graecina, herself becomes a Christian. On Labeo's return, Hegio's dishonesty comes to light and Labeo dismisses him. Having delivered his report on the British campaign to Nero, Labeo is given new duties that require the household to move into Rome, and against a background of the intrigues of the imperial court, the life of the family continues. Labeo takes Marcus to view the gladiatorial combats, and the boy, repelled by the violence and bloodshed, insists on saving the life of a British slave, Galdus, who has fought particularly bravely and been injured, and on taking him to the household. Cineas renews his acquaintance with Lucius, a centurion who has returned to Rome as escort to Paul and Luke, and becomes intrigued with what Lucius tells him about the Christian religion. They set out to observe the Christian community, and are instrumental in saving the life of Eubulus and his daughter Lydia, with whom Lucius falls in love and for whose sake he converts to Christianity. The great fire engulfs Rome, and Nero, seeking to avoid the anger of the Romans, puts the blame on the Christians and mounts a wave of persecution, forcing the Christians to retreat into the catacombs. At this point, the vengeful Hegio, who has entered the service of Nero's accomplice Tigellinus, betrays Helena and Marcus as Christians and they are arrested. They are rescued and hidden with the other Christians, notably Lucius, Eubulus, and Lydia, in the catacombs, until the persecution is over. Labeo, having given Isaac his freedom, then removes Helena and Marcus from Rome, and, accompanied by Cineas, takes them to Britain where he intends to settle. But their health has been seriously undermined by their ordeal, and Marcus soon dies, followed immediately by his mother. After attempting suicide and being prevented by a vision of his son, Labeo decides to return to military life, and he and Cineas join in the Emperor Vespasian's campaign in the Middle East, under the command of Titus. They take part in the battle of Jotapata, where Labeo's life is saved by Isaac, who is in command of the Jewish forces, and who is later, in turn, saved and released by Cineas. Cineas and Labeo then take part in the siege and destruction of Jerusalem, during which Isaac dies in the flames. After Titus returns to Rome, Cineas and Labeo travel on to Pergamos (Pergamum?), where they are converted to Christianity. Cineas then returns to Greece to spread the gospel, and Labeo returns to Britain to do the same. Here he is reunited with Galdus, who also becomes a Christian, and he eventually dies, much venerated by the local Christian community.

CHAPTER 8

The Satirical Romances and the Novels of Sensation

The majority of De Mille's novels, although little known now, were well known in their time, but only as popular fiction: there is nothing that differentiates them from other popular fiction of their time. These frothy and improbable comedies and lurid and melodramatic novels of sensation would offer, as they were intended to offer, light entertainment only. Even De Mille seems to have recognised this, as a remark recorded by Burpee indicates: "A member of De Mille's family once said to him, picking up a copy of *Cranford*, 'James, why don't you write this sort of thing?' He glanced at the book, then looked at her in a pitying sort of way, and replied, 'Don't I wish that I could!' " ("Appreciation" 1; H). Together, as a sample of their genre, they interest the literary historian; but individually, they elude interpretation by the critic.

De Mille began by writing humorous novels, and there are few bibliographic problems with this group. All those that were published appeared, with the possible exception of *A Castle in Spain*, during De Mille's lifetime, and are clearly identified as his own in his letters.[1] In addition, there are two other novels that appear to fall into this category and that we know he wrote at least in part: "America Dissected" and "Ashdod Webster and His Starring Tour" (C1; B1).

From what we know of the lost "America Dissected," it was a comedy in the same vein as his others. De Mille describes it, in some detail, in a letter of 7 May 1868 to a correspondent at Harper Brothers:

> I have been for a long time at work at my "Frenchmen", and at length forward you part of it, amounting to about one half, for your inspection. It is unnecessary for me to explain the idea of it, since that will sufficiently explain itself. This first half refers to New York, Boston, & and Philadelphia. The remainder takes in the West, & consists of duels in Canada, extravagant adventures, and whimsical impressions; while the whole ends with the flight of the party from the country. They are only *three weeks* in America, yet in that time they of course see everything, learn everything, and understand everything.
>
> I have called it *"America Dissected"*. Another title which I have thought of is *"Three Weeks in America,"* another *"American Notes"* by several Frenchmen. . . .
>
> You may perhaps think that it would be better not to have such *uniform depreciation* [sic] and that some bright American character should be developed. I have not been unmindful of that. "Carri Metcaf" is to be developed into a bright, impulsive, generous being, very different from what she seems to be at first She is the heroine of the piece, and figures largely in the second part. She marries De la Poussiere. H[iram?] Adams is to grow into the best type — the true hearted, unsophisticated American, — one who is shrewd, passionate, averse to shams, soft hearted and brave. He loves Paris, like all Americans, and is captured by his wife, while making an effort to go back with the Frenchmen. Before that he figures largely in the scene in the West and in Canada. My Irishmen I do not think out of place. I find that Frenchmen have a weakness for them. "The Malloni" is a mixture of "Father Prout" and Thackeray's "Capitain Costigan[.]" (To Harper Brothers; B3)

In spite of De Mille's promise to avoid *"uniform depreciation,"* Harper Brothers evidently decided that the novel would not suit them, and it was

Illustrated manuscript page of "Eggs Eggs Eggs," which later appeared in The Dodge Club *as "A Nightmare"*

never published. The manuscript, probably incomplete, has disappeared, along with most of De Mille's other manuscripts and papers.

"Ashdod Webster and His Starring Tour" also resembles his other comedies. It reverses the pattern of "America Dissected," however, sending a young American hero to Europe for a tour that becomes the occasion for satiric humour. "Ashdod Webster," which might have suited Harpers better, De Mille chose to send to *Blackwood's Magazine*. In his letter of 23 July 1879 to the editor, he writes:

> I send you herewith per mail the first half of a story entitled "Ashdod Webster's Starring Tour" which I submit to your inspection. It is a Satirical Romance and refers chiefly to the practise [sic] frequently indulged in by distinguished Americans of making a "starring tour" in Europe. (To the editor of *Blackwood's*; B3)[2]

The manuscript has survived, although it seems only to consist of the half that De Mille sent to *Blackwood's*, and may never, therefore, have been completed after they refused it.

The first comedy novel to appear in book form was *The Dodge Club* (1869),[3] and it was quickly followed by "The Minnehaha Mines" (which appeared in serial form only [1869–70]) and *The Lady of the Ice* (1870). These were followed by four examples of what De Mille calls, in the same letter to *Blackwood's*, the "Satirical Romance": *The American Baron* (1871), *A Comedy of Terrors* (1872), *The Babes in the Wood* (1875), and *A Castle in Spain* (1878).

The Lady of the Ice and "The Minnehaha Mines" are somewhat different from De Mille's other humorous novels. What particularly distinguishes them from *The Dodge Club*, and from the satirical romances that were to follow them, is their setting (Canada, in the former, and America in the latter) and their use of a first-person narrator. De Mille speaks in the persona of his hero in *The Lady of the Ice*, and that persona is much more developed than any third-person character he presents in the third person in *The Dodge Club*. In chapter 1, for example, under the title, "Consisting Merely of Introductory Matter," the hero introduces himself:

> This is a story of Quebec. Quebec is a wonderful city.
>
> I am given to understand that the ridge on which the city is built is Laurentian; and the river that flows past it is the same. On this (not the river, you know) are strata of schist, shale, old red sand-stone,

trap, granite, clay, and mud. The upper stratum is ligneous, and is found to be very convenient for pavements.

It must not be supposed from this introduction that I am a geologist. I am not. I am a lieutenant in her Majesty's 129th Bobtails. We Bobtails are a gay and gallant set, and I have reason to know that we are well remembered in every place we have been quartered. (*Lady* 5; A1)

The studied ingenuousness of this opening ("not the river, you know"), the tantalizing statement, "I have reason to know that we are well remembered," and the choice of the regimental nickname, the Bobtails (not a real regiment, but a name intended to suggest ragtag and bobtail or rabble), immediately signal De Mille's good-humoured irony. But the voice of this opening, however much it offers irony, also reveals the engaging and not very bright persona of the hero. Lieutenant Alexander Macrorie then describes himself, using the third-person for modesty:

Tall, straight as an arrow, and singularly well-proportioned, the picturesque costume of the 129th Bobtails could add but little to the effect already produced by so martial a figure. His face was whiskerless; his eyes gray; his cheek-bones a little higher than the average; his hair auburn; his nose not Grecian — or Roman — but still impressive: his air one of quiet dignity, mingled with youthful joyance and mirthfulness. Try — O reader! — to bring before you such a figure. Well — that's me.

He adds that his character was "bold, yet cautious; brave, yet tender; constant, yet highly impressible" (*Lady* 6; A1). The story follows Macrorie's fortunes in his search for the mysterious woman whom he has rescued from the breakup of the ice on the river. The description of the rescue is a powerful and dramatic piece of writing. Macrorie also saves Phaylim O'Halloran, a suspected Fenian, from an angry mob, and meets O'Halloran's two daughters, Nora, whom Macrorie thinks is the woman he rescued from the ice, and Marion, with whom he falls in love, although she seems to be in love with Jack Randolph, Macrorie's friend. Marion finally reveals that she, not Nora, is actually the lady of the ice; Macrorie forgives her for her deception and marries her. Alongside this story runs the story of the overly susceptible and tenderhearted Jack Randolph, who manages to become engaged to three women simultaneously, while actually being in love with a fourth who turns him down until each of the other three has taken her revenge on him, but who finally accepts his proposal. The story moves well, although De Mille indulges himself by inflicting far too much of O'Halloran's exaggerated Irish brogue and stereotypical behaviour on the reader.

The Lady of the Ice was not, however, particularly well received. It lacked the popular appeal of *The Dodge Club*, possibly as a result of its Canadian setting. Consequently, it was not reprinted during De Mille's lifetime, and, until the facsimile edition of the Toronto Reprint Library appeared in 1980, was also overlooked after his death. Rather oddly, however, it was, according to De Mille's letter to the publishers of *Literary World*, one of the two (the other being *Cord and Creese*) that were dramatized during his lifetime (To Messrs G. H. Harnes; B3).

"The Minnehaha Mines," De Mille's other attempt at first-person narration, failed even to achieve publication in book form. Although it clearly draws on De Mille's experiences in Cincinnati as bookkeeper with the West Columbia Mining and Manufacturing Company, it is clearly not in the least autobiographical. The protagonist and narrator, Bob Laidlaw, is a good-natured but not very bright young man, and the development of his personality does not demonstrate any apparent attempt on De Mille's part to individualize and develop his creation. Florence Huntingdon, the main female character, is developed in a much more interesting way; she is a capable and determined woman, who is far better at dealing with the fraudulent director of the company than are any of the clerics and academics who make up the balance of the shareholders. There are some interesting sketches of a trip down the river to a small and squalid mining settlement on the riverbank, of shareholders meetings, and of a timber yard where Laidlaw sometimes takes refuge from his problems. Essentially, however, De Mille cannot make the story of a manufacturing company in difficulties interesting, let alone very funny: the plot limps along to a *deus ex machina* ending, and the attempts at humour are forced and thin. The failure of "The Minnehaha Mines" to achieve book publication is quite justified.

The Dodge Club, on the other hand, which immediately followed "The Minnehaha Mines," is not only the earliest and the best known of De Mille's comedies, but is also deservedly the most popular. Although *The Dodge Club* was published in 1869, it may have been written much earlier. According to MacMechan, it was written "before going to Acadia" ("James De Mille"; 413; F), which would mean, if MacMechan is correct, that it was written sometime before the middle of 1861. Like many of De Mille's subsequent novels, it ran as a serial in *Harper's Magazine*, appearing there in 1867, before it was published as a book in 1868 (Edwards 14; D). Even if MacMechan is wrong, if De Mille in 1867 had had the manuscript at least half-finished before offering it to Harper Brothers for serial publication (as he did with the manuscript of "Ashdod Webster"), this timing would indicate that it was written no later than early 1867. *The Dodge Club* has something in common with the later satirical romances, notably the author's delight in the Italian setting, and the use of a third-person narration that is frequently interrupted by the author who mocks what he is writing or introduces a digression. De Mille himself grouped *The Dodge Club* with the satirical romances in his letter to Messrs. Harnes (B3).

But as Gwendolyn Davies points out in her excellent introduction to a recent reprint of the novel, it has much more in common with the nineteenth-century travel literature it is engaged in mocking (Introduction; F). It traces the adventures of the Dodge Club (Buttons, Dick Whiffletree, Doctor Snakeroot, Senator Jones, and Mr. Figgs) through France and Italy. They call themselves the Dodge Club, as Buttons explains to Dick when Dick joins them, "Because our principle is to dodge all the humbugs and swindles, which make travelling so expensive generally. . . . Neither the Doctor nor the Senator understand a word of any language but the American" (*Dodge* 6–7; A1). De Mille's satiric intent is already evident here, in his implication of the absurd notion that a group with two members who speak only English could really succeed in avoiding "humbug and swindles" — as indeed they do not. The novel has very little in the way of plot, for the action proceeds in a series of loosely related incidents, including the celebrated encounter between the bashful Senator Jones and the far-from-bashful Countess de Notterino, two separate encounters between the club members and brigands, one unsuccessful romance (Dick and Pepita), and one successful one (Buttons and Ida). What plot there is, however, acts as a framework for a great deal of satiric anecdote and comment by De Mille as he describes the travels of the club. In the opening chapter, in which Dick watches the departure of the French army from Paris to the battlefront in Italy, De Mille takes a potshot, as he does occasionally throughout the novel, at the behaviour of the local people: "A great many tears are shed, and a great deal of bombast uttered. For the invincible soldiers of France are off to fight for an idea; and doesn't every one of them carry a marshal's baton in his knapsack?" (*Dodge* 5; A1). De Mille also makes one or two sharp remarks about the level of the accommodation provided: "They took lodgings near the Piazza di Spagna. This is the best part of Rome to live in, which every traveller will acknowledge. Among other advantages, it is perhaps the only clean spot in the Capital of Christendom" (*Dodge* 56; A1). But most of the satire is reserved for his pompous, naïve, and insular American travellers, and the invincible chauvinism of Senator Jones is a favourite target. Senator Jones thinks Italians are "a singular people. They're deficient. They're wanting in the leading element of the age. They haven't got any idee of the principle of pro-gress. They don't understand trade" (*Dodge* 56; A1). After he has met the countess, however, he is at least prepared to admit that "The Italians, or at any rate the people of Florence, have just about as much cuteness as you will find anywhere" (*Dodge* 109; A1), and he admires the size of St. Peter's Basilica, although he cannot imagine the "utility" of it: " 'This,' said the Senator, 'is about the first place that has really come up to my idee of foreign parts. In fact it goes clean beyond it. I acknowledge its superiority to any thing that America can produce. But what's the good of it all?' " (*Dodge* 58; A1). The senator is not a simple buffoon, however: arrested by the authorities on suspicion of spying, he retains a certain dignity, and he is warmhearted in caring for Buttons when the latter is injured by brigands. It is a balance maintained only with difficulty, but nevertheless maintained.

At the same time, De Mille is also having fun with the conventions of the genre in which he is writing. The conventional long-winded chapter headings, which list the topics covered in the chapter, are mocked in the heading for chapter 20: "The glory, grandeur, beauty, and infinite variety of the Pincian Hill; narrated and detailed not columnarily but exhaustively, and after the manner of Rabelais" (*Dodge* 60; A1). And, true to his promise, after a single paragraph, the chapter continues as a truly Rabelaisian list of relevant and irrelevant items that the reader must contemplate from the Pincian Hill, from "the Tiber" to "Soda-Water."[4] A similar list of topics (taking up 3 5/8 column inches) in the heading for chapter 37, which begins with "Rome. — Ancient History" and ends with "Concluding Remarks of a Miscellaneous Description," is followed not by the promised chapter, but by a parenthetical note addressed to the reader, explaining the impossibility of writing such a chapter:

> There! as a bill of fare I flatter myself that the above ought to take the eye. It was my intention, on the departure of the Club from

> Rome, to write a chapter of a thoroughly exhaustive character, as will be seen by the table of contents above; but afterward, finding that the chapter had already reached the dimensions of a good-sized book before a quarter of it was written, I thought that if it were inserted in this work it would be considered by some as too long. . . . And if any of my readers prefer to wait till they read that chapter before reading any further, all I can say is, perhaps they'd better not, as after all it has no necessary connection with the fortunes of the Dodge Club. (*Dodge* 88; A1)

The jokes are designed to be shared with the reader, and the reading public seems to have appreciated them very much, for the book had at least 12 editions between 1868 and 1897 (Edwards 16–18; D).

Critics, too, thought highly of it. George Stewart refers to "those rollicking merry sketches . . . vivacious and sprightly, and brimful of rich fun and rare humour" (404; F). R.W. Douglas praises its "genuine verve and irrepressible humour" (41; F), and Wylie Mahon calls that humour "as rich and pure as can be found almost anywhere else" (321; F). Only MacMechan, not well known for his sense of humour, offered less than warm praise:

> The faults in construction are many. . . . The writing is flimsy; there is no plot; the adventures with the brigands form no part of the story; the very title is a misnomer. But all deductions made, *The Dodge Club* is a readable book. It displays genuine verve and ease, and irrepressible boyish humour. ("James De Mille" 413; F)

In fact, despite MacMechan's "deductions," the book is not merely "readable," but very enjoyable: the reviewer for *Harper's Magazine* called it "spicy" (Crockett, "As Writer" 135; E). For some tastes, it can hold up well in competition with the more celebrated *Innocents Abroad* of Mark Twain.

After the publication of *The Dodge Club*, De Mille wrote his four remaining humorous novels in very similar fashion. His concept of what he calls the "satirical romance," as manifest in *The American Baron, A Comedy of Terrors, The Babes in the Wood,* and *A Castle in Spain,* is described by De Mille in his letter to Messrs. Harnes:

The chief characteristic . . . is the union of sensationalism with extravagant humour: the most tragic incidents are brought forward only to be dismissed with playful mockery; the plot is highly elaborated, tragedy & comedy exist side by side, the pervalent [sic] atmosphere is one of mock seriousness; and the author while he freely uses the most startling and harrowing details never fails to turn them into ridicule, and thus appears to satirize and burlesque the whole sensational school of fiction. The chief works of this class are the "Dodge Club," — "Babes of the Wood," "Comedy of Terrors," and the last of his products . . . "A Castle in Spain" in which the above characteristics are very strikingly manifested. (B3)

It is clear from this description that he wrote his comedies with a precise aim in mind.
The American Baron, although De Mille omits any mention of it in the letter, is nevertheless probably the best example of what he intends, and it is highly enjoyable. The plot, which follows the romantic entanglements — all of which are complicated by the interference of the villain, Count Girasole — of three women (Kitty Willoughby, Minnie Fay, and Ethel Orne) with three men (Scone Dacres, Baron Atramonte, and Lord Hawbury), is certainly "elaborated," but without ever becoming too confusing.[5] "Startling and harrowing" certainly describe Hawbury's rescue of Ethel from a forest fire, Girasole's rescue of Minnie from a fall into a crevasse while crossing the Simplon Pass, and Dacres's discovery of his wife's insanity. All of these incidents in turn are certainly "turned . . . into ridicule": Hawbury discovers that his hair, beard, and moustache have been burned away; Girasole's rescue of Minnie is revealed to be only one of a series of incidents in which Minnie is rescued from disaster by a man who promptly falls in love with her; and Dacres meets Kitty Willoughby, and, although he thinks she is his mad wife, nevertheless finds himself in love with her. The climactic episode, in which Girasole kidnaps Minnie and Kitty Willoughby, in an attempt to force the former into marrying him, is extremely dramatic, but is followed immediately by the ridiculously neat and tidy ending in which the three couples are carefully united. The difficulties of the lovers are made both more suspenseful and more ridiculous by the fact that they are taking place in a country that is in the middle of considerable political unrest, and the situation keeps them on the edge of being arrested, but never actually plunges them into any serious political danger.

De Mille's plot formula is similar in *A Comedy of Terrors*, *A Castle In Spain*, and *Babes in the Wood*. In each, two or more pairs of lovers are first brought together (this is usually narrated in flashback towards the beginning of the book), then separated by confusions (in *A Comedy of Terrors*, Maudie Heathcote, responding to two simultaneous proposals of marriage, sends her acceptance to the wrong man), misunderstandings, and manipulation by the villain, and, after some mildly dangerous adventures (Seth Grimes rescues Maudie Heathcote from the Siege of Paris in a hot-air balloon, which is then blown off course in a storm and lands in Norway), are finally reunited. The background of political turmoil is also present in each of the novels. None of the three is as consistently humorous as *The American Baron*: the ending of *A Comedy of Terrors*, for example, is distinctly perfunctory, and the action of *Babes in the Wood* perhaps overcomplicated. The plots, although formulaic, are carefully constructed and they work without loose ends, although they require more than their fair share of suspension of disbelief.

Similarly, the characterization of major characters is also formulaic. In each novel, there is a contrasted pair of heroines, the sensible one (Kitty Willoughby in *The American Baron*, Georgie Lovell in *A Comedy of Terrors*, Kitty Patterson in *Babes in the Wood*) and the silly one (Minnie Fay in *The American Baron*, Maudie Heathcote in *A Comedy of Terrors*, Rosette in *Babes in the Wood*), although "sensible" and "silly" are differently defined from one novel to another (Kitty Willoughby is more sensible than Georgie Lovell). There is a rough-hewn but good-hearted hero (Rufus Gunn in *The American Baron*, Seth Grimes in *A Comedy of Terrors*) who is always American, and a more genteel one (Lord Hawbury in *The American Baron*, Paul Carrol in *A Comedy of Terrors*), who is usually British or possibly Canadian. The villain is a French or Italian aristocrat (Count Girasole in *The American Baron*, the Count de Potiron in *A Comedy of Terrors*). Nevertheless, there are occasional minor characters who are more sharply drawn: in *The American Baron*, the Reverend Saul Tozer, a bible-thumping Protestant missionary to what he considers to be the sadly misled Catholic people of Italy, is presented humorously, and it is possible to suspect that he may have been drawn from life. He may not be based on an individual, but he may be a composite of some of the ministers De Mille knew.

Similarly, the satire in the comedies is usually directed at a stock range of targets. The lives of wealthy travellers to Europe, of a sort De Mille may have met with on his own visit, and their interactions with each other and with a surrounding culture not their own, are what De Mille is interested in. But he mocks not only the behaviour of the real-life wealthy visitors to Italy, but also their fictional versions, who would be familiar, as De Mille points out, to readers of sensational fiction, so that the satire is constantly double-edged. Generally speaking, his satire is good-natured, but effective, at least as long as he stays within certain limits. When he departs from them, in *Babes in the Wood*, he is less successful, and the portrait of the upwardly mobile Pattersons (Bill Patterson, manufacturer of "Patterson's pills," is an Englishman who has made his fortune and aspires to become a member of the gentry) is tedious and laboured, and is disfigured by De Mille's attempt to represent a working-class English accent. *Babes in the Wood*, in fact, is by far the weakest novel of the group.

Although, strictly speaking, *A Castle in Spain* is also a part of this group, in fact, it marks a divergence from De Mille's description of his satirical romance. Mahon's comments make the book sound very much like *The American Baron*:

> The love-complications of the story are a rare study in the philosophy of the heart. Each of the six principal characters of the book is madly in love with two of the remaining five. This is exceptional in novels, perhaps also in life. If each of the three young men had fallen in love with the three young ladies while they were at it, and each of the three young ladies had acted in a similar way towards the three young men it would have simplified matters greatly; but as it is we are constantly harassing our brains to keep the love-affairs straight, something indeed which the lovers themselves could never do. (322; F)

Mahon is right to a certain extent, for the plot and the principal characters resemble, at least superficially, those of the three satirical romances already discussed. While travelling in Spain at the time of the Carlist uprising, Miss Katie Westlotorn, Mr. and Mrs. Russell (Katie's guardians), Dolores, Mr. Ashby (Katie's fiancé, formerly in love with Dolores), and Harry Rivers (a friend of Ashby's and an acquaintance of Mr. Russell's, in love with, and engaged to, Miss Sydney Talbot) are captured by a group of brigands under the leadership of an Irishman, O'Toole, who is masquerading as Don Carlos (the claimant to the Spanish throne). O'Toole's headquarters are in an isolated castle, which gives the novel its title. While the travellers are imprisoned in the castle, Katie and Ashby quarrel, the latter finds himself falling in love with Dolores for the second time. Dolores is revealed to be still in love with Ashby, and Katie is very attracted to Harry Rivers, who falls in love with her. Outside the castle, Captain Lopez (Katie's rejected suitor and a member of the Spanish Republican Army) captures Raleigh Brooke (an American journalist) and Sydney Talbot, who is in search of her fiancé, Harry Rivers, and who, after meeting Brooke, disguises herself as a priest to travel with him. Lopez's troops take the castle, but instead of releasing the prisoners, Lopez tries to force Katie to marry him in a ceremony that he orders the supposed priest he has captured to conduct. During the argument about the marriage, however, Dolores releases some of the imprisoned Carlists, and Lopez is captured and his troops thrown out of the castle. The real Don Carlos arrives to guarantee the travellers protection for the rest of their journey through Spain, and the three rearranged couples (Katie and Harry, Paul and Dolores, and Brooke and Sydney) are married.

But there are considerable differences between this novel and its predecessors, principally because *A Castle in Spain* is much less farcical than the other three. Certainly there is much humour, which can be as well appreciated today as at the time of writing. O'Toole in his disguise as King Carlos, for example, threatens Mr. Russell with confiscation of his "bonds," and the latter disguises himself as a Hungarian Countess his attempt to escape from the castle, under the guidance of Rita, of whom he then becomes afraid because she seems to want him to marry her in return for her help. Mrs. Russell, too, is deluded by O'Toole, in her case into thinking that her husband is dead and that "Don Carlos" intends to make her Queen of Spain. Nevertheless, the comic and satiric elements of the novel are largely confined to the subordinate characters and the subplot, and the humour in the shifts of allegiance among the wavering lovers, who are the major characters, is subdued, and designed to provoke smiles rather than outright laughter. The danger faced by the lovers, too, is real and convincing. Brooke and Sydney are in real danger when they are in Lopez's hands, and Brooke's subsequent injury and Sydney's revelation of her love for him, although conventionally melodramatic, are not presented in as ridiculous a light as Mahon's remarks suggest. Lopez, too, represents a considerable advance in subtlety in relation to De Mille's previous villains: he is not a buffoon (like Girasole or Potiron) although he is touchy, self-important, and conscious

THE SATIRICAL ROMANCES AND THE NOVELS OF SENSATION

of his own dignity in a slightly foolish way, and his villainy has to be taken very seriously. He is perfectly serious, for example, about shooting Brooke and Sydney as spies, but is restrained by his own feeling that shooting a helpless and unarmed pair is not work for a soldier. He is also ready to force marriage on an unwilling Katie by any means at his disposal, and is only prevented by the overthrow of his troops and his own capture. Moreover, he is not wholly villainous: in final defeat he is generous. When he is captured, he promises to help treat the dangerously wounded Brooke, if released from his bonds, and he carries out his promise, making sure Brooke is out of danger before making his escape. Other characters, although in general resembling their counterparts in the other novels, are also subtly different. Among the men, for example, Brooke, the American journalist, is much more sophisticated than Rufus Gunn, just as Harry Rivers is less of the aristocrat than Lord Hawbury; and among the women, Katie Westlotorn is less frivolous than Minnie Fay but less serious than Kitty Willoughby, and Dolores is much stronger and more assertive than Ethel Orne. If anything, characterization in this novel is closer to characterization in the novels of sensation than it is to that of the other romances. It is tempting, because *A Castle in Spain* appears to have been composed so late in De Mille's life, to describe it as an attempt by De Mille to synthesize the two different types of novel he had been writing up to this point, but to do so is probably an overstatement. Yet the differences certainly suggest a shift in his approach at this time.

None of the comedies, except *The Dodge Club*, has succeeded in attracting critical attention. Even MacMechan offers only a few general remarks:

> [T]here are several comic novels of adventure. Here he succeeded much better [than with the novels of sensation]. But even here we must not expect anything like the fun of Lever or Marryat, or anything approaching a faithful representation of life or manners. We must simply surrender ourselves to our author, acquiesce in his melodramatic world, or "stageland," and then we can enjoy the entertainment he provides for us.... The action is always lively and bustling. Even in the most tragic scenes we feel that the manager of the puppets is too good-natured to let his dolls come to harm.... We are never more than comfortably alarmed. Then, after the puppets have danced a sufficient length of time, the showman reaches down his hand and

Arthur De Mille, James's youngest brother, and Alice

sweeps them off the stage with scant ceremony. After a certain amount of complication the knot is cut rather than untied, the sky clears and the three or *more* pairs of lovers are made happy for evermore. Stories like *The Dodge Club, A Castle in Spain, The American Baron* . . . are in his happiest vein because he could give free vent to his talent for burlesque and good-natured caricature. They are to be regarded as literary practical jokes on the public. They might be curtailed with advantage. . . . But neither situations nor characters are fully worked out. They might easily have been made so much better. ("James De Mille" 414–15; F)

Elsewhere, if there is any mention of the "comic novels of adventure" at all, there is little agreement. Wylie Mahon, for example, thought them very good, particularly *The American Baron*, in which, he writes, "we have De Mille at his best in depicting character and in creating ludicrous situations" (321–22; F). H.P. Scott, however, called *The American Baron* "a poor novel, but containing good bits of description, and one or two bits of melo-dramatic situations" (135; F). Mahon also liked *A Castle In Spain* in spite of its complicated plot, and described it as "full of humor which would do no discredit to Dickens himself" (322; F). Scott, on the other hand, disliked it, dismissing it as "a burlesque" (135; F).

The other novels are largely ignored, even *The Lady of the Ice*. Burpee, however, in preparing his projected book on De Mille, mentions *The Lady of the Ice* (although only in passing) in his description of De Mille's trip to Europe. He comments simply that James and Elisha "spent three weeks in and about the ancient capital [Quebec], some of the results of which James afterwards embodied in his novel *The Lady of the Ice*" ("Appreciation" 7; H). MacMechan ignores the novel entirely. It did, however, receive a quite favourable review in the *Atlantic*, which called it "a cheerful little novel" and a "pleasant study of manners and characteristics," and a more enthusiastic one in *Harper's Magazine*, whose reviewer praised its "rollicking humor" and pointed out that "James DeMille is an author who gives you a double laugh — one at the folly of the book, and another at your own folly in being interested in it" (qtd. in Crockett, "As Writer" 138; E). It is puzzling that it should have been ignored so consistently by Canadian critics, at least until the publication of the University of Toronto Reprint Series edition, since it might have been considered of particular interest to them, and to Canadian readers.

After his first comedies, De Mille quickly turned his attention to another type of popular fiction. The first of his novels of sensation appeared soon after *The Dodge Club*, and the two types of work were thereafter written concurrently. Four of the novels of sensation were published first in serial, and then in book form: *Cord and Creese* (1869), *The Cryptogram* (1871), *An Open Question* (1873), and *The Living Link* (1874). All four are clearly identified as De Mille's by letters and receipts in the Harper Brothers Archives, and by contemporary critics. Problems with this group are limited to a fifth novel attributed to De Mille (*Old Garth* [1883]), a lost manuscript ("The Isles of Greece"), and an unidentifiable work ("Under a Spell").

Old Garth appeared in 1883, apparently without prior serial publication. The book is listed as De Mille's by Watters, presumably on the authority of the title page, and the Edwards's checklist concurs (D). It is not mentioned anywhere in De Mille's surviving papers, however, or in the correspondence immediately following De Mille's death between Dr. Pryor, Arthur De Mille, and Alfred De Mill, when they were settling his affairs. It is not included in Knowles's list, in the list supplied to the Legislative Library, or in McFarlane's entry on De Mille in his bibliography of New Brunswick writers, published in 1895 (26; F), and MacMechan, writing in 1906, does not refer to it in his remarks on De Mille's novels of sensation ("James De Mille" 414; F). There is, however, no internal evidence to suggest that the novel is not De Mille's, since it shares many of the characteristics of the other four in the group, and it is always possible that it had been completed and sent before his death to Munro, who had simply not got around to publishing it. The attribution of *Old Garth* to De Mille, therefore, has to remain somewhat questionable in the absence of any firm evidence other than the title page, but his authorship cannot be ruled out altogether.

"The Isles of Greece," known to exist in manuscript, has been lost. If *Old Garth* were not clearly subtitled "A Story of Sicily," however, it would be tempting to assume that it was the published version of the lost manuscript. In the correspondence between Pryor and De Mille's brothers, it is clear that they found, among De Mille's papers, the manuscript of a novel that they refer to as "The Isles of Greece," and that they sent to Harper Brothers in an attempt to get it published. It was rejected, however, and returned to the family, and has since disappeared. If the title was not on the manuscript itself, it might have been invented for convenience, probably by Arthur, without anybody having actually read the manuscript

THE SATIRICAL ROMANCES AND THE NOVELS OF SENSATION

(after all, they certainly submitted the manuscript of "Ashdod Webster and His Starring Tour" for publication without realizing that it was not finished). But if he had read it, even Arthur cannot have supposed that Sicily was a Greek island.

"Under a Spell" is known only from a reference made by De Mille himself. In the letter to Harper Brothers dated 7 May 1868, in which he describes "America Dissected," he refers to another manuscript that he submitted to Harper Brothers: "In the meantime I should like to have 'Under a Spell' back again for the sake of meditating over it. I intend to rewrite it once more so that not a vestige of its original self will appear" (B3). It is possible that this rewriting resulted in something we now know by another title; there are no other references to "Under a Spell." But since De Mille does not describe it at all, there is no way of checking, as there is with "America Dissected," whether or not "Under a Spell" corresponds to any of the known titles.

When, with the publication of *Cord and Creese* in serial form in 1868, De Mille began his series of novels of sensation, he was attempting a novel in a flourishing subgenre devoted to the depiction of "lurid, implausible, or sensational events, and frequently involving guilty secrets" ("Sensation" 884; G).[6] De Mille would certainly have been familiar with the work of writers of such novels, particularly that of Wilkie Collins. In addition, what appears to be De Mille's own tongue-in-cheek comment on the novel of sensation is conveniently set out in *Cord and Creese* itself, in an ironic conversation between the Reverend Courtenay Despard and Mrs. Thornton, when the former claims the advantages to the reader of not reading novels one at a time:

> in each novel there are certain situations. Perhaps on an average there may be forty each. Interesting characters also may average ten each. Thrilling scenes twenty each. Overwhelming catastrophes fifteen each. . . but where you read according to my plan you have the aggregate of all these effects in one combined — that is to say, in ten books which I read at once I have two hundred thrilling scenes, one hundred and fifty overwhelming catastrophes, one hundred interesting characters, and four hundred situations of absorbing fascination. . . . By following this rule I have been able to stimulate a somewhat jaded appetite, and to keep abreast of the literature of the day. (*Cord* 82–83; A1)

Mrs. Thornton's response is even more deconstructively mischievous: "Why, one could write ten novels at a time on the same principle, and if so he ought to write very much better," to which Despard replies: "I think I will try it some day." Regardless of this fun at the expense of what he is writing, De Mille produces a respectable example of the genre.

Cord and Creese traces in typical looped and convoluted narrative style the adventures of Louis Brandon in his attempts to recover the family fortune and clear his father's name, after the latter has fallen victim to the activities of the villain, John Potts.[7] The complications of the plot almost proved too much for De Mille: the introduction of the events that have preceded the opening of the novel is accomplished only by a heavy reliance on letters (the letter found on Colonel Despard's skeleton), journals kept by the characters (Langhetti's journal of the plague at Quebec), and long accounts given by one character to another. To keep the narrative going, De Mille relies heavily on coincidence: it is, for example, coincidental that Brandon should come ashore on the same tiny island in the Indian Ocean where the *Vishnu* was wrecked, that Beatrice should be on the ship that the *Falcon*, with Brandon on board, rescues just after Brandon has himself been rescued, that Langhetti is on board the same ship as the Brandons on the voyage to Quebec, and so on. The transitions from one group of characters to another are often absurdly frequent and sudden: at one point, the narrative leaps from the stranded Louis Brandon on Coffin Island to Mrs. Thornton's drawing room, for a conversation that is so different in style and content (light, sophisticated, humorous banter between old friends) that many readers, even those accustomed to sudden changes of direction, must have wondered if they were reading the same story. The characters are almost pure examples of the stereotypes found in the novel of sensation: Louis Brandon is handsome, clever, and passionate, his brother Frank only slightly less so; their sister, Edith, and Louis's beloved, Beatrice, are pure and virtuous; the villains, Potts and Clark, are wicked and cunning, but in the end no match for the hero. Moreover, as they are in *Helena's Household*, the characters are seen only from the outside, and there is no attempt at an internal point of view. The narrative is interrupted by digressions, such as a discussion of church music between Mrs. Thornton and Despard, another on singing between Brandon and Beatrice, a description of Sable Island while Brandon is discovering the wreck of the *Vishnu*, and a complete description of the plot and staging of the opera composed by Langhetti.

Nevertheless, the book has some points of merit. Although the characters are, for the most part, stereotypes, there are some attempts at individuality: Beatrice is pure and virtuous, but she is also spirited enough to face down the villain whom she believes to be her father and to make a number of independent attempts to escape before being rescued by Brandon. Potts is not just wicked and greedy: he is also shown to be, atypically, both vulgar and stupid. In addition, his background as a villain is more exotic than usual, for he has been a member of Thuggee, the cult of religious stranglers devoted to the worship of the goddess Kali, and the cord of the title is their weapon;[8] and Clark, Potts's associate, is an escapee from an Australian penal settlement, who, in the course of an earlier attempt to escape, has turned to cannibalism to survive. The locations of much of the action, notably Coffin Island, the wreck of the *Vishnu*, and the expedition from a Caribbean island to dive for the treasure, are exotic and admirably described. Many of the descriptions of action, such as storms at sea, Brandon's fight to avoid drowning after being pushed overboard, the wreck and evacuation of the *Falcon*, the epidemic of ship fever, and even the forced bank failure, are handled vividly and economically.

De Mille's remaining novels of sensation do not resemble *Cord and Creese* very closely, although they are very similar to each other. *The Cryptogram* (1871), *An Open Question* (1873), *The Living Link* (1874), and *Old Garth* (1883, if it really is De Mille's), appear almost formulaic in their use of coincidence, stock plot events (ciphers, old documents leading to the discovery of treasure, missing relations, concealment of crimes, disguises and impersonations, attempted murders, secret marriages, presumed deaths, and so on), and stock characters (the beautiful, wilful heroine, for example, and the handsome, noble, and clever hero who wins her). In each of them, moreover, the plot is so ingeniously convoluted that it almost defies intelligible summary, yet, at the same time, being much stronger and more neatly articulated than the plot of *Cord and Creese*. There are noticeably fewer implausibilities, although there are still one or two (such as the marriage in the dark in *The Living Link*), and far fewer digressions (again, there is an exception in the historical discussion in *Old Garth*). There is less attention to originality of plot (that of *The Cryptogram* turns on the solution, first erroneous and then correct, of a cryptogram, as does the plot of Poe's the *Gold Bug*, although De Mille develops the process of solution in a much more interesting way). There is also less attention to the development of character (although the ambiguous Belinda, in *An Open*

Question, who may be either a simpleminded tool of the villain or a profoundly cunning villain in her own right, is an important exception). There are signs of inattention to detail, and the endings are abrupt and hurried (especially in *Old Garth*, which concludes with several pages of what reads like a synopsis). Moreover, in conforming, as it were, more closely to the conventions of the subgenre, this group seems to have lost much of what is attractive in *Cord and Creese*. The exotic locales have disappeared: Italy, Switzerland, and Sicily replace the Indian Ocean, Australia, Africa, and the Caribbean. There are few passages of De Mille's excellent descriptions of complex action, and many long passages of implausible, stilted, and melodramatic dialogue. There are no flashes of genuine humour (such as the discussion of the novel of sensation in *Cord and Creese*). Consequently, although they remain marginally readable, they lack much in the way of distinct appeal.[9]

Among De Mille's earlier critics, *Cord and Creese* attracted a certain amount of attention. The reviewer for *Harper's Magazine* was delighted by it:

> *Cord and Creese* by the author of *The Dodge Club* is one of those stories of perfectly impossible adventure, so plausibly told and with a succession of absurdly interesting incidents that you read it in spite of yourself, and after galloping through its pages, lay it down in a state of mental exhaustion, surprised at yourself for being interested in it. (Crockett, "As Writer" 135–36; E)

An anonymous reviewer for the *Acadian Recorder* wrote, at the time of its publication, that

> This novel, it is said, has been read in manuscript by several competent critics, who unanimously pronounce it, in point of interest of plot, variety of adventure, and graphic delineation of character, to be fully equal to any of the novels of Wilkie Collins. (Rev. of *Cord*; F)

The same writer also includes a favourable assessment of De Mille, when he notes that "The Professor had previously become somewhat popular as the writer of the very clever 'Dodge Club' papers, which ran through Harper's Magazine lately, and was pronounced by an eminent literary authority to be the best thing of the kind which had appeared since the *Pickwick Papers*" (Rev. of *Cord*; F). The notice is therefore of interest in showing not only that De Mille was highly regarded by some contemporary critics, but also that he was already known locally as an author at a very early stage of his career.

Certainly, the comparison with Collins is an exaggeration of the quality of the novel, but it was not the only time the comparison with Collins was made. Mahon, for example, writes that "in after years he found it easy to write sensational stories, as sleep-disturbing as those of Wilkie Collins. 'The Living Link,' and 'Cord and Crease' [sic] are of this class" (320; F).[10]

MacMechan, however, in mentioning Collins, says merely that De Mille responded to the popularity of Collins and other writers such as Charles Reade, Jules Verne, and Eugène Sue, and "wrote stories in their manner," and that their influence "accounts for the existence of such novels as *The Cryptogram, Cord and Crease* [sic], *The Living Link*." *Cord and Creese*, in particular, MacMechan calls "a lurid romance, somewhat resembling in places Sue's *Le Juif Errant*" ("James De Mille" 414; F). George Stewart appears to be ambivalent about *Cord and Creese*, calling it "much too sensational for our taste, yet a novel in which rein is given to a strong and fertile imagination" (404; F).

Later critics, such as they were, tended to be very much influenced by MacMechan, who managed, in his previously cited essay "James De Mille, the Man and the Writer," to constitute himself an authority on De Mille. MacMechan's discussion of the novels of sensation as a group, therefore, is worth looking at. It is clear that he is, above all, extremely embarrassed by them. He describes them caustically as "sensational stories of the wildest kind, abounding in impossible adventures, angelic heroines, and villains of the deepest dye. They are weak in construction, not seldom 'padded,' and spun out to an undue length" ("James De Mille" 414; F). And he tries to excuse what he considers to be De Mille's lapse. His argument, briefly, is that De Mille did not take these novels very seriously, but deliberately wrote below his best to conform to public taste because he had no literary ambition to do better, but that, nevertheless, his cultivated nature as "a gentleman and scholar" is always evident in what he writes.[11] In support of this, MacMechan says that the novels were "written at top speed from notes, and not revised," and points to two of the digressions — Langhetti's opera and the discussion between Courtenay Despard and Mrs. Thornton on church music — as evidence of De Mille's "cultured taste" revealing itself.

There are two points at which MacMechan's account must be considered cautiously. His first questionable assertion occurs at the point where, quoting from evidence gathered from De Mille's acquaintances, he says that

De Mille "disparaged" his own novels "calling them his 'trash,' his 'pot-boilers' " (MacMechan; H). There are two relevant items recorded in MacMechan's notes: "*Mrs Lawson* called his books 'pot-boilers'," and "*Mr W.B. Grey*, lawyer. pleasant, old-fashioned[,] stupid. . . Confirmed the 'pot-boiler' story his '*trash*' " (MacMechan; H). What MacMechan seems to mean is that Grey and Mrs. Lawson said that De Mille himself called the novels "pot-boilers" and "trash." But it should be pointed out that one of the sources is a man whom even MacMechan considered (rightly or wrongly) "stupid," and that Mrs. Lawson, as previously noted, could not have known De Mille for very long. Certainly, this evidence is in sharp contrast to De Mille's remark that he wished he could write like Mrs. Gaskell (Burpee, "Appreciation" 1; H). This reported remark has a much more circumstantial ring to it, although it must be admitted that, according to Burpee, he was told the story by a member of the family (whom he does not name, but who was probably his mother, De Mille's sister Alice) who could be considered a less-than-impartial witness. Burpee, at least, does not seem to feel any need to defend De Mille's status as a scholar and a gentleman of cultured taste.

MacMechan's second questionable assertion is that the novels were "written at top speed from notes, and not revised." It is possible that MacMechan's estimate of De Mille's speed in writing was influenced by previous mentions of it. It was commented on admiringly, while De Mille was still alive and writing, in a *Toronto Leader* notice of De Mille quoted by the *Dalhousie Gazette*:

> Prof. James DeMill, who won his first fame four years ago by the "Dodge Club" in Harper's is a rapid worker. He is under contract to furnish four serial stories to various magazines in the coming year; it is related that one of his books, "The B.O.W.C." was finished in six days; and he completed, in six weeks, a manuscript which he sold for $2,000. All this is in addition to his regular occupation as Professor of Dalhousie College, Halifax, and the use of his leisure in preparing a textbook on Rhetoric. (5 Jan. 1871: 30; H)

Moreover, one of MacMechan's own correspondents appears to confirm the rapidity of De Mille's composition:

> James would drop in to the book-store, and Budd would ask him for some copy. He would pick up perhaps some wrapping paper, and

without looking at the part of his story written last, would dash off a fresh instalment of it, keeping up a running conversation all the time, and then, tossing it to his brother, ask "Here, Budd, will that do?" This my wife had from her father, who was an intimate friend of Budd De Mill. (MacMechan; H)

The reliability of this is perhaps open to some question: it is not clear, for example, why De Mille would "drop in" to the bookstore, since it was he, not Elisha, who owned it, unless the store is simply mistaken for the office of the *Christian Watchman*. On the other hand, it seems fairly safe to assume that a certain amount of speed was required to account for the volume of De Mille's writing. But the picture conjured up of De Mille scribbling as fast as he could is not supported by the appearance of De Mille's only surviving novel manuscript, "Ashdod Webster." Here, the handwriting is careful and legible, with only a very few minor corrections, the contents are fully and appropriately punctuated, and the pages are neatly set out in double column. It is, in fact, as neat as the manuscript of *Behind the Veil*, and a great deal neater and more legible than his letters.

Letters to his publishers, furthermore, make it quite clear that De Mille certainly revised his manuscripts. In a letter about *The Living Link* to Miss Booth of Harper Brothers, for example, he writes:

> Your favourable opinion about the story I left with you gives me very great pleasure. Since I saw you last I have thought of certain elements which can be combined with the story so as to improve it very much[.] . . . I should like to know whether, if I were to rewrite this story, you would like it for the Bazar, or prefer a *new one altogether*. (B3)[12]

In fact, in his letter of 7 May 1868 about "America Dissected," also to Harper Brothers, he seems almost too eager to revise: "I am always ready to alter anything if it may be deemed best." It is in this letter too, that he requests the return of the manuscript of "Under a Spell" for what he implies would be extensive revisions (B3). This willingness to revise may have lent some credence to the notion that he was a "thorough hack" writing only for the money, which is what H.P. Scott called him (136; F). It is an opinion clearly shared by George Grant, who wrote to MacMechan that,

> Much as I admired & liked him, I could not pretend to rate his writings very highly, except the Dodge Club. . . . The others were written, hurriedly & to order, I think — He was in debt, & and had

found that he could get out of debt in that way — He gave the public such wares as they were willing to pay for. (MacMechan; H)

Grant must be referring only to the popular novels here, having either forgotten or not heard of *Helena's Household*.

Certainly his public was willing to pay him and pay him well. Harper Brothers' "List of Payments" records that he received $2,000 each for *The Living Link* and *The American Baron*, $1,000 each for *Cord and Creese* and *The Cryptogram*, $750 for *A Castle In Spain*, and $712.50 for *The Dodge Club* (Harper, Memorandum 203; H). But in spite of these earnings, which were excellent by the standards of the time, and whatever else he may have earned for his other work for which no record exists, De Mille was not well-off, and after his death his family was left almost without resources. Grant may at least have been right in saying that he required the money to pay off his debts, for although Mrs. De Mille was under the impression that all his debts had been paid off — or so she told MacMechan (H) — before they came to Halifax, Alfred De Mill, writing to Dr. Pryor during the time they were attempting to settle his brother's affairs in early March 1880, shortly after De Mille's death, contradicts this: "His troubles I always attributed to his *book store* & I believe that he did not get rid of the last of *those debts* until about 8 years ago" (To Dr. John Pryor; H). If H.P. Scott is right in thinking that these debts were "in the neighborhood of $20,000," which is the only estimate we have (136; F), De Mille's attempts to pay off his creditors would easily have swallowed everything he earned by his pen. Moreover, in the same letter to Pryor, Alfred discusses his brother's unwise speculation in American bonds, which suggests an alternative or supplementary reason for De Mille's financial problems.

On balance, however, the evidence is in De Mille's favour. He may well have written with the expectation of being paid, but neither his attitude to his work, as suggested in the letters, nor the quality of the work itself suggest that it was turned out mechanically and abnormally fast. He was a craftsman of popular literature, not the great artist that MacMechan would have liked him to be, but he wrote competently and professionally within the conventions and demands of that craft. The various satirical romances and novels of sensation, like his children's books and the two religious novels, offer ample evidence of that professionalism.

THE SATIRICAL ROMANCES AND THE NOVELS OF SENSATION

NOTES

1 In 1878, when De Mille wrote to Messrs. Harnes of *Literary World* (B3), he was clearly expecting that *A Castle in Spain* would be published almost immediately, since he had just handed over the manuscript to Harper Brothers the same month (this according to a list of "Payments to J. De Mille," which forms part of the Harper Brothers Archives [vol.7, 1887-93, 203; H], now in Columbia University's Butler Library, Special Manuscript Collection, and used by permission). The copyright notice of the copy that is described by Watters as the 1878 edition (in the possession of the Halifax Regional Library), however, reads, "Copyright, 1878, by James De Mille — Copyright, 1883, by Harper & Brothers," which suggests that publication was in fact delayed until 1883 (Watters 273; D).

2 As far as can be determined, this letter, which has survived in the National Library of Scotland (and is used by permission), represents De Mille's only attempt to publish anywhere except the United States.

3 *The Dodge Club Abroad*, which appears on some lists and on the title page of some of De Mille's other books, is clearly an error, and should be, simply, *The Dodge Club*. There is no trace of a second Dodge Club book in the Harper Brothers archival records. The subtitle is given variously as *Italy in 1859* (which was used in the first book edition) or "Italy in MDCCCLIX" (which was used in the serial publication).

4 "The Tiber, The Campagna, The Aqueducts, Trajan's Column, Antonine's Pillar, The Piazza del Popolo, The Torre del Capitoglio, The Hoar Capitoline, The Palatine, The Quirinal, The Viminal, The Esquiline, The Caelian, The Aventine, The Vatican, The Janiculum, St. Peter's, The Lateran, The Stands for Roast Chestnuts, The New York *Times*, The Hurdy-gurdys, The London *Times*, The Raree-shows, The Obelisk of Mosaic Pharaoh, The Winecarts, *Harper's Weekly*, Roman Beggars, Cardinals, Monks, Artists, Nuns, The New York *Tribune*, French soldiers, Swiss Guards, Dutchmen, Mosaic-workers, Plane-trees, Cypress-trees, Irishmen, Propaganda Students, Goats, Fleas, Men from Bosting, Patent Medicines, Swells, Lager, Meerschaum-pipes, The New York *Herald*, Crosses, Rustic seats, Dark-eyed Maids, Babel, Terrapins, Marble Pavements, Spiders, Dreamy Haze, Jews, Cossacks, Hers, All the Past, Rags, The original Barrel-organ, The original Organ-grinder, Bourbon Whisky, Civita Vecchia Olives, Hadrian's Mausoleum, *Harper's Magazine*, The Laurel Shade, Murray's Hand-book, Cicerones, Englishmen, Dog-carts, Youth, Hope, Beauty, Conversation Kenge, Bluebottle Flies, Gnats, *Galignani*, Statues, Peasants, Cockneys, Gas-lamps, Dundreary, Michiganders, Paper-collars, Pavilions, Mosaic Brooches, Little Dogs, Small Boys. Lizards, Snakes, Golden Sunsets, Turks, Purple Hills, Placards, Shin-plasters, Monkeys, Old Boots, Coffee-roasters, Pale Ale, The Dust of Ages, The Ghost of Rome, Ice Cream, Memories,

Soda-Water. Harper's Guide-Book." (*Dodge* 60; A1)

5 *The American Baron* opens with a party of ladies, consisting of the Dowager Lady Dalrymple, the childlike Minnie Fay, her sensible widowed sister Kitty (Mrs. Willoughby), Ethel Orne, and their maids, crossing the Simplon Pass by horse-drawn sled. When Minnie's sled is swept into a crevasse by an avalanche, she is rescued by the Count Girasole, who immediately proposes to her. It is then revealed that her life has previously been saved by a Captain Kirby and by Rufus K. Gunn, each of whom has afterwards proposed to her, and to escape from whom she is travelling in Italy. The party moves on to Naples, where Minnie is rescued again from a fall into the crater of Vesuvius by Scone Dacres, an act that brings Dacres and his friend Lord Hawbury into contact with the dowager's party. Complications now develop when Dacres becomes very attracted to Minnie. When he calls on Minnie he meets Kitty Willoughby, and mistakes her for the mad wife from whom he has separated and who, unknown to him, has since died. At the same time, Hawbury is also courting Minnie, under the impression (unwittingly created by Dacres in his description of the rescue of Minnie, and perpetuated by Ethel herself who is avoiding him under the impression that he has forgotten about her) that Ethel Orne is Minnie's sister and therefore cannot be the Ethel whose life he saved in a forest fire in Canada several years previously and still hopes to find. To add further to the confusion, Count Girasole first catches up with the women in order to renew his attentions to Minnie, and then follows them, as do Hawbury and Dacres, when they move on to Rome. Here, when Minnie goes to see the Pope in procession on his way to the Church of the Jesuits — during which Saul Tozer, an American Protestant minister, pushes forward in an attempt to confront the Pope and is arrested — she is recognized by Rufus K. Gunn. Gunn calls on Minnie later the same day, revealing that he is now Baron Atramonte ("the American Baron") and an officer in the Zouaves, and claims her affections in what Kitty Willoughby and the dowager consider a very vulgar fashion. Count Girasole also arrives, and becomes very jealous of the baron, and so does Lord Hawbury, who is, nonetheless, pleased to renew an old friendship with the Baron. Girasole, convinced that Hawbury has won Minnie's affections, hires some brigands and kidnaps Minnie and Mrs. Willoughby when the dowager's party is driving through the Campagna; he releases Ethel and the dowager, but imprisons Hawbury and Dacres, when they try to rescue the women. After a certain amount of confusion, during which Hawbury is temporarily buried alive, Ethel disguises herself as an Italian maid with the assistance of a priest, Minnie is rescued and proposed to by Saul Tozer, Count Girasole is killed in a fall over a cliff, and the baron arrives with a company of Zouaves to complete the rescue. All the misunderstandings are resolved and the three heroines (Mrs. Willoughby, Minnie, and Ethel) are united with their respective suitors (Scone Dacres, Baron Atramonte, and Lord Hawbury).

6 According to the *Oxford Companion to English Literature*, novels of sensation "flourished from c.1860 onwards," and included as "classics of the genre" such works

as Wilkie Collins's *The Woman in White* (1860), Mrs. H. Wood's *East Lynne* (1861), and M.E. Braddon's *Lady Audley's Secret* (1862). In addition, "Many of the novels of the period (e.g. those of Mrs. Gaskell and Dickens) include sensational elements, and the genre later developed into the thriller and detective novel" ("Sensation" 884; G). Critical comparisons made at the time between De Mille and Collins, although they may exaggerate De Mille's abilities, demonstrate that his work was clearly understood to be a part of a recognized genre.

7 In 1828, Colonel Despard captures a Thuggee band, among them John Potts, who subsequently murders Despard by leaving him alone aboard the *Vishnu* in the Indian Ocean, and steals Despard's baby daughter Beatrice, putting her in the care of a Mary Lawton (who appears later in the story under the false name of Mrs. Compton) in Hong Kong. Having framed Despard's servant, Uracao, for the murder of his employer, Potts goes to England, taking with him his son Johnnie, an accomplice named Clark, and Edgar Lawton. In order to enrich himself, he causes the financial ruin of Ralph Brandon, an important businessman and landowner, and takes his country estate from him. While this is happening, Ralph quarrels with his older son, Louis (the hero of the novel), who goes to Australia. After Ralph Brandon's death in the workhouse, Potts arranges for Brandon's wife, and his two other children, Frank and Edith, to emigrate to Quebec. On arrival at the quarantine station of Grosse Ile, Mrs. Brandon dies in an outbreak of "ship fever," and Frank and Edith are separated, the latter being rescued by Paolo Langhetti after having been buried alive.

This material is revealed at intervals in flashbacks throughout the narrative. The novel actually opens in 1846 in Sydney, when Louis receives a letter from his dying father, warning him against Cigole (an agent of Potts), and enclosing an old letter concerning a sunken ship with treasure on board. Louis sails for England, and during a hurricane in the Indian Ocean, Cigole pushes him overboard. He lands on Coffin Island, where he finds the wreck of the *Vishnu* and Colonel Despard's remains, a letter explaining the circumstances of Despard's death, and a length of cord. He is rescued by crew of a ship called the *Falcon* and is almost immediately involved in rescuing two survivors (Beatrice and the servant, Asgeelo) from another ship that is under attack by the pirate Zangorri, from whom Louis takes a creese (or *kris*, a Malay or Indonesian dagger) with Potts's name carved on the handle. While continuing its journey, the *Falcon* is sunk by a storm off the African coast. Only Louis, Beatrice, and Asgeelo survive and reach London where Beatrice and Louis, already in love, separate. In disguise, Louis goes back to Brandon Hall, the family home that is now occupied by Potts, from whom he discovers his family's fate. He leaves for Quebec, taking with him the letter concerning the treasure, eventually finds his brother Frank in New York, goes with him to the Caribbean, and there retrieves the treasure. Meanwhile, Beatrice has gone to Brandon Hall to join Potts, whom she believes is her father, and is held prisoner. Langhetti has taken Edith back to England, where he intends stage his new opera, *Prometheus*, and they visit Langhetti's sister, Mrs. Thornton, at Thornton Grange. Louis and Frank, now very rich, return to England disguised as American bankers to begin the process of ruining Potts. Beatrice escapes, takes refuge at Thornton Grange, and agrees to sing the lead in *Prometheus*, which becomes so successful that the publicity reveals Beatrice's whereabouts to Potts, who then kidnaps her. Louis finds out, and arranges for her to be rescued. Afterwards, he arranges for Potts's private bank to fail, ruining him. Louis then reveals his identity, and ejects Potts from Brandon Hall, giving him the cord found on Despard's body. Potts then sends Vijal, his Malayan servant, to kill Louis with the cord, telling him Louis had framed Vijal's father, Uracao, for Despard's murder. Vijal confronts Louis, who convinces him Potts has lied and gives him the creese with Potts's name on it. Vijal strangles Potts's son with the cord. Louis visits Langhetti and Beatrice and explains what has been happening and why. Mrs. Compton reveals that Beatrice is actually Colonel Despard's daughter and sister to the Reverend Courtenay Despard, Mrs. Thornton's friend, who immediately goes in search of Potts to kill him, but finds him murdered by Vijal with the cord and the creese. Louis and Beatrice are finally united.

8 De Mille does not seem to have done research into the cult, for his descriptions of its weapons and the behaviour of its members do not agree with the popular account of the British police administrator responsible for the cult's suppression. The account, which first appeared in the United Kingdom, was also available in the United States as early as 1839 (see Sleeman; G).

9 This difference between *Cord and Creese* and De Mille's other novels of sensation may have been noticed by the reading public of the time, because none of the other novels became at all popular, if relative popularity may be judged by the existence of reprints. Neither *The Living Link* nor *An Open Question* achieved more than a couple of printings, and *Old Garth* was never reprinted at all (Edwards 26, 31, 30; D). There is, however, a third, modern reprint of *The Cryptogram* in the Toronto Reprint Series. *Cord and Creese*, by contrast, became enough of a popular success to be reprinted a number of times, and 10 reprints are recorded between 1869 and 1897 (Edwards 13–14; D). In addition, the serial publication was copied in Halifax, from *Harper's Bazaar* by the *Acadian Recorder* between 15 November 1867 and 6 June 1868.

10 Mahon's misspelling of the title is typical, and suggests that De Mille, if the title was his own choice, might have been wiser to choose a less exotic word, or use the more obviously foreign spelling, *kris*.

11 "Yielding half in joke to a public taste, not perhaps of the highest order, De Mille did not condescend unduly. His stories are impromptus, written at top speed from notes, and not revised, but they bear everywhere the marks of unusual talent. . . . The style of his novels is peculiarly light and non-resistant. There is a distinguished air about them, bespeaking the gentleman and the scholar. *Cord and Crease* [sic] is a lurid romance, somewhat resembling in places Sue's *Le*

Juif Errant. ... But the description of Antigone in the Greek play, the music of Langhetti and the scene between the lovers in the church reveal the cultured taste. They could not have been written except by a genuine lover of the things that are lovely in literature and life. They suffice to show how much greater the man was than his work. They make you feel that he might have done much better. But he did not choose. His ambitions do not seem to have been literary. His own work he continually disparaged, calling them his 'trash,' his 'pot-boilers.' No one could take them less seriously than their author." (MacMechan, "James De Mille" 414; F)

12 This letter of 26 October 1870 to Miss Booth of Harper and Brothers is in the Gratz Collection of the Historical Society of Pennsylvania, and is used by permission.

CHAPTER 9

A Strange Manuscript Found in a Copper Cylinder

A Strange Manuscript Found in a Copper Cylinder is De Mille's best-known and best-liked work. Published anonymously in 1888, eight years after De Mille's death, it initially attracted much popular attention, and has recently begun to attract a new wave of critical attention, so that there were two editions in print in its centenary year. The novel deserves its popularity, since there is a great deal to enjoy in the satiric adventure story of the amiable, but dense hero, Adam More, during his captivity in the warm, beautiful, and fertile land at the South Pole inhabited by the strange race who call themselves the Kosekin.

The history of *A Strange Manuscript Found in a Copper Cylinder* is itself a little strange. As with some of De Mille's other works, a date for the composition of the novel can be suggested only approximately. When Mrs. De Mille, acting as her husband's executor with Dr. Pryor's assistance, found the manuscript among De Mille's papers almost immediately after his death, and wrote to Harper Brothers about it, she referred to it as "the last book my husband ever wrote" (Mrs. James De Mille; H).[1] She is contradicted, however, by Alfred De Mill, whom Dr. Pryor had consulted about it, in his letter concerning the manuscript's publication prospects. In his response, dated 6 March 1880, Alfred asserts not only that "The 'Copper Cylinder' MS is one of the first stories ever written by James," but also that he himself had "read it over some years ago & told him that the concluding chapter could be re-written with advantage, & he entirely agreed with me" (To Dr. John Pryor; H). Much depends on what Alfred meant by the words "first stories ever written" and "some years" in his letter. By the former, he appears to mean books written and published, since he refers to James having "endorsed a note" for Nathan De Mill "in 1865 or 1866 long before he began to write," although (as Alfred very well knew) James had been writing verse, magazine articles, and short stories since his junior year at Brown University (1852–53) and had also written pieces of serial fiction for the *Christian Watchman* in 1861.[2] If the first edition of *Helena's Household* was published in 1866 (as De Mille himself suggests) or 1867, then this makes 1866 the earliest possible date for the composition of *Strange Manuscript*. Alfred's phrase about "some years" is equally unsatisfactory, since he could mean anywhere between five and ten, which would suggest that a version at least somewhat resembling the version we have now existed (since we do not know what De Mille did about the last chapter even if he "entirely agreed" with Alfred about rewriting it) by 1875 at the latest, but more probably as early as 1870. On the existing evidence, therefore, Malcolm Parks's assertion that "the composition of *A Strange Manuscript*, then, can be assigned to the mid- to late 1860s" must be considered definitive (Introduction xx; F).[3]

The progress of *Strange Manuscript* from manuscript to published book is also rather strange. In his letter to Dr. Pryor, Alfred, although he admitted that he did not think that his brother "ever offered it for sale," was enthusiastic about *Strange Manuscript*'s chances of publication:

> I think that a purchaser might be found for it among the publishers of the great monthlies & when I heard from Willie that you intended offering it to Lea and Shepard I thought that possibly you were not alive to the fact of its being a work of considerable merit. It might be changed a little at the end with advantage & offered either to Harpers or in England. Perhaps as the book market is poor in the States now owing to the Seaside Library run London might be the best to try at first. (H)

An engraving from the first edition of
A Strange Manuscript Found in a Copper Cylinder

For some reason, Alfred's advice was not taken, and the manuscript was packed away. In June or July of 1887, however, it was rediscovered by Mrs. De Mille among her husband's papers. She sent it to Harper Brothers, to whom she explained that she "thought it had been sent away for publication & so mislaid, but on opening a trunk lately found the manuscript just as I sent it to you" (Mrs. James De Mille; H). Harper Brothers bought it from her for $800, less than the $900 she first asked for (as her letter makes clear), but more than they had originally offered. The serial publication began in *Harper's Weekly* on 7 January 1888 and ran until 12 May, when the book was apparently ready for distribution, and the first review appeared just under two weeks later.[4] By mid-June, the novel was well launched: in addition to its North American publication, it also appeared as a serial and as a book in England, and as a serial in Australia.[5] Further editions appeared up to 1910, but then there was a long break, ended finally in 1959 by the publication of the New Canadian Library edition (Parks, Introduction xxxvii–xxxviii; F).

Ironically, in view of the fact that *Strange Manuscript* was to become his best-known work, the various serial publications and the early book editions all appeared without De Mille's name on the title page. This omission, at least from the first edition, clearly upset Mrs. De Mille very much, for she wrote about it to Harper Brothers. In reply, they explained that the omission was necessary to avoid having the novel pirated by other publishers:

> if we had anounced [sic] the author's name, the story might have been reprinted on us, on the ground that Professor de Mille having been a British subject, he might have been considered as not entitled to the protection of copyright in the United States. We would be obliged if you would kindly preserve the secret of the authorship. (Harper, To Mrs. De Mille; H)

The request, however, seems to have been a case of the left hand at Harper Brothers not knowing what the right hand was doing, for the "secret" was clearly already no secret at all. Indeed, it seems never to have been a secret, since De Mille had been named as the author in reviews from the very beginning. In the *New York Times*, for example, on 21 May, only a fortnight after the serial version of *Strange Manuscript* had been completed in *Harper's Weekly*, the reviewer began by stating "It is now an open secret that this story ... is the work of the late Prof. De Mille" ("Novel"; F) and a later review in the *Critic* includes the statement that,

Foreseeing that the author would be charged with imitating Mr. Haggard, the publishers authorized a statement, some time ago, that the book was written long before Mr. Haggard was heard of in the literary world. The general opinion is that it is the work of the late James De Mille." (Rev. of *Strange Manuscript*; F)

It is possible, however, that the omission of the author's name from the title page may have constituted a sufficient protection against unauthorized reprints, regardless of anybody's knowledge of who the author was.

The reviews that greeted the novel on its publication are mixed, but on the whole approving. The previously cited review from the *New York Times* is not only the earliest known review, but also by far the most thoughtful. Writing in a tone of gently ironic appreciation, the reviewer discusses *Strange Manuscript* as a "wonder book" of the sort "done by assuming that novel readers, instead of being students of scientific or aesthetic or psychological problems, are simply grown-up children." The reviewer makes the inevitable comparison with Haggard, but suggests also the resemblance of atmosphere in certain parts of the novel to works by Poe, and to Coleridge's "Ancient Mariner," and draws attention to the author's originality in choosing the Antarctic rather than Africa for a location, as well as to the "reckless prodigality of invention" ("Novel"; F). Most of the other American reviewers followed this lead, commenting variously on the novel's "thrilling adventure . . . [and] vein of speculative philosophy" (Rev. of *Strange Manuscript*, *Brooklyn Daily Eagle*; F), "sly satire" (*Morning Journal*; F), and "amazing conceits and vivid descriptions" (*Critic*; F). Some of the reviewers had minor reservations, but only one (at least among those whose comments have come to light) took a totally negative view of *Strange Manuscript*. The reviewer for the *Times* of Philadelphia, almost incoherent with anger and disgust, asserts that the purpose of *Strange Manuscript*, "seems to be to make science grotesque and story telling repulsive . . . and every page of the book is unwholesome. . . . No man can read it without feeling that his manhood has been degraded" (Rev. of *Strange Manuscript*, *Times*; F).[6] The reviewer was also far too disturbed to explain to his readers what the story was actually about. Fortunately, however, the extreme hostility of this reviewer seems to have been an isolated occurrence. Most reviewers in American papers were extremely careful, in making the comparison between De Mille and Haggard, to explain that a delay in publication meant that *Strange Manuscript* was written before Haggard's

She and *Allan Quartermain*. When they did make it, the comparison was by no means always to De Mille's disadvantage.

British reviewers, however, either were not informed of, or failed to understand, the publication delay that made De Mille Haggard's precursor rather than merely his imitator. Nevertheless, they seem to have enjoyed *Strange Manuscript*, calling it, for example, "thrillingly interesting, intensely satirical, and undoubtedly clever in its execution" (Rev. of *Strange Manuscript, Perthshire Advertiser*; F) and "exciting and absorbing" (*Leeds Mercury*; F), although the reviewer for the latter found the abrupt end "provoking," and so anticipated much of the later critical argument about the novel. Curiously, the reviewer for the *Athenaeum* ignored the more obvious comparison with Haggard, and accused De Mille of plagiarizing, in 1888, from *Erewehon*, "the same ideas of topsy-turvydom which occurred to Mr. Butler in 1872" (Rev. of *Strange Manuscript, Athenaeum*; F). Although it would not have been impossible for De Mille to have borrowed from Butler before 1880, a comparison of the two novels suggests that the *Athenaeum*'s reviewer has left himself or herself open to the charge of not having read either book very thoroughly.

Canadian criticism of *Strange Manuscript* got off to a shaky start. The book was reviewed on publication in Goldwin Smith's periodical, the *Week*, which had recently been established, but clearly the reviewer (like the British reviewers) either ignored or had been left uninformed about its author's identity. He or she damned it with very faint praise in an offhand opening remark: "This anonymous novel will gratify lovers of the marvellous to their heart's content." After a plot summary, the review continues more abrasively:

> The story seems to be a sensational satire. It has some of the characteristics of the *Arabian Nights*, and the works of Jules Verne and Rider Haggard. It ends abruptly, and without disposing of some of the principal characters. The illustrations are numerous and striking. The last one represents More standing on the summit of a pyramid, rifle in hand, after he has been hailed "Father of Thunder and Ruler of Clouds and Darkness." By the way, he must have gone on his sealhunt with a magazine of ammunition. The supply seems to have been inexhaustible. (Rev. of *Strange Manuscript, Week*; F)

In its anxiety to carry out the intention announced in its prospectus to promote "the free and healthy development of the Nation" (Daniells 197;

G), the *Week* missed a golden opportunity to evaluate a major work by an interesting and lively contributor to that nation's literature. The reviewer may well have had reason to dislike the novel (the points made about the ending and about the endless supply of ammunition are well taken), but it may be surmised that he or she might have been willing to give it more serious attention had its author been identified as a Canadian and an established writer.

Almost immediately, however, writers concerned with De Mille began to offer more serious and, occasionally, more detailed criticism of *Strange Manuscript*. In 1895, in his annotated *New Brunswick Bibliography*, W.G. McFarlane was quick to recognize the difference between *Strange Manuscript* and De Mille's other fiction:

> Unlike his other work it is a novel with a purpose, it has a sociological bearing. . . . He satirizes the race for wealth and fame, the eager desire for life. . . . The book abounds in lurid, powerful description of this enchanted land . . . with its strange people and hideous customs. (25; F)

In 1906, this point was also emphasized by Lawrence Burpee, De Mille's nephew, in a letter to the editor of the *Nation*: "Despite the surface gayety of this curious story, there is a serious undercurrent that appeals to the student of modern problems of living" ("Novels"; F).[7] Mahon had already, a year earlier, pointed out the didactic element and the sombre quality of *Strange Manuscript*: "This powerfully written story is a sermon which haunts the memory and the heart" (322; F). Not until 1922, however, was the importance of *Strange Manuscript* seriously acknowledged, when R.W. Douglas, writing in the *Canadian Bookman*, asserted that this was the work that would give De Mille "a distinguished position in the literature of his time which the years are sure to confirm and render impregnable," and called it "a biting, blistering satire on the restlessness of humanity" (42, 43; F). Ironically, and unfortunately in view of the fact that this first serious discussion of the book was so enthusiastic, his recommendation that *Strange Manuscript* "never should be allowed by Canadians to lie unread and unregarded to gather dust on the highest book shelves of their libraries" was completely ignored by Canadians for the next 47 years (Douglas 43; F).[8]

The disregard of the novel by readers, and the critical silence about it, were broken simultaneously in 1969 with the publication of R.E. Watters's

New Canadian Library Series edition, with its critical introduction. Some criticism followed this edition, and Parks's previously cited critical edition of the book was published in 1986. Generally speaking, however, serious critical study of the novel has been inexplicably scarce, if it is true, as Richard Cavell asserts, that "De Mille is ranked as one of our most important novelists on the basis of *A Strange Manuscript Found in a Copper Cylinder*" (205; F). The place of the novel in the tradition of social and moral criticism, and in particular in the tradition of utopian fiction has attracted most of the critical attention, but some consideration has been given to the question of De Mille's literary influences, and to the problem of the structure of the novel.

The question of the relationship of *Strange Manuscript* to the traditional novel of ideas, and to nineteenth-century utopian literature was first considered by George Woodcock in the year in which Watters's edition appeared. Writing about the utopian novel in Canadian literature and referring to *Strange Manuscript*, Woodcock pointed out that "in the whole of Canadian writing there has appeared only one utopian novel of any real interest; it is significant in terms of our society as much as of our literature" ("Absence" 3; F). In the following year, Crawford Kilian examined *Strange Manuscript* in the context of the utopian tradition, giving a very useful and careful account of the author and of the composition of the novel, including an argument for an early date of composition (in the 1860s). Kilian argues, on the basis of Frye's theory of genres, that the novel is "primarily a Utopian satire" in the form of a " 'Menippean satire' or 'anatomy' — 'a vision of the world in terms of a single intellectual pattern,' " offering the reader, in turn, "a vision of a society whose altruism is insane because it is godless" (62; F). Subsequent criticism has not succeeded in refuting Kilian's very convincing argument.

Woodcock, it is true, later reconsidered his idea about *Strange Manuscript*. In an article entitled "De Mille and the Utopian Vision," in which he largely ignores Kilian (particularly on the date of composition), Woodcock argues that *Strange Manuscript* is not "in the strict sense, a utopia or an anti-utopia, since these genres portray complete societies which show respectively the positive and the negative results of carrying out certain theories of social reconstruction to their practical and logical conclusion" (177; F). Although the "mad and masochistic" society of the Kosekin is presented in the dystopic mode, Woodcock maintains, it does not develop any theory of social reconstruction; instead, "by portraying it De Mille is seeking to isolate and expose self-destructive elements in his own society," and is offering "an exposure of the anti-vitalist attitudes that shadowed [his] own world" (178, 179; F). Woodcock's argument is seriously damaged, as Parks later indicates, by its assumption of a late (towards the end of the 1870s) date of composition, in order to account for the influence of Bulwer-Lytton's *Coming Race* (1871), Butler's *Erewhon* (1872), and Mallock's *New Republic* (1877), which Woodcock sees as being important to De Mille's novel.

In 1976, when Parks first presented evidence for the early date of composition (the mid- to late 1860s) he did so in the course of an article, "Strange to Strangers Only," which is, like those of Kilian and Woodcock, primarily concerned with *Strange Manuscript* as a novel of ideas. In it, he argues that the satire in *Strange Manuscript* is "double-edged, an assault upon extremes of opposite kinds" and that it is "as crucial to see Adam as the impercipient and unwitting apostle of Western materialism as it is to recognize the painfully obvious imperfection of the Chief Pauper. Both put forth recipes for the death of the spirit" (76; F). Parks's article, in addition, clarifies the importance of De Mille's reading of More and Swift as utopian satirists, giving particular prominence to the influence of Swift (through De Mille's knowledge of the fourth book of *Gulliver's Travels*) as the key to "the welter of ironies and cross-purposes" that De Mille is offering to the reader (Parks, "Strange" 76; F).

Regrettably, Kenneth Hughes's contribution to the debate on *Strange Manuscript* as a novel of ideas ignores both Parks's careful examination of those "ironies and cross-purposes" and Kilian's earlier discussion of it as Menippean satire. In "A Strange Manuscript: Sources, Satire, a Positive Utopia," following Woodcock in preferring a late date of composition, but contradicting him concerning the nature of the utopia portrayed, Hughes offers an interpretation of *Strange Manuscript* as

> a positive Utopia which satirizes an aristocratic class that serves no useful social function. . . . Utopia is here not a place . . . but the process of progress itself. . . . the novel comes to an end with the rest of the manuscript unread: not because De Mille could not make a proper ending as some have suggested, but because, according to Buckle's thesis, history is open-ended and progress never ceases. (123; F)

Hughes's argument presents Adam More as a "Promethean" figure "bringing the Kosekin up to the stage of social development characteristic of the Renaissance, including the development of capitalism and class society" (120; F). This line of argument requires Hughes not only to ignore the evidence of Alfred's testimony to his brother's difficulty with the ending (as set out by Kilian), but also to do considerable critical violence to the text. Hughes does suggest, however, the names of some previously unconsidered sources of influence on De Mille, in the form of travel literature (Sir John Mandeville, whose work De Mille had read in his student days at Brown University), history (Henry Buckle), anthropology (Sir Edward Tylor), and science (Charles Darwin and Sir Charles Lyell).

Although this discussion of *Strange Manuscript* as a novel of ideas made it necessary for De Mille's critics to consider literary influences, at least in passing, only one such critic has directed attention primarily to specific works. In "The American Antecedents of James De Mille's *A Strange Manuscript Found in a Copper Cylinder*," Wayne Kime examines the "overwhelming evidence of its author's indebtedness to the works of three American writers . . . Edgar Allan Poe, William H. Prescott, and Herman Melville" in a convincing attempt to bring into focus De Mille's "intentions and strategies in the novel," and to discern "some of the dominant patterns of his mind and art" (281; F). Kime concludes with the suggestion that De Mille

> appears to have conceived of the work as in part what we might now call a Nabokovian amusement: a succession of more or less exact literary echoes, perceivable only to the fit audience who might be familiar with the range of works thus alluded to, but providing for those persons a series of pleasant recognitions. (300; F)

In this Kime is correct, but the intensity of his argument for the influence of these three American writers in particular obscures, to some extent, the considerable range of other influences De Mille drew upon, and severely limits the richness of the Nabokovian amusement Kime proposes.

Consideration of the problem of *Strange Manuscript*'s structure has concentrated from the very beginning on its abrupt ending. The problem, in fact, was identified even before the novel was published. Although his abilities as a literary critic should not be overestimated, Alfred De Mill, in his previously cited letter to Dr. Pryor, is the first to address the problem squarely:

> James . . . was never able to make a satisfactory *denouement* to the plot in it. . . . I read it over some years ago & told him that the concluding chapter could be re-written with advantage, & he entirely agreed with me. I do not know whether he has ever touched it since, or not. (H)

The ending of the novel was also identified as problematic by at least one of the critics who reviewed the book when it first appeared. As mentioned earlier, the reviewer for the *Leeds Mercury* complains briskly:

> we have a crow to pluck with the unknown author, for he actually drops the curtain just as More is about to make his escape with a beautiful maiden called Almah from the weird and terrible land of the Kosekin! What could be more provoking than such a conclusion as this? (Rev. of *Strange Manuscript*; F)

Other critics agreed. It is even one of the few points of criticism that the reviewer for the *Week* troubled to make about *Strange Manuscript*.

In view of this common reaction, it is not surprising that only two attempts have been made to argue that, in spite of the abruptness of the ending, the text as we have it is complete. The first of these attempts is Kenneth Hughes's previously mentioned argument for considering *Strange Manuscript*, "a positive Utopia" that requires a positive conclusion (123; F). This requirement, Hughes claims, is fulfilled by leaving Adam and Almah at the peak of their triumph. At the same time, according to Hughes, the ending also provides, in Lord Featherstone's breaking off with a yawn and a demand for his dinner, "a last satirical jab" at the aristocratic yachtsman (123; F), who is the representative of the reactionary and outworn aristocracy that is to be replaced by the vigorous and Promethean Adam More (120–21; F). This argument, however, depending upon the flawed positive-utopia theory, is totally unconvincing.

The second attempt (more recent and more careful than the first) to argue for the completeness of the text, is made by Camille La Bossière, in "The Mysterious End of James De Mille's Unfinished Strange Manuscript." La Bossière maintains that the abruptness and unsatisfactoriness of the novel's ending is a deliberate rhetorical strategy, and argues that De Mille has deliberately set up a pattern of iteration, but that the novel's governing idea, the "obvious mirror-reversal of values," of light and darkness, life and death, as unambiguous as the division of the polar year into two seasons, is not permitted to be enriched significantly beyond the logic of simple antithesis. (51–52; F)

Consequently, he continues, "Once the master concept is put in motion, its author is unable to do much more than repeat it time and again, in character, place, thought, and event," and eventually De Mille, tiring of "endlessly predictable iteration . . . playfully passed on the awkward task of . . . ending the book to his pleasure-loving host" at the highest point of Adam More's career (52; F). Nevertheless, although La Bossière's argument is attractive and much closer to the text than Hughes's, it is not altogether convincing.

Readings of *Strange Manuscript*, therefore, must take into account the abruptness of the ending and its lack of formal closure, although there will obviously be some readings for which it is less important than others.[9] Any reading that depends on considering *Strange Manuscript* as a finished text must find itself on thin ice, as does that of Hughes. Even a reading that takes the apparent lack of closure to be a particular (and peculiar) form of closure, as La Bossière's does, may in the end be vitiated by the fact that we do not have definitive proof of a finished text. All interpretations, however, would be, if not on sure ground, at least on an equal footing, perhaps, if it could be demonstrated that the book is — exactly as it appears to be — unfinished.

In the face of all arguments to the contrary, when the novel is being read, and even reread, the experienced general reader and the critic can still find themselves, like the reviewer for the *Leeds Mercury*, turning over the last page to look for more, and being brought up short in disappointment. My contention here, therefore, is that *A Strange Manuscript* is indeed unfinished. It is a fragment, not a complete novel — a beginning without an end — albeit an intriguing fragment.[10] This fragmentary state can be argued on a number of grounds besides Alfred's remark about the ending. The formal organizing patterns — of structure, action, symbol, characterization, and theme — all support the argument for an unfinished text, particularly when compared to patterns established in De Mille's other novels.

To begin with, even the length of *Strange Manuscript* is suggestive. In comparison with De Mille's other novels of sensation, the novel is peculiarly short. Running to about 89,900 words, it is shorter than any of them, for by a rough word count, the shortest, *Old Garth*, exceeds it by approximately 11,000 words, and the longest, *The Cryptogram*, which runs to 289,000 words, is more than three times as long. If length alone is weak evidence, since the plot of *The Cryptogram* is almost Byzantine in its complexity and accounts for almost all the length of the novel, *Strange Manuscript* can also be compared to *Cord and Creese*. The latter is, among De Mille's novels of sensation, the only one that effectively adds some narrative density (ideas, setting, and character) to the mechanics of the plot, just as *Strange Manuscript* attempts to add some satiric and philosophical depth. *Cord and Creese*, too, is much longer than *Strange Manuscript*, and although the sense of closure in its final chapter is not strong, the novel nevertheless reaches a definite, calculated, and perfectly standard conclusion.

As far as internal evidence is concerned, the novel's structure offers some support to the notion that it is unfinished. *Strange Manuscript* has an outer (frame) narrative concerning the finding of the cylinder and manuscript by the four yachtsmen, and an inner narrative, contained in that manuscript, concerning the adventures of Adam More among the Kosekin. Again, the only remotely similar structure in De Mille's work is that of *Cord and Creese*, a great deal of which is told in flashback. There is, however, no other true double narrative in anything else De Mille wrote.

Moreover, the double narrative itself is unbalanced. The typical response to the arrangement of inner and outer narrative is suggested by Fred Cogswell, in his discussion of De Mille in the *Literary History of Canada*:

> This pseudo-scientific commentary is interspersed with the action and is thus designed to make the book more suspenseful as well as more credible. Although ingenious, the commentary is often more boring than convincing and takes up a disproportionate number of pages. (113; F)

In fact, the frame narrative occupies only five chapters and part of a sixth (the last) out of a total of 30. The effect of disproportion is created by the fact that two complete frame narrative chapters (plus the fragment of frame-narrative tacked on to the end of the last chapter of the inner narrative) fall within the last five chapters of the book, heavily weighting the last pages of the novel towards the discourse of the outer story and away from the action of the inner story. Since the frame narrative, unlike the inner narrative, has no natural narrative trajectory, the emphasis that falls on it in the closing pages, even without the abruptness of the final paragraphs, leaves the ending without any suggestion of finality or closure. Consequently, if Watters's comment that the yachtsmen "provide a kind of Greek chorus to the main narrative" correctly identifies an aesthetic pattern (in the form of Greek classical drama with which De Mille was extremely familiar) in the working of the story (xi; F), then *Strange Manuscript* ends, improbably, without the extremely important final chorus.

Furthermore, if the frame narrative is, by this evidence, unfinished, there is also clear evidence from the last few lines of the frame narrative that the inner narrative, too, is unfinished. It lacks its own conclusion, breaking off after a speech by Almah that suggests future action, and when Featherstone stops reading, it is clear that at least some portion of the manuscript remains unread. It should be noted, too, that the shift from inner to outer narrative occurs here in the same chapter, although all previous shifts between the two narratives have been marked by a new chapter opening. The pattern here is all too suggestive of outside interference: an ending cobbled together by someone who was unfamiliar with the manuscript and who, accidentally or on purpose, juxtaposed pages from drafts of separate chapters that had been left as they were when De Mille had either given up trying to revise the novel or been prevented from finishing it by his sudden death.

In addition, when the inner narrative breaks off at the point at which Adam More and Almah are at the peak of their triumph, the break disrupts a symbolic structure within Adam More's inner narrative: the parallel between More and his original companion, Agnew. To begin with, as has been pointed out by a number of critics, Agnew's name is clearly symbolic — deriving from the Latin *agnus* (lamb), and suggesting the *agnus dei* of the Christian tradition — for Agnew is actually a sacrifice. Not only is he sacrificed at a cannibal feast by the savages he tries to befriend, he is also, according to Watters, "sacrificed" by De Mille in a prefiguration of the adventures of Adam himself, who is destined to be sacrificed by the Kosekin (xii; F). But Adam's sacrifice is hard to read, as the story ends. Adam is faced with being sacrificed physically for the benefit of the Kosekin — being killed on the altar and later eaten so that the Kosekin may obtain a share of his holiness — but he escapes this form of sacrifice, by agreeing to rule the Kosekin and, for their sake, to accept all their wealth, which they consider sinful. From the Kosekin point of view, therefore, More is sacrificed spiritually for the Kosekin by giving up his chance for sanctity (poverty). At the end of the book, however, it is not clear whether the physical or the spiritual sacrifice is the other of the comparison with Agnew. If it is the physical one, More's fate, from his own (and the reader's) point of view, is contrasted with Agnew's, since More escapes death to live in luxury with the woman he loves, and is therefore not sacrificed at all. If it is the spiritual sacrifice, More's fate parallels Agnew's, for a sacrifice does take place: in accepting the wealth of the Kosekin, which by his standards is no sacrifice at all, More also accepts a lifetime of captivity among them, which because of their strangeness to him, is a considerable sacrifice, even if he has not realized it.[11] In this case, De Mille is sacrificing More to the closure of the symbolic pattern, just as he has earlier sacrificed Agnew to the prefiguration of it. The ambiguity, therefore, of the ending of this symbolic pattern contributes to the lack of closure and supports the argument for an unfinished text.

Another disrupted pattern is the pattern of plotting within More's own narrative. More's interaction with the Kosekin involves two distinct, but related subplots, in both of which Layelah is a key figure. One of these interrupted subplots is the conflict between Layelah and Almah for Adam's affections. The two women embody the traditional battle between the light (good) and the dark (evil) elements of the hero's soul in Jungian interpretations of romantic narratives (a useful example from De Mille's own reading is Scott's *Ivanhoe*, in which a conflict arises between blonde Rowena and dark Rebecca for the love of the eponymous hero), although De Mille rather blurs the distinction by giving both of his women dark hair. Almah, the image of More's better nature, offers an example of patient submission to a strange culture, even in the face of death. Layelah, however, offers a temptation to More by reinforcing his reaction to the Kosekin way with her own strong dislike for it. But although it is proper for More, as an outsider, to dislike certain elements of the religious philosophy of the Kosekin nation, for Layelah to do so is a manifestation of rebellion, which leads her, because she is emotionally drawn to More, into treachery to her own people, when she helps him try to escape. Her propensity for treachery is then turned against Adam himself when he tries to escape with Almah, leaving Layelah behind.

The second of these interrupted subplots is a more subtle version of Layelah's conflict with Almah and with her own people. It is the treachery of ideas, or (to use a word foreign to De Mille that nevertheless applies to his whole purpose in *Strange Manuscript*) subversion, which De Mille explores through More's conversations with Layelah's father, the Kohen Gadol. The Kohen Gadol is, as De Mille suggests through these conversations, an example of the way in which the Kosekin society, like its Western counterpart, is open to corruption from within. He, of all the Kosekin whom More encounters, with the exception of Layelah herself, is the most susceptible to moral failure, having already been tempted and having fallen. Consequently he is, it might be extrapolated, the most susceptible, through his continued exposure to More's ideas, to an intellectual treachery parallel to Layelah's treachery of feeling.

Both subplots, however, are left unfinished when Featherstone, the last reader in the frame narrative, breaks off his reading. As Woodcock has pointed out, neither Layelah nor her father is present in the final chapters of More's account, so that, "If one can judge by the skilful interweaving of plot and sub-plot in the earlier part of the novel, it seems unlikely that De Mille would have wished to end it without bringing these important figures back on stage" ("De Mille" 174; F). In each of the subplots concerning them, therefore, the action is left hanging: Layelah disappears without a full confrontation with Almah over More, and her father disappears without having done anything except talk. This abandonment of plot action once it has been set up is without parallel in De Mille's novels of sensation, where plots are always very tightly, almost obsessively finished. *An Open Question*, it is true, deliberately finishes with the authorial voice reiterating the question to which the title refers: whether the beautiful Belinda, who is the heroine's confidante and yet betrays her into extreme danger, is the real villain in her own right, or simply the innocent dupe of the apparent villain (Belinda's father). But with the exception of this clearly special case, De Mille never leaves loose ends to his plots. Moreover, in *Strange Manuscript*, in addition to interrupting the action of the subplots, the abrupt ending also leaves the symbolic patterns of both subplots unresolved in the absence of their central characters, since no final acts of emotional or intellectual treachery are completed, to be either rewarded or defeated. Consequently, yet another argument for an unfinished text falls into place.

An analysis of characterization, it is true, makes little contribution to such an argument. Even so, it is worth noticing that the wrangling of the yachtsmen, as it reveals their characters initially, seems designed to provide the basis for some later development in the action, although no such development occurs. The doctor's obsession with "preserved meat"

(*Strange* 5–6; A1), for example, during the discovery of the floating cylinder, which contains only the remains (albeit the literary remains) of Adam More, is curiously suggestive of the cannibalism that characterizes the savages and the Kosekin within the narrative that the cylinder contains, and both are related to the entirely symbolic cannibalism of the Christian Communion of the Body and Blood of Christ. But the pattern, although reinforced by repeated descriptions of the meals taken aboard the yacht that punctuate the reading of the manuscript, remains unresolved at the end. In individual character development even less happens: Almah, at least, shows signs of developing towards the end into a stronger personality than the delicate and passive figure More first encounters, as though to balance her more satisfactorily with Layelah in preparation for the confrontation that never happens. But the personality of the central character, Adam More, seems, although wooden, firmly established, and no sign of further developments beyond his inveterate, but amiable density can be discerned. This piece of evidence, however, cannot be used to infer that De Mille had finished not only the development of the protagonist but also that of the whole book.

The most convincing evidence of an unfinished text, nevertheless, comes from the interruption in De Mille's thematic development of the satiric commentary on the difference between Western and Kosekin values and between their associated moral codes. The difference is not simply that the Kosekin inhabit, as Allan Bevan claims, "a world of inverted values," preferring death to life, darkness to light, poverty to wealth, and separation to marriage (209; F). That such simple inversion is not the point is signalled unmistakably by De Mille, on at least one occasion, in one of Adam More's classic blunders. In a conversation with Layelah, More blurts out in the face of her firm determination to separate him from Almah and marry him herself, "See here . . . why can't I marry both of you? . . . Let me marry her and you too." Layelah's response to this suggestion is to exclaim that "that's downright bigamy!" (*Strange* 180, 181; A1). A straightforward inversion of values would require that Adam's response be right according to Kosekin values, since it is wrong according to Western values. That bigamy is wrong according to both sets of values indicates that although there are inversions between the value sets, there are parallels between the supporting moral codes. The effect of this proposition is to alter considerably the thrust of the satire: De Mille is progressing, as the narrative develops, towards an assertion that it does not matter what the value set is, the moral code will be inadequate to uphold it.

This assertion is not only a much harsher judgement of Western society than that offered by the satire of simple inversion, it is also more complex — and more likely to be responsible for what Parks describes as "the welter of ironies and cross-purposes" of the novel ("Strange" 76; F). But the ironies and cross-purposes remain a welter rather than falling into an orderly web, only because they remain unresolved at the end of the book as we have it. In the final pages of More's narrative, it is because the Western moral code is inadequate that More is able to save his life by taking advantage of the Kosekin, and it is because the Kosekin moral code is inadequate that the Kosekin can give up to him their moral responsibility to avoid wealth. The implication of the central argument for the failure of all moral codes, however, remains unasserted, for it is at the precise point where the pattern of the commentary in the frame narrative should logically address itself to this argument that the text ends. Moreover, it is difficult to imagine what De Mille could have done to extract More from his difficulties, and even more difficult to imagine how he could solve what might be called the Kosekin dilemma. Having set up a satirical demonstration of the inadequacy of moral codes, he is without a mechanism to argue for the correction of human folly — at least, human folly defined (in the usual sense of the term) as a failure to adhere to a moral code. Given this technical dilemma and the spiritual bleakness of the notion that all moral codes are inadequate, the abrupt ending of both parts of the double narrative cannot possibly be considered as any form of closure, and the thematic pattern is as unfinished as the patterns of structure, action, symbol, and characterization. De Mille was clearly very far from ready to offer the manuscript for publication.

In conclusion, therefore, *Strange Manuscript*, De Mille's most important and popular work, is inarguably unfinished. But although the Kosekin dilemma could not have been satisfactorily resolved by the mere rewriting of the last chapter, as De Mille's brother Alfred suggested, the book could possibly have been finished eventually. Given time, the technical expertise developed in De Mille's popular fiction, if put to the service of his more mature personality, might have enabled him to solve the technical and thematic problems of *Strange Manuscript* and to finish it as it deserves to have been finished. De Mille's time, however, ran out before he could do so, and *A Strange Manuscript Found in a Copper Cylinder* remains a fragment as strange as its title suggests.

NOTES

1 Annie De Mille's letter of July 1887, to Harper and Brothers is undated, but since it refers to the receipt of a letter dated 16 July from Harper, it must have been written towards the end of the month. The letter, which is in the Special Manuscript Collection in Columbia University's Butler Library, is used by permission.

2 The remark also weighs against the earlier edition of *Helena's Household* claimed by Watters, as well as against the early problematic novels, *The Arkansas Ranger*, *John Wheeler's Two Uncles*, and the publication in book form of *Andy O'Hara*, unless Alfred simply did not know about them, even though during the period of their alleged publication he and James were living in the same city, if not under the same roof.

3 Parks's fullest argument for this approximate publication date is part of his meticulous account of the publishing history of *Strange Manuscript* in his introduction to the 1986 standard edition. He suggests that the discrepancy between Mrs. De Mille's remark and that of her brother-in-law may be reconciled by assuming that Mrs. De Mille, unfamiliar with her husband's methods of writing, did not realize that in 1879 he was revising an existing manuscript, rather than writing a new one (Introduction xxii; F). All quotations from and references to *Strange Manuscript* in this chapter use the 1986 edition.

4 There is no record of the date of copyright deposit for *Strange Manuscript* in Harper Brothers' records, but the first review appeared in the *New York Times* on 21 May 1888 ("Novel"; F), suggesting that bound copies must have been available in the first or second week of May, at the latest.

5 With considerable generosity, Harper Brothers made additional payments to Mrs. De Mille from the proceeds of these foreign editions, although, since she had sold the copyright to them outright, she was not legally entitled to anything further.

6 The sheer vehemence of this review has a certain charm:

> A very different kind of essay in fiction is "A Strange Manuscript Found in a Copper Cylinder" . . . the purpose of which seems to be to make science grotesque and story telling repulsive. Whoever reads this book must have a patient, plodding mind, predisposed to delight in horrors. As a story it is not interesting, and every page of the book is unwholesome. It is a travesty on life and death — an awkward attempt at using the speculations of science as the elements of fiction. Since Mrs. Shelley's "Frankenstein" English literature has not been polluted by a tale so unworthy. The thing is an offense to scientific thought, to refinement of feeling, even to a heathenism that has in it any of the instincts of the divine nature. No man can read it without feeling that his manhood has been degraded.
>
> [The author's] conceptions are as awkward as his title. He has no imagination to begin with. He paints a huge canvas with a whitewash brush and fills it with

hideous figures that are only the outlines of distorted realities. He reverses the order of nature and thinks he has created a new world. He . . . causes horrors upon horrors to accumulate, and yet we do not shudder because the trick is so bald and the device intellectually so feeble that it only excites our contempt.

It is strange that such a tale found a publisher at all. . . . There is no possible or adequate explanation of it unless it is that the distorted and the hideous in this age have the power to blind us to beauty and truth — that the bald images of the blackguard have become our standards of culture, poetry and fiction. (Rev. of *Strange Manuscript*, *Times*; F)

7 At the time of this letter, however, Burpee did not realize that *Strange Manuscript* was an early work. He calls it "the very last one [James] wrote," and uses the occasion to suggest that

Had James De Mille lived a few years longer . . . there is little doubt that he would have written novels worthy to stand beside the best product of his generation. He had the equipment. He was a thinker; he had read widely, and absorbed what he read; he had the indespensable [sic] insight into human nature and a keen appreciation of the humorous side of things; above all, he possessed imagination. ("Novels"; F)

8 *Strange Manuscript* received occasional mention in the United States as an example of early science fiction and utopian fiction, in studies such as J.O. Bailey's *Pilgrims Through Space and Time* (1947).

9 Woodcock, in particular, argues very strongly on the basis of the abruptness of its ending that *Strange Manuscript* is an incomplete text: "A writer as experienced in the craft of Victorian popular fiction as De Mille would not have deliberately made so lame an end, which even as an anticlimactic device is ineffective. One senses a tired hand abandoning an unfinished task" ("De Mille" 174; F). But his reading of the novel in terms of utopian and antiutopian fiction is not affected by the unfinished state of the text.

10 The story opens in the year 1850. Lord Featherstone and three of his friends — Noel Oxenden, Dr. Congreve, and Otto Melick — are on board the yacht *Falcon*. While becalmed near Madeira, the four men find a copper cylinder floating in the sea, which, when opened, proves to contain a letter from Adam More to the finder, together with a narrative of the events that have led him to write it and set it afloat. They begin to read the manuscript, with Melick as the first reader. More's narrative relates how he and a companion, Agnew, go ashore, while becalmed off the ice fields of Antarctica to shoot seals, and are unable to return to their ship. In their small boat, they drift towards two volcanoes, but before they reach them, come to land, where they find the long-dead corpse of a sailor. They bury him, and continue along the channel towards the volcanoes. They encounter a group of savage cannibals, who murder Agnew. More escapes and

continues his journey alone in their boat, passing between the volcanoes and being swept into a natural tunnel, where he encounters a sea monster. His boat emerges finally onto a warm sunlit sea surrounded by a fertile country that appears to resemble the Earth as it was in the age of the dinosaurs, and is inhabited by a race called the Kosekin. He is rescued by a sea captain who takes him ashore. (At this point, More's narrative is interrupted for a discussion between the yachtsman, after which the reading is continued by Congreve.) Among the Kosekin in their underground city, he is treated like an honoured guest, and is introduced to Almah, a beautiful young woman who has come here as a stranger, but who is able to teach him the language and explain the customs and ideas of the Kosekin to him. He shares her duties of tending the corpses of the honoured dead, and participates in two hunts. He discovers from conversations with Almah and the Kohen (one of the Kosekin officials) that the Kosekin prefer death, misery, darkness, and poverty to life, happiness, light, and wealth, and that they worship death and practise cannibalism. After he finds out that the Kosekin intend to sacrifice him and Almah, he determines to escape. (At this point, More's narrative is interrupted for more discussion between the yachtsman, after which the reading is continued by Oxenden.) More and Almah are taken to the capital city of the Kosekin to prepare for the sacrifice, and there More meets the Kohen Gadol (a more important official than the Kohen), from whom he learns more about the Kosekin way of life; he also meets the Kohen Gadol's beautiful daughter Layelah, who falls in love with him and whom he persuades to help him escape. Intending to leave with him herself instead of letting him take Almah, she shows him how to manage the *athalebs* — the winged monsters that the Kosekin use for travel. More escapes, taking Almah with him, but they are pursued by the Kosekin with Layelah, who catch up with them after they land on the Island of Fire. On the way back to the capital, Layelah causes the *athaleb* on which she and More are riding to fall behind and they become separated from the rest of the party. More kills the monster. They fall into the sea, and come ashore on a small island, where the Kosekin find them. (At this point, More's narrative is interrupted for more discussion between the yachtsman, after which the reading is taken up by Featherstone). More and Almah are taken back to the capital, and prepared for the sacrifice by undergoing a ceremony of separation (the Kosekin version of betrothal). Finally they are taken out to the top of a pyramid in the city square. At the moment Almah is about to be killed, More turns the tables on the Kosekin by killing their leaders. The Kosekin immediately begin to regard him as a hero, and he and Almah are declared the rulers of the Kosekin. They promise to rule benevolently, according to the reversed values of Kosekin philosophy, by accepting all the wealth of their subjects. (The novel ends with a declaration by Featherstone that he is too tired to read any further.)

11 Since the balance between captivity and riches seems, at least in More's closing remarks, not to be too disagreeable, it is probably not this problem, therefore, which is, in his own words, the "fate" from which "escape is as impossible as from the grave,"

that he describes in the letter accompanying the manuscript (*Strange* 8; A1). Although we may take this as part of the ironic structure of the book, is clearly not intended as such by More, who is incapable of irony. The fact that we do not know, at the conclusion, what it is that More considers to be his terrible and inescapable fate, is yet another loose end that signals an unfinished structure.

Conclusion

"The work of this writer [James De Mille] demands notice in any sketch of Canadian literature however brief, because he was prominent as a Canadian author when these were few in the land," wrote his son, singling out for particular mention *The Dodge Club*, *A Castle in Spain*, and *A Strange Manuscript Found in a Copper Cylinder* (Alban De Mille 324; F). Perhaps the modesty of this comment was due to Alban's fear of overstating his father's claim to recognition, for certainly James De Mille deserves attention not only for the fact of his existence as a Canadian writer but also for the kind of work he produced and for the kind of person he was.

Born 34 years before Confederation, he was not, of course, a Canadian by birth in the modern sense. But he came of Loyalist stock on both sides of the family, and certainly considered himself a Canadian. Apart from brief visits — one to Europe and a number to the United States — he spent his whole life in the Maritime provinces, and when he presented the region of his birth to the Canadian and American public in his children's books, he did so with affectionate pride.

But it is not merely his family and residence that make him Canadian, it is also his personality. For, in a very peculiar way, De Mille's personality seems to anticipate the stereotypical Canadian, the definition of which is now debated in literary and historical studies, and in the media. To begin

CONCLUSION

with, like many Canadians he spent a great deal of time observing Americans, whom for the most part he liked. He wrote a great deal about them, introducing them as characters in his fiction, and producing one or two shrewd portraits. Nevertheless, he remained unshakably Canadian, no more wanting, apparently, to be an American because of his liking for them than a forester wants to be a tree.

Moreover, he spent a great deal of his life trying to reconcile the discordant elements of his personality, much as modern Canadians are trying to reconcile the various regions and provinces of their country into a harmonious confederation. A man of wide scholarship, with a passion for study, he tried to turn himself into a businessman in order to support his family. Even when he found a suitably intellectual niche for himself, first at Acadia College and then at Dalhousie College, we can see him still trying to balance the writer and the academic, the satirist and the teacher, the critic of society and the responsible citizen.

His reputation as a writer is, in addition, tinged by a very Canadian irony. He achieved only a local reputation during his lifetime, for the greatest part of his work was published anonymously in the United States. Fame was achieved only posthumously, with the publication of *A Strange Manuscript Found in a Copper Cylinder* — a book that may not have been intended to be published in its present form. Today, however, if Canadians recognize the name of James De Mille, it is probably because they have read this book.

Finally, again like many Canadians, he was (and still is) a very elusive personality. He never gave himself away in his writing, even in the deeply serious poem *Behind the Veil*, or in apparently autobiographical fiction such as "The Minnehaha Mines," and even in fiction he only twice wrote in the first person. He left very little in the way of personal documents, although it is probably due more to bad luck than to any effort on his part that fire destroyed many of the records for the periods of his life that he spent in Saint John and at Acadia College. Even the one existing photograph of him reveals very little. Three previous attempts to write a biography of De Mille have been interrupted by the author's death before the work was finished.

Certainly, his life, as described in the preceding pages, illustrates very clearly the difficulties and dilemmas facing the Canadian writer in De Mille's lifetime. Given the time and place of his birth, he lived in a community without possibilities for the companionship of other writers, who might have given him encouragement and assistance, possibly by steering him in other directions. If, for example, at the time he was working on *Strange Manuscript*, he had had the support and advice of another writer close at hand, he might have been persuaded not to leave it unfinished (assuming that it was not left unfinished because work on it was interrupted by his sudden death). De Mille also lived without a serious market for his work in his own country, and was, therefore, forced to conform to the standards and tastes of the United States: *The Lady of the Ice*, with its Quebec City setting, is ample demonstration (not to mention the books of the B.O.W.C. Series) that he could find material for his fiction in his own country, if only people were interested in reading it. His full-time academic work took time and energy from his writing, regardless of how fast he might write, and the academic pressure seems to have stimulated efforts to escape to full-time writing that, in the end, left him more dependent on his salary from Dalhousie. His perseverance in continuing to write in these circumstances deserves applause, not the charge of being a hack who wrote only for mercenary reasons.

The work that he produced was by no means the trash that it has often been made out to be. Within the limitations of popular fiction, of both the comic novel and the novel of sensation, he wrote capably and entertainingly, and he gave his readers good value for their money. A reader in search of entertainment can find it even today in much of his work. *The Cryptogram* and *Cord and Creese*, for example, if due allowance is made for changing tastes in popular thrillers since the 1870s, are very readable, and deserve to be more widely known. Among his comic novels, *The Dodge Club* and *The American Baron* can still make readers laugh. Moreover, the attempt (mentioned earlier) in *A Castle in Spain* to amalgamate comedy and suspense, and the apparent attempts to finish *A Strange Manuscript Found in a Copper Cylinder*, suggest that De Mille had a great deal of potential for further development. The latter novel, even in its unfinished state, is not only entertaining but thought provoking. His novels should be read for their entertainment value and their interest: regardless of where they were published, they were part of what Canadian readers of the time thought was worth reading, as well as what a Canadian writer thought was a worthwhile contribution to their genre.

Just as importantly, however, De Mille deserves to be remembered because he was worth remembering. In person, James De Mille was a good father and husband, a conscientious and careful teacher, a stimulating and supportive colleague, and a pleasant and good-humoured acquaintance. If Alban De Mille did not touch on his father's personality in his essay, it was either because he was writing only about his father's professional career, or because his father died when the boy was too young to remember him clearly. During James De Mille's life, colleagues and students alike responded to him with affection, and long after his death and long after they had left Dalhousie, they continued to remember him affectionately and to regret their loss. Among them, George Patterson alone offers the sort of verbal snapshot that can give the modern reader glimpses of De Mille in life. As a student of De Mille in the last year of De Mille's life at Dalhousie, he presents a brief classroom portrait:

> In his Rhetoric class taken in our first year we used as a textbook his *Elements of Rhetoric*. One day we were discussing "alliteration." In the book, after giving the usual illustrations . . . he goes on to say that alliteration was frequently used in the titles of books citing as examples — *The Pilgrim's Progress*, *The Dairyman's Daughter*, *Pride and Prejudice*. It happened that when we reached this subject in class, I was asked to tell what I knew about alliteration. I tried to do so and, following the book, went on to say that it was used frequently in the titles of books. I quoted the examples given and added to them *Helena's Household, Cord and Creese*, and *The Living Link*. . . . I thought myself very clever, but if I expected to impress DeMille with my cleverness, I was doomed to disappointment. He took no notice whatever, and when the class gave me a bit of a "hand," he did not seem to know what it was all about. ("As Teacher" 147–48; G)

Similarly, he gives us a rare glimpse of De Mille the writer caught incidentally in the spotlight of another performer:

> In the late fall of 1879, the great Mrs. Scott Siddons gave a recital in Halifax. . . . One of her funny selections was that from DeMille's *The Dodge Club*; where the American Senator at the Italian Countess' request, undertook to teach her some English poetry. . . .
> The audience was convulsed with laughter; time after time the reader had to pause to allow the applause to die down. DeMille was the only one who showed no sign of appreciation. He was seated in

Annie De Mille (third row, right) at the wedding of her youngest son Frank (front) to Cecilia Humphreys, Vancouver, 1908. Alban De Mille is immediately behind her.

CONCLUSION

the front row of the first gallery in the Old Academy of Music directly opposite the stage, his hands on his cane and his chin resting on his hands. He never even smiled, though he must have been highly delighted, not only at the way the selection was given, but because a selection from his writings had been chosen by the most celebrated actress of her time as worthy to illustrate her genius. ("As Teacher" 148; G)

Patterson also offers a brief account of a personal encounter with De Mille outside the classroom:

When I [came] back for my second year, I met DeMille and his son, William Budd, walking arm in arm across the Parade. I, of course, touched my hat to him, but for a moment there was no response — no sign of recognition. I have no doubt the son told him who I was, for DeMille quickly turned around, called me by name, shook hands with me, kindly inquired what I had been doing during the summer, and gave me such a welcome as made me very happy. ("As Teacher" 148; G)

The warmth of Patterson's recollections is more than sufficient to bring De Mille, however briefly, to life.

In conclusion, it must be admitted that James De Mille leaves a great deal to be desired as the subject of a biography. We have, regrettably, no way of learning as much as we would like to know about him. Most of his papers, as previously mentioned, have disappeared, and the remaining ones contain very little personal material: what can be gathered, from them and from the recollections of those who, like Patterson, knew him personally, has been presented here. Even to his biographer, however, James De Mille reveals as little as possible, and judging from the expression — of reserve and quiet amusement — in his portrait, this is as he would have wished it to be.

APPENDIX A

De Mille's Contributions to the *Christian Watchman*

This appendix constitutes a preliminary checklist only, since, as pointed out in chapter 4, articles, fiction, and usually the verse that appeared in the *Watchman* were anonymous in the sense that they appeared either without any form of identification at all, or with identification consisting of initials or obvious pseudonyms. Items listed here are those I am sure, beyond all reasonable doubt, were written by De Mille. Some of the other contributed material is possibly his, and some is completely unattributable to anybody in particular. (These problems, however, will have to await discussion elsewhere.) The *Watchman* only existed for one year — 1861 — so all the following pieces appeared in that year.

#	Date	Title
1.	2 January	"Dies Irae. A New Translation"
		"The Conquest of India" 1
2.	9 January	"The Conquest of India" 2
		"The Missionary's Son" 1
3.	16 January	"The Conquest of India" 3
		"The Missionary's Son" 2
4.	23 January	"The Conquest of India" 4
		"The Missionary's Son" 3
		"Havelock's March"
5.	30 January	"The Conquest of India" 5
		"The Missionary's Son" 4
6.	6 February	"Horton Sketches, No. 1"
		"The Missionary's Son" 5
		"A Trip to Wales"
7.	13 February	"Horton Sketches, No. 2"
		"The Missionary's Son" 6

8.	20 February	"Horton Sketches, No. 3"
		"The Missionary's Son" 7
9.	27 February	"Horton Sketches, No. 4"
		"The Missionary's Son" 8
10.	6 March	"Horton Sketches, No. 5"
		"The Missionary's Son" 9
11.	13 March	"Horton Sketches, No. 6"
		"The Missionary's Son" 10
		"Among the Dutchmen" 1
12.	20 March	"Horton Sketches, No. 7"
		"The Missionary's Son" 11
		"Among the Dutchmen"
13.	27 March	"Horton Sketches, No. 8"
		"The Missionary's Son" 12
		"Among the Dutchmen" 3
		"The Death of Havelock"
14.	3 April	"Horton Sketches, No. 9"
		"The Missionary's Son" 13
		"Among the Dutchmen" 4
15.	10 April	"The Missionary's Son" 14
		"Recollections of Naples 1, 'Fair Parthenope' "
16.	16 April	"Andy O'Hara" 1
		"Recollections of Naples 2, 'Life in Naples' "
17.	24 April	"Andy O'Hara" 2
		"Recollections of Naples 3, 'Arts and Antiquities' "
		"Among the Dutchmen" 5
18.	1 May	"Andy O'Hara" 3
		"Recollections of Naples 4, 'Ascent of Vesuvius' "
		"Female Education" 1
19.	8 May	"Andy O'Hara" 4
		"Recollections of Naples 5, 'Tomb of Virgil, Grotto of Posilippo, Pozzuolo' "
		"Among the Dutchmen" 6
		"Female Education, Its Necessity" 2
20.	15 May	"Andy O'Hara" 5
		"Recollections of Naples 6, 'Baiae and Its Environs' "
21.	22 May	"Andy O'Hara" 6
		"Recollections of Naples [7], 'Pompeii' "
		"Female Education, Its Necessity" 3

APPENDIX

22.	29 May	"Andy O'Hara" 7
		"Recollections of Naples 8, 'Salerno and Paestum' "
		"Among the Dutchmen" 7
23.	5 June	"Andy O'Hara" 8
24.	12 June	"Andy O'Hara" 9
		"Female Education, Its Character" 4
		"A Horton Sketch"
		"Inaugural Discourse" (Acadia College)
25.	19 June	"Andy O'Hara" 10
		"Recollections of Naples 9, 'Sorrento' "
26.	26 June	"Andy O'Hara" 11
		"Recollections of Naples [10], 'From Naples to Albano' "
27.	3 July	"Andy O'Hara" 12
		"Acadia College"
		"Female Education. Its Results" 5
28.	10 July	"Andy O'Hara" 13
		"Brown University"
29.	17 July	"Andy O'Hara" 14
		"Recollections of Rome I. 'From Albano to Rome' "
		"Report of Committee on Education" (Eastern New Brunswick Baptist Association)
30.	24 July	"Recollections of Rome [II]. 'Life in Rome' "
31.	31 July	"Recollections of Rome III. 'The Modern City — Its Repulsions' "
32.	7 August	"Recollections of Rome IV. 'The Modern City, Its Attractions' "
33.	14 August	"Recollections of Rome V. 'Bird's Eye View of Modern Rome' "
34.	21 August	"Recollections of Rome VI. 'Bird's Eye View of the Ancient City' "
35.	28 August	"Recollections of Rome VII. 'The Environs of Rome' "
36.	4 September	"Recollections of Rome [VIII]. 'Associations — The Kingly Period' "
37.	11 September	"Recollections of Rome [IX]. 'Associations — The Republican Period' "
38.	18 September	"Recollections of Rome [X]. 'Associations — The Imperial Period' "
39.	26 September	"Recollections of Rome [XI]. 'Associations —

		The Rise of the Church' "
40.	2 October	"Recollections of Rome [XII]. 'Associations — The Papacy' "
41.	9 October	"Recollections of Rome [XIII]. 'The Roman' "
		"Acadia College"
42.	16 October	"Recollections of Rome [XIV]. 'Roman Government' "
43.	23 October	
44.	30 October	"Recollections of Rome [XV]. 'Antiquities in the Modern City' "
45.	6 November	"Recollections of Rome [XVI]. 'Antiquities — A Walk Through the Campo Vacchino' "
46.	13 November	"Recollections of Rome [XVII]. 'Antiquities — A Stroll on the Appian Way' "
47.	20 November	"Recollections of Rome [XVIII]. 'Christian Antiquities — The Catacombs' "
48.	27 November	"Recollections of Rome [XIX]. 'Ancient Churches' "
		"Hebrew Poetry, No. I. 'Sources of National Poetry' "
49.	4 December	"Recollections of Rome [XX]. 'Basilica — St. John Lateran — Sta Maria Maggiore' "
		"Hebrew Poetry, No. II. 'Circumstances in the History of the Hebrews Favourable to the Growth of a National Poetry' "
		"Acadia College"
50.	11 December	"Recollections of Rome [XXI]. 'The Basilica of St. Peter's' "
		"Hebrew Poetry, No. III. 'Its Growth — Variety — Form, and Use' "
		"Acadia College"
51.	18 December	"Hebrew Poetry, No. IV. 'Temple Worship' "
		"The Powers of Conscience Illustrated"
52.	26 December	"Recollections of Rome [XXII]. 'Churches' "

APPENDIX B

De Mille's Contributions to the *Christian Visitor*

Although it is practically certain that the pieces listed in appendix A were, in fact, written by De Mille, there may remain some small doubt about the contributions to the *Visitor* listed below. They are probably De Mille's, since the Reverend I. E. Bill had no other assistant at this time, and they are certainly not written in Bill's style.

"Encourage Your Minister"
This series of general articles on the relationship between congregations and their pastors ran for 13 instalments, beginning in the issue for 3 January 1855 and concluding in the issue for 18 April 1855, thus coinciding with the dates De Mille worked at the paper. They were usually signed "Amicus," and although De Mille, does not use the pseudonym "Amicus" in the *Christian Watchman*, his "Recollections of Rome" and other travel articles are signed "A," as though he had a particular attraction to this letter.

"Three Days in North Wales"
This contribution by De Mille, without attribution, appeared in two issues of the *Visitor*: 1 June and 8 June 1855. The trip recounted is clearly De Mille's version of one that is recorded in the first few pages of volume 1 of Elisha's journal.

"Faith, Hope, and Love"
This is piece of fiction (in the style of a fable) about the archangel Israfel, published in the *Visitor* 21 February 1855. It is labelled "written for the *Christian Visitor*" and attributed to "Aleph."

Selected Bibliography

The selected bibliography is divided into sections, as follows:

A. Published Works by James De Mille
  1. Novels
  2. Short Stories
  3. Verse
  4. Miscellaneous Prose
B. Manuscripts and Papers of James De Mille
  1. Novels
  2. Verse
  3. Letters
  4. Other Documents
C. Lost or Disputed Works of James De Mille
  1. Novels
  2. Short Stories
  3. Verse
D. Bibliographical Sources for James De Mille's Published Works
E. Biographical Material on James De Mille
F. Criticism on James De Mille
G. General References: Published Material
H. General References: Manuscripts, Collections, and Public Records

Notes

In section A of the selected bibliography, the dates of serial publication of the novels are not included, except when serialization was not followed by publication in book form (in the case of *Andy O'Hara*, no copy of the book has been located), and only first editions of the book form are included, except for the two currently available editions of *A Strange Manuscript Found in a Copper Cylinder*, and the modern paperback edition of *The Martyr of the Catacombs*, since this is the only extant edition. In section

B, items marked with an asterisk are transcriptions, not manuscripts in De Mille's own hand. The selection of biographical references and critical material in sections F and G does not include entries in general reference books or mention in dissertations and theses (unless these have been cited in the text), or discussion in newspaper or periodical articles not of historical or critical significance.

For an explanation of the parenthetical reference system used in this book see "A Note on the Citation of Research Materials," p. 12.

A. Published Works by James De Mille

1. Novels

The American Baron. New York: Harper, 1871.
Among the Brigands. Young Dodge Club Series 1. Boston: Lee, 1871.
"Andy O'Hara." [By the author of *The Missionary's Son.*] *Christian Watchman* 16 Apr. 1861 through 17 July 1861.
Andy O'Hara: Or, the Child of Promise. New York: Carlton, 1861.
"*The B.O.W.C.*": *A Book for Boys.* B.O.W.C. Series 1. Boston: Lee [1870].
The Babes in the Wood: A Tragic Comedy. A Story of the Italian Revolution of 1848. Boston: Gill, 1875.
The Boys of Grand Pré School. B.O.W.C. Series 2. Boston: Lothrop, [1870].
A Castle in Spain. New York: Harper, [1878].
A Comedy of Terrors. Boston: Osgood, 1872.
Cord and Creese: Or, the Brandon Mystery. New York: Harper, [1869].
The Cryptogram. New York: Harper, [c. 1870].
The Dodge Club: Or, Italy in 1859. New York: Harper, 1869.
"The Earl's Daughter." *Dalhousie Gazette* 8 Feb. through 22 Mar. 1869.
Fire in the Woods. B.O.W.C. Series 4. Boston: Lee [1871].
Helena's Household: A Tale of Rome in the First Century. New York: Carter, 1867.
The Lady of the Ice. New York: Appleton, 1870.
The Lily and the Cross: A Tale of Acadia. Boston: Lee, 1874.
The Living Link. New York: Harper, 1874.
Lost in the Fog. B.O.W.C. Series 3. Boston: Lee, [1870].
The Martyr of the Catacombs: A Tale of Ancient Rome. New York: Carlton, [1865].
The Martyr of the Catacombs. Chicago: Moody, 1970

"The Minnehaha Mines." *Boston Commercial Bulletin* 1 Jan. 1870 through 28 May 1870.

———. *New Dominion and True Humorist* [Saint John] 8 Jan. through 25 June 1870. [The microfilm is missing the issues containing the first and twelfth instalments.]

"The Missionary's Son." [By "X."] *Christian Watchman* 9 Jan. 1861 through 10 Apr. 1861.

Old Garth: A Story of Sicily. New York: Munro, [c. 1883].

An Open Question. New York: Appleton, 1873.

Picked Up Adrift. B.O.W.C. Series 5. Boston: Lee, 1872.

The Seven Hills. Young Dodge Club Series 2. Boston: Lee, [c.1872].

A Strange Manuscript Found in a Copper Cylinder. New York: Harper, 1888.

A Strange Manuscript Found in a Copper Cylinder. Ed. and introd. R.E. Watters. New Canadian Library Series 68. Toronto: McClelland, 1969.

A Strange Manuscript Found in a Copper Cylinder. Ed. and introd. Malcolm G. Parks. Ottawa: CEECT–Carleton UP, 1986.

The Treasure of the Seas. B.O.W.C. Series 6. Boston: Lee, [1872].

The Winged Lion: Or, Stories of Venice. Young Dodge Club Series 3. Boston: Lee; New York: Dillingham, 1877.

2. Short Stories

"The American Trooper: A Page in the History of the Revolutionary War." *Gleason's Pictorial Drawing-Room Companion* 17 June 1854: 378–79.

"The Artist of Florence." *Flag of Our Union* 5 Aug. 1854: 246–47.

"The Australian Footman: A Romance in the Antipodes." *Flag of Our Union* 29 July 1854: 238–39.

"The Balloon Ascent." *Flag of Our Union* 25 Mar. 1854: 96.

"The Captive's Flight." *Flag of Our Union* 20 May 1854: 160.

"The Castle and Crucible." *Flag of Our Union* 27 May 1854: 164.

"The Circassian's Revenge." *Gleason's Pictorial Drawing-Room Companion* 18 Feb. 1854: 103.

"The Contrabandist." *Flag of Our Union* 22 Apr. 1854: 124.

"The Corsair of Scio: A Tale of the Isles of Greece." *Flag of Our Union* 22 July 1854: 230–31.

"The Goblin Tower: A Tale of Tuscany." *Gleason's Pictorial Drawing-Room Companion* 14 Oct. 1854: 230.

"Hugo von Ehrenfels: A Rhenish Tale." *Flag of Our Union* 25 Feb. 1854: 62.

"The Loss of the Hector: Or, the Transformation." *Godey's Lady's Book* May 1862: 253–59.

"The Priestess of the Sun: A Tale of Peru." *Flag of Our Union* 3 June 1854: 176.

"The Rose of Acadie." *Flag of Our Union* 4 Nov. 1854: 351.

"Rudolph the Burgess: A Legend of Noyais." *Gleason's Pictorial Drawing-Room Companion* June 1854: 358–59.

"The Spanish Knight." *Flag of Our Union* 8 Apr. 1854: 100–11.

"The Traitor's Doom." *Gleason's Pictorial Drawing-Room Companion* 29 Apr. 1854: 266–67.

"The Were Wolf." *Flag of Our Union* 24 June 1854: 200.

3. Verse

Behind the Veil. Halifax: privately published, 1893.

"A Bray from a Dunkie." *Morning News Double XXtra* [Saint John] Apr. 1861: n. pag.

"The Death of Havelock." [By "Lamed."] *Christian Watchman* 27 Mar. 1861: 4.

"Dies Irae: A New Translation." *Christian Watchman* 21 Jan. 1861: 4.

"A Fenian Song." *Morning News Double XXtra* [Saint John] Apr. 1861: n. pag.

"The Gallant Highwayman." *Songs of the Maritimes: An Anthology of the Poetry of the Maritime Provinces*. Ed. Eliza Ritchie. Toronto: McClelland, 1931. 207

"Havelock's March." *Christian Watchman* 16 Jan. 1861: 4.

"The Indian Names of Acadia." *Songs of the Great Dominion*. Ed. W.D. Lighthall. London: Walter Scott, 1889. 285–86.

"In New Brunswick You'll Find It." *Atlantic Advocate* 47 (1956): 65.

"James De Mille's 'Class Poem 1854.'" Ed. and introd. Patricia Monk. *Canadian Poetry* 15 (1984): 61–75.

"Lines: To Florence Huntingdon, Passamaquoddy, Maine." *Boston Commercial Bulletin*. 26 Mar. 1870: 1.

———. *New Dominion and True Humorist* [Saint John] 16 Apr. 1870: 171.

"Lord Hilbert: A Ballad." *Flag of Our Union* 29 Apr. 1854: 135.

"The Maiden of Passamaquoddy." *Journal of Education* [Halifax] 4th ser. 3.7 (Dec. 1932): 147–48.

"The Maranon." *Gleason's Pictorial Drawing-Room Companion* 28 Jan. 1854: 58.

"The Mic-Mac Chief." *Morning News Double XXtra* [Saint John] Apr. 1861: n. pag.

"Moses Et Ingens Dux." *Morning News Double XXtra* [Saint John] Apr. 1861: n. pag.

"A Nightmare." *The Dodge Club: Or, Italy in 1859.* New York: Harper, 1869. 30–31. [In manuscript form, this poem is untitled, and I have listed it under the first line, "Eggs Eggs Eggs" in section B2)

"A Oad Detaylin a Resint Visit Till the Club's Domain." [By "Goliah O'Gahaghan, Late Bombardier of the Ty-a-a-l Artillery."] *Morning News Double XXtra* [Saint John] Apr. 1861: n. pag.

"A Oad! To an Angle. Hon Angelus sed Anglin est." [By "Goliath O'Gahachan. Bombadier in the R-r-r-oyal Artillery."] *Morning News Double XXtra* [Saint John] Apr. 1861: n. pag.

"A Oad on the Late Struggle." [By "Goliah O'Gahaghan, Late Bombadier in the R-r-r-oyal Artillery."] *Morning News Double XXtra* [Saint John] Apr. 1861: n. pag.

"A Oad Porthrayin the Tory Party." [By "The Spicial Reporter till the 'Fraymen' " . . . Goliah G'Gahagan, Late Bombardier in the R-r-r-oyal Artillery."] *Morning News Double XXtra* [Saint John] Apr. 1861: n. pag.

"The Oaken Tree." *Gleason's Pictorial Drawing-Room Companion* 20 May 1854: 318.

"A Ode to the Great Confederation." By "Goliah O'Gahaghan." *Humorist* [Saint John; formerly *New Dominion and True Humorist*] 10 Dec. 1864: 3.

"Phi Beta Kappa Poem." *Providence Daily Journal* 18 June 1879: 16.

"Phi Beta Kappa Poem." Ed. and introd. Patricia Monk. *Canadian Poetry* 9 (1981): 89–99.

"A Raggedy Gang." *Songs of the Maritimes: An Anthology of the Poetry of the Maritime Provinces.* Ed. Eliza Ritchie. Toronto: McClelland, 1931. 206.

"Song." ["Hearken to the Loud Resounding."] *Songs of the Psi Upsilon Fraternity.* New York: Burnett, 1857.

"Song" ["Ye whimpering coves assembled here."] Junior Burial Programme, 1853. John Hay Library Archives. Brown University.

"Thoughts of Home: Dedicated to Florence Huntingdon." *Boston Commercial Bulletin* 9 Apr. 1870: 1.

⸺. *New Dominion and True Humorist* 30 Apr. 1870: 186.

"Throned Beside the Yellow Tiber." *Christian Watchman.* [This verse appears in various instalments of "Recollections of Naples" and "Recollections of Rome" by "A." See appendix A, nos. 31–40.

Untitled. "[3,000,000 bushels Coal!"] *Boston Commercial Bulletin* 28 May 1870: 1.

──────. *New Dominion and True Humorist* 25 June 1870: 254.

4. Miscellaneous Prose

"Acadia College." *Christian Watchman*. [See appendix A, nos. 20, 27, 37, 41, 49, and 50.]

"Among the Dutchmen." *Christian Watchman*. [See appendix A, nos. 11, 12, 13, 14, 17, 19 and 22.]

"Brown University." *Christian Watchman* 10 July 1861: 2.

"Convocation Address." *Dalhousie Gazette* 15 Nov. 1878: 1–6.

"Acadia: The Home of Evangeline." *Gleason's Pictorial Drawing-Room Companion* 4 Nov. 1854: 278.

"Acadie, and the Birth-place of Evangeline." *Putnam's Monthly* Aug. 1853: 140–45.

The Early English Church: A Paper Read Before the Church of England Institute. Halifax: privately published, 1877.

The Elements of Rhetoric. New York: Harper, 1878.

"Hebrew Poetry." *Christian Watchman*. [See appendix A, nos. 48–51.]

"Horton Sketches." [By "Gamma."] *Christian Watchman*. [See appendix A, nos. 6–14.]

"Imagination and Fancy Among the Arabs." *Godey's Lady's Book and Magazine* May 1861: 425–26.

"Inaugural Discourse." *Christian Watchman* 12 June 1861: 1–2. [Delivered at Acadia College.]

"Inaugural Discourse." *Dalhousie Gazette* 15 Nov. 1873: 1–6.

"Recollections of Naples." [By "A."] *Christian Watchman*. [See appendix A, nos. 15–22, and 25–26.]

"Recollections of Rome." [By "A."] *Christian Watchman*. [See appendix A, nos. 29–42, 45–50, and 52.]

"Reminiscences of St. John: Things That Are Not Generally Known." [By "Old Times."] *Morning News* [Saint John] 18 Feb. 1861: 2; 25 Feb. 1861: 2; 18 Mar. 1861: 2; 3 Apr. 1861: 3; 5 Apr. 1861: 2; 8 Apr. 1861: 2; 12 Apr. 1861: 2; 15 Apr. 1861: 2; 19 Apr. 1861: 2; 24 Apr. 1861.

Report of Committee on Education [of the Eastern New Brunswick Baptist Association]. ["J.[ames] De Mill, Chairman."] *Christian Watchman* 17 July 1861: 2.

B. Manuscripts and Papers of James De Mille

1. Novels

"Ashdod Webster and his Starring Tour." Thirty-five chapters. Killam Library Archives, Dalhousie University.

2. Verse

*"And Dost Thou Hope My Favour." Fragment. Killam Library Archives. Dalhousie University.
"Behind the Veil." Six pages, incomplete. Killam Library Archives. Dalhousie University.
*"The Brunensian Hippodrome." John Hay Library Archives. Brown University.
"Class Poem 1854." Original drawings by De Mille. Nineteen pages. John Hay Library Archives. Brown University.
*"The Cook He Flung His Dipper Down." Killam Library Archives. Dalhousie University.
"Eggs Eggs Eggs." Original drawings by De Mille. One page. Killam Library Archives. Dalhousie University.
*"The Fisher." Fragment. Killam Library Archives. Dalhousie University.
*"A Gallant Highwayman." Killam Library Archives. Dalhousie University.
*"In Barbary." Killam Library Archives. Dalhousie University.
*"In That High Hall." Fragment. Killam Library Archives. Dalhousie University.
"Jesus — After the Manner of 'Stabat Mater.' " Newspaper clipping. Killam Library Archives. Dalhousie University.
"The [Sweet] Maiden of Quoddy." Newspaper clipping. Killam Library Archives, Dalhousie University.
*"Oh Its Ferra Wet in Ta Highlands." Killam Library Archives. Dalhousie University.
*"Oh Meet Me by Moonlight." Fragment. Killam Library Archives. Dalhousie University.
*"Oh the Chieftain is Gone." Fragment. Killam Library Archives. Dalhousie University.
*"Oh the Fashions Are Queer." Killam Library Archives. Dalhousie University.
*"Oh What Is That Glides Softly." Killam Library Archives. Dalhousie University.
*"Phi Beta Kappa Society Reunion Poem." Killam Library Archives. Dalhousie University.

SELECTED BIBLIOGRAPHY

"Sympathy." Killam Library Archives. Dalhousie University.
*"There Was a Captive in a Prison." Fragment. Killam Library Archives. Dalhousie University.
*"Thy Friend He is False." Fragment. Killam Library Archives. Dalhousie University.

3. Letters and Other Documents

To the editor of *Blackwood's Magazine*. 23 July 1879. MS 4,389 f. 156. National Library of Scotland, Edinburgh.
To Miss [Mary L.] Booth. 26 Oct. 1870. Gratz Collection :3.31. Historical Society of Pennsylvania Library.
To the secretary of the Dalhousie Board of Governors. 2 July 1865. Killam Library Archives. Dalhousie University.
To Alfred Henry De Mill. 24 Feb. 1856; 12 Oct. 1857; 4 Dec. 1857; [late 1859 or early 1860]; 19 May 1860; [after July 1865]. Killam Library Archives. Dalhousie University.
To John Goforth. 21 Jan. 1875. Dreer Collection 104: 1.44. Historical Society of Pennsylvania Library.
To Messrs. G.H. Harnes and Co. *Literary World*. 31 May 1878. Za letter file. Beinecke Library, Yale University.
To Harper Brothers. 7 May 1868. [This is a copy, and is kept in the Killam Library Archives, Dalhousie University. The original is believed to be in the possession of T.B. Higginson, Burk's Falls, Ontario.]
To Harper Brothers. 2 Apr. 1869. Massachusetts Historical Society Library.
To Harper Brothers. 11 May 1872. Harper Brothers Special Manuscript Collection. Butler Library, Columbia University.
To Harper Brothers. 18 Mar. 1878. Harper Brothers Special Manuscript Collection. Butler Library, Columbia University.
To Ralph ———. N.d. Killam Library Archives. Dalhousie University.
To Michael Laird Simons. 2 July 1873. Za letter file. Beinecke Library, Yale University.

4. Other Documents

Memorandum of a business discussion made for Nathan De Mill and William Short. 10 Nov. 1856. Killam Library Archives. Dalhousie University.
Notebook used for chemistry and rhetoric notes. Illustrated. Killam Library Archives. Dalhousie University.

C. Lost or Disputed Works of James De Mille

1. Novels

"America Dissected." Lost.
The Arkansas Ranger. [1865?] Disputed.
The Dodge Club Abroad. Mistaken for *The Dodge Club.*
"The Isles of Greece." Lost.
John Wheeler's Two Uncles: Or, Launching into Life. New York: Carlton, [1860]. Lost.
The Soldier and the Spy. [1865.] Disputed.
A Week at Forestdale; Being a Summer Idyll, That Is, an Idle Tale, As a Mere Trifle For an Idle Dinner Writ. [By "Idle Sinner."] New York: Westcott, [1868]. Disputed.

2. Short Stories

"Bend or Break; A Story for Boys." *Christian Watchman* 14 Aug. 1861: 4. Disputed.
"The Highwayman." *Christian Watchman* 24 July 1861: 4. Disputed.

3. Verse

"A Forlorn Stave." [By "W."] *Morning News* [Saint John] 15 Nov. 1854: 2. Disputed.
"New Brunswick Land Jobbing." [By "Shakespeare."] *Morning News* [Saint John] 25 Mar. 1861: 2. Disputed.
"A Solemn Dirge." [By "W."] *Morning News* [Saint John] 8 Nov. 1854: 2. Disputed.

SELECTED BIBLIOGRAPHY

D. Bibliographical Sources for De Mille's Published Works

Allibone, S. Austin. *A Critical Dictionary of English Literature and British and American Authors.* Supplement by John Foster Kirk. Philadelphia: Lippincott, 1891.
American Catalogue of Books. 1861–1910.
Edwards, Dr. Mary Jane, et al. "James De Mille (1833–1880) — Preliminary Checklist." Ottawa: CEECT–Carleton UP, 1982.
Watters, Reginald Eyre. *A Checklist of Canadian Literature and Background Materials, 1628–1960.* 2nd rev. ed. Toronto: U of Toronto Press, 1972.

E. Biographical Material on James De Mille

Crawley, Edmund A., et al., eds. *Memorials of Acadia College and Horton Academy for the Half-Century, 1828–1878.* Montreal: Dawson, 1881.
Crockett, A.J. "A Pictonian Looks at His Attic." *Dalhousie Review* 5 (1925–26): 65–75.
———. "As Writer." "Concerning James De Mille." *More Studies in Nova Scotian History.* Ed. George Patterson. Halifax: Imperial, 1941. 120–43.
"Dallusiensia." *Dalhousie Gazette* 5 Jan. 1871: 30.
Eaton, Arthur W.H. *The History of King's County.* Salem, MA: The Salem Press, 1910. 488, 787
General Catalogue and Historical Records of Acadia College 1838–1888. Halifax: S. Selden, 1888.
Harvey, D.C. *An Introduction to the History of Dalhousie University.* Halifax: n.p., 1938.
"James De Mille." *Canada School Journal* 4 June 1880 125.
Koopman, Harry Lyman. "Literary Men of Brown, III: James De Mille." *Brown Alumni Monthly* July 1907: 27–30.
Oxley, J. MacDonald. "Some Reminiscences of the Men of '76." *Dalhousie Gazette* 12 Jan. 1903: 159–63.
"A Professorial Who's Who." *Dalhousie Gazette* 12 Jan. 1903: 176–80.
Scott, Ephraim. "The First Ten Years of Dalhousie, 1863–1873." *Dalhousie Gazette* 12 Jan. 1903: 152–59.
Scott, H.P. "James De Mille." *Dalhousie Gazette* 10 Apr. 1885: 135–36.

F. Criticism on James De Mille

Bailey, James Osler. *Pilgrims through Space and Time: Trends and Patterns In Scientific and Utopian Fiction.* New York: Argus, 1947.

Rev. of *Behind the Veil*, by James De Mille. *Dial* 1 Feb. 1906: 44.

Bevan, A.R. "James De Mille and Archibald MacMechan." *Dalhousie Review* 36 (1955–56): 201–15.

Burpee, Lawrence J. "Canadian Novels and Novelists." *Sewanee Review* 11 (1903): 385–411.

———. "Novels of James De Mille." *Nation* 16 Aug. 1906: 138.

———. "James De Mille." *Nation* 11 Oct. 1906: 303.

———. "James De Mille." *Canadian Bookman* 8 (1926): 230–36.

Cavell, Richard. "Bakhtin Reads De Mille: Canadian Literature, Postmodernism, and the Theory of Dialogism." *Future Indicative: Literary Theory and Canadian Literature.* Reappraisals: Canadian Writers 13. Ed. John Moss. Ottawa: U of Ottawa P, 1987. 205–10

Cogswell, Fred. "Literary Activity in the Maritime Provinces, 1815–1880." *Literary History of Canada.* Ed. Carl F. Klinck. 1965; Toronto: U of Toronto P, 1970. 102–24.

Rev. of *Cord and Creese*, by James De Mille. *Acadian Recorder* 25 Oct. 1867: 2.

"D.H." "A Letter of James De Mille." *Canadian Notes and Queries* 12 (1973): 9.

Davies, Gwendolyn. "George Stewart's Comments on James De Mille." *Canadian Notes and Queries* 26 (1980): 10.

———. "*The Dodge Club* and the Tradition of Nineteenth-Century American Travel Literature." *The Dodge Club: Or, Italy in MDCCCLIX.* By James De Mille. Maritime Literature Reprint Series 3. Sackville, NB: Ralph Pickard Bell Library, 1981.

De Mille, Alban Bertram. *Literature in the Century.* Nineteenth Century Series 2. Ed. Justin McCarthy. Philadelphia: Lippincott, 1900.

Douglas, R.W. "James De Mille." *Canadian Bookman* Jan. 1922: 39–44.

Ellsworth, R.C. "Utopian Literature of Canada." *Canadian Notes and Queries* 12 (1973): 4.

Gerson, Carole. "Three Writers of Victorian Canada." *Canadian Writers and Their Works.* Ed. Robert Lecker, Jack David, Ellen Quigley. Fiction Series vol. 1. Downsview, ON: ECW, 1983. 195–256. 17 vols. to date. 1983- .

Higginson, T.B. "A Letter of James De Mille." *Canadian Notes and Queries* 10 (1972): 4.

Hughes, Kenneth J. "A Strange Manuscript: Sources, Satire, a Positive Utopia."

SELECTED BIBLIOGRAPHY

The Canadian Novel. Beginnings. A Critical Anthology. Ed. John Moss. Toronto: New Canadian, 1980. 11–115.

Kilian, Crawford. "The Cheerful Inferno of James De Mille." *Journal of Canadian Fiction* 1 (1972): 61–67.

Kime, Wayne R. "The American Antecedents of James De Mille's *A Strange Manuscript Found in a Copper Cylinder.*" *Dalhousie Review* 55 (1975): 280–306

La Bossière, Camille R. "The Mysterious End of James De Mille's Unfinished Strange Manuscript." *Essays on Canadian Writing* 27 (1983–84): 41–54.

Liechti, James. Rev. of *Behind the Veil*, by James De Mille. *Dalhousie Gazette* 25 Nov. 1893: 79–83.

McFarlane, William G. *New Brunswick Bibliography.* Saint John: Sun, 1895.

MacLeod, Douglas E. "A Critical Biography of James De Mille." Diss. Dalhousie U, 1968.

MacMechan, Archibald. "An Important Canadian Poem." *Week* 9 Dec. 1892: 36–37.

———. "Concerning James De Mille." *Canadian Bookman* 4 Apr. 1922: 125–26.

———. "James De Mille, the Man and the Writer." *Canadian Magazine* 27 Sept. 1906: 404–16.

———. Introduction. "A Voyage of Long Ago." *Canadian Geographical Journal* 11 Sept. 1935: 148–60.

———. *Headwaters of Canadian Literature.* Toronto: McClelland, 1924. 46–50.

Mahon, A. Wylie. "James De Mille." *Westminster: A Paper for the Home* Nov. 1905: 320–23.

Monk, Patricia. "James De Mille as Mystic: A Reconsideration of *Behind the Veil.*" *Canadian Poetry* 3 (1978): 38–55.

Murray, W.C. Rev. of "Behind the Veil," by James De Mille. *Dalhousie Gazette* 25 Nov. 1893: 78.

"The Novel of Adventure." Rev. of *A Strange Manuscript Found in a Copper Cylinder*, by James De Mille. *New York Times* 21 May 1888: 3.

Parks, Malcolm G. Introduction. *A Strange Manuscript Found in a Copper Cylinder.* By James De Mille. Ottawa: CEECT–Carleton UP, 1986. xvii–lix.

———. "Strange to Strangers Only." *Canadian Literature* 70 (1976): 61–78.

Pierce, Lorne. *An Outline of Canadian Literature (French and English).* Toronto: Ryerson, 1927. 164–67.

Rhodenizer, Vernon B. *A Handbook of Canadian Literature* Ottawa: Graphic, 1930. 137–39.

Roberts, C.G.D. "De Mille's *Behind the Veil*." *Week* 23 Feb. 1894: 301.

Russell, B. "De Mille in Halifax." *Nation* 30 Aug. 1906: 181.

Scott, H.P. "James De Mille." *Dalhousie Gazette* 14 Apr. 1885: 135–36.

Scott, S.D. "James De Mille, Prolific Writer." *Vancouver Province*, 21 Oct. 1921:

Stewart, George. "Canadian Literature." *Stewart's Literary Quarterly* Jan. 1870: 403–07.

Rev. of *A Strange Manuscript Found in a Copper Cylinder*, by James De Mille. *Times* [Philadelphia] 31 May 1888: 5.

Rev. of *A Strange Manuscript Found in a Copper Cylinder*, by James De Mille. *Brooklyn Daily Eagle* 3 June 1888: 7

Rev. of *A Strange Manuscript Found in a Copper Cylinder*, by James De Mille. *Morning Journal* [Boston] 5 June 1888: 4.

Rev. of *A Strange Manuscript Found in a Copper Cylinder*, by James De Mille. *Week* 26 July 1888: 561.

Rev. of *A Strange Manuscript Found in a Copper Cylinder*, by James De Mille. *Critic* 15 Sept. 1888: 125.

Rev. of *A Strange Manuscript Found in a Copper Cylinder*, by James De Mille. *Leeds Mercury* 1 Oct. 1888: 8.

Rev. of *A Strange Manuscript Found in a Copper Cylinder*, by James De Mille. *Perthshire Advertiser and Strathmore Journal* [Perth] 1 Oct. 1888: 4.

Rev. of *A Strange Manuscript Found in a Copper Cylinder*, by James De Mille. *Athenaeum* 15 Dec. 1888: 811.

Watters, R.E. Introduction. *A Strange Manuscript Found in a Copper Cylinder*. By James De Mille. Toronto: McClelland, 1969: vii–xvii.

Woodcock, George. "De Mille and the Utopian Vision." *Journal of Canadian Fiction* 2.3 (1973): 174–79.

———. "Possessing the Land: Notes on Canadian Fiction." *The Canadian Imagination*. Ed. David Staines. Cambridge: Harvard UP, 1977: 69–96.

———. "An Absence of Utopias." *Canadian Literature* 42 (1969): 3–5.

SELECTED BIBLIOGRAPHY

G. General References: Published Material

Acadia University. *General Catalogue and Historical Records of Acadia College 1838–88*. Halifax: Selden, 1888.

Allison, David. *History of Nova Scotia*. 3 vols. Halifax: Bowen, 1916.

Archer, Andrew. *A History of Canada for the Use of Schools*. London: Nelson; Saint John: McMillan, 1875.

———. *Canada: A Short History of the Dominion of Canada*. New Brunswick School Series. Saint John: McMillan, 1884.

Benham, W. Gurney. *Benham's New Book of Quotations, Proverbs, and Household Words*. London: Ward Lock, 1924.

Bill, I.E. *Fifty Years with the Baptist Ministers and Churches of the Maritime Provinces*. Saint John: Barnes, 1880.

Blakeley, Phyllis. *Glimpses of Halifax, 1867–1900*. Halifax: Public Archives of Nova Scotia, 1949.

Boggs, W.E. *The Genealogical Records of the Boggs Family: The Descendants of Ezekiel Boggs*. Halifax: Royal, 1916.

Boswell, James. *The Life of Dr Samuel Johnson*. Everyman's Library 2. 2 vols. London: Dent, 1949.

Bowes, John A. *Historical Sketch of the St John Grammar School, 1805–1884*. Saint John: George Day, 1885.

Bronson, Walter C. *The History of Brown University, 1764–1914*. Providence: Brown University, 1914.

Brown, Robert P., et al. *Memories of Brown*. Providence: Brown Alumni, 1909.

Burns, Robert. "To A Mouse." *Poems and Songs of Robert Burns*. Ed. and introd. James Kinsley. Everyman's Library 94. London: Dent, 1958. 61–62.

Cameron, J.H. "Valedictory." *Dalhousie Gazette* 1 May 1878: 134–37

Chipman, Eliza Ann. *Memoir of Mrs Eliza Ann Chipman*. Halifax: Ritchie, 1885.

Chute, Arthur Crawley, and William Bambrick Boggs. *The Religious Life of Acadia*. Wolfville, NS: n.p., 1933.

Christian Watchman [Saint John].

Christian Messenger [Halifax].

Christian Visitor, [Saint John].

Collections of the New Brunswick Historical Society. 2 vols. Saint John: Sun, 1899.

Coldwell, Albert. "The Vaughan Prize Essay." *Memorials of Acadia College and Horton Academy for the Half-Century, 1828–1878*. Ed. Edmund A. Crawley, et al. Montreal: Dawson, 1881. 55–120.

Crawley, Edmund A., et al., eds. *Memorials of Acadia College and Horton Academy*. Wolfville: n.p., 1881.

———. "The Rise and Progress of Higher Education in the Maritime Provinces." *Memorials of Acadia College and Horton Academy for the Half-Century, 1828–1878*. Ed. Edmund A. Crawley, et al. Montreal: Dawson, 1881. 5–52.

Daniells, Roy. "Confederation to the First World War." *Literary History of Canada: Canadian Literature in English*. Ed. Carl F. Klinck. 1965. Toronto: U of Toronto P, 1970. 191–207.

Eaton, Arthur W.H. *The History of King's County*. Salem, MA: Salem Press, 1910.

Eaton, Brenton H. *Reply of the Granville Street Baptist Church to the Letter Addressed to Them by the Hon. J.W. Johnston, Judge in Equity*. Halifax: privately published, 1868.

Flew, Antony. "Immortality." *The Encyclopedia of Philosophy*. Ed. Paul Edwards. Vol. 4. New York: Macmillan–Free Press; London: Collier-Macmillan, 1967. 139–50. 8 vols. 1967.

Fortescue, John W. *1763-1793*. London: Macmillan, 1911. Vol. 3 of *A History of the British Army*. 14 vols. 1906–17.

Fraser, Duncan C. "Reminiscences of 1872." *Dalhousie Gazette* 25 Jan. 1908: 112–18.

"Garneau, François-Xavier." *The Oxford Companion to Canadian Literature and History*. 1967 ed.

Gesner, Abraham. *New Brunswick with Notes for Emigrants*. London: Simmons, 1847.

Gray, Thomas. "Elegy Written in a Country Churchyard." *Gray and Collins: Poetical Works*. Ed. Austin Lane Poole. Oxford Standard Authors. Oxford: Clarendon, 1919. 91–97.

Griffin-Allwood, Philip G.A. " 'Joseph Howe is Their Devil': Controversies among Regular Baptists in Halifax, 1827–1868." Moody, *Repent and Believe*. 71–68.

Halifax and Dartmouth City Directory 1869– .

Harris, Reginald. *The Church of St Paul's in Halifax*. Toronto: Ryerson, 1949.

Harvey, D.C. *An Introduction to the History of Dalhousie University*. Halifax: n.p., 1938.

Higgins, T.A. *The Life of John Lockett Cramp, D.D.* Montreal: Drysdale 1887.

Hopkins, H.W. *City Atlas of Halifax, Nova Scotia*. Halifax: Provincial Survey, 1878.

Jack, David Russell. *Centennial Prize Essay on the History of the City and*

SELECTED BIBLIOGRAPHY

County of Saint John. Saint John: McMillan, 1883.
Johnston, John W. *Letter to the Granville Street Church*. Halifax: privately published, 1867.
―――. *Memorial to the Central Baptist Association of Nova Scotia*. Halifax: privately published, 1868.
King, Edwin D. and Gordon J. Quigley. *History [of the] First Baptist Church, Halifax N.S., Canada: 1827–1977*. Halifax: n.p., 1977.
Kirkconnell, Watson. *The Acadia Record*. Rev. ed. Wolfville, NS: Acadia University, 1953.
Lee, G. Herbert. *The First Fifty Years of the Church of England in the Province of New Brunswick*. Saint John: Sun, 1880.
Lighthall, W.D. *Songs of the Great Dominion*. London: Walter Scott, 1889.
Logan, J.W. "Recollections of Professor Macdonald." *Dalhousie Gazette* Apr. 1901: 55–57.
Longley, Ronald Stewart. *Acadia University, 1838–1938*. Wolfville, NS: n.p., 1939.
Millar, E.D. "The Rev. James Ross, D.D." *Dalhousie Gazette* 12 Jan. 1903: 144–52.
Minutes of the 17th Session of the Central Baptist Association of Nova Scotia. Halifax: Christian Messenger Office, 1867.
Minutes of the 18th Session of the Central Baptist Association of Nova Scotia. Halifax: Christian Messenger Office, 1868.
Moody, Barry M., ed. *Repent and Believe: The Baptist Experience in Maritime Canada*. Baptist Heritage in Atlantic Canada Series 2. Hantsport, NS: Lancelot, 1980.
Morning Herald [Halifax].
Morning News [Saint John].
Neatby, Hilda. *Queen's University: To Strive, to Seek, to Find, and Not to Yield, 1841–1917*. Montreal: McGill–Queen's UP, 1978. Vol. 1 of Queen's University. Ed. Frederick W. Gibson and Roger Graham. 2 vols. 1978–83.
Nova Scotian Institute of Natural Science. *The Proceedings and Transactions of the Nova Scotian Institute of Natural Science of Halifax, Nova Scotia*.
Novascotian [Halifax].
Obituary. Nathan Smith De Mill. *Christian Visitor* 5 Jan. 1865: 2.
Obituary. George Lawson. *Dalhousie Gazette* 22 Dec. 1895 75–79.
O'Callaghan, E.B. *The Documentary History of the State of New York; Arranged under the Direction of the Hon. Christopher Morgan, Secretary of State*. 4 vols. Albany, NY: Weed, 1849–51.

Otto, Rudolf. *The Idea of the Holy: An Inquiry into the Non-Rational Factor in the Idea of the Divine and its Relation to the Rational.* Trans. John W. Harvey. 6th ed. London: Oxford UP, 1931.

Patterson, George. "As Teacher." "Concerning James De Mille." *More Studies in Nova Scotian History.* Ed. Patterson. Halifax: Imperial, 1941. 143–48.

──────. *The History of Dalhousie College and University.* Halifax: Morning Herald, 1887.

Plato. "Apology." *Plato: Euthyphro, Apology, Crito, Phaedo, Phaedrus.* Ed. and trans. Harold N. Fowler. 1914. Loeb Classical Library. London: Heinemann; Cambridge, MA: Harvard UP, 1966. 1–16.

Prebble, Paul H., ed. *One Hundred Years: Brief Histories of the Brussels Street United Baptist Church, Leinster Street United Baptist Church and the Central United Baptist Church.* Saint John: Lingley, 1950.

Preston, R.A. "Presidential Address." *Canadian Historical Association Report.* Ottawa: Canadian Historical Association, 1962.

Roberts, Richard L. Foreword. *The Martyr of the Catacombs.* By James De Mille. Chicago: Moody: 1970. 5–6.

Ritchie, Eliza, ed. *Songs of the Maritimes: An Anthology of the Poetry of the Maritime Provinces.* Toronto: McClelland, 1931.

Roe, F.B., and N. Geo. Colby. *Historical Atlas of York County, N.B., and St. John, N.B. (City and County).* 1875. Belleville, ON: Mika, 1973.

Sabine, Lorenzo. *The American Loyalists: Or, Biographical Sketches of Adherents to the British Crown in the War of the Revolution.* Boston: Little, 1847.

Saint John and Its Business. Saint John: Chubb, 1875.

Saint John City Directory. Saint John: McAlpine, 1863–1864.

"Sensation, Novels of." *The Oxford Companion to English Literature,* 5th ed. 1985.

Songs of the Psi Upsilon Fraternity. New York: Burnett, 1857.

Saunders, Edward Manning. *History of the Baptists of the Maritime Provinces.* Halifax: John Burgoyne, 1902.

Sleeman, Captain William H. *The Thugs or Phansigars of India: Comprising a History of the Rise and Progress of that Extraordinary Fraternity of Assassins.* Philadelphia: Carey, 1839.

Smeed, J.W. *Jean Paul's "Dreams."* London: Oxford UP, 1966.

"The Statistician at Large." *Dalhousie Gazette* 12 Jan. 1903: 172–73.

Tennyson, Alfred, Lord. "In Memoriam." *Tennyson: Poems and Plays.* Oxford Standard Authors. London: Oxford UP, 1965. 230–66.

──────. "Oenone." *Tennyson: Poems and Plays.* Oxford Standard Authors.

SELECTED BIBLIOGRAPHY

London: Oxford up, 1965. 38–41.
Thomas, Clayton L., ed. *Taber's Cyclopedic Medical Dictionary*. 15th ed. Philadelphia: Davis, 1981.
Wallace, Frederick William. *Record of Canadian Shipping: A List of Square-Rigged Vessels, Mainly 500 Tons and Over, Built in the Eastern Provinces of British North America from the Year 1786 to 1920.* Toronto: Musson, 1929.
Whidden, D.G. "Horton Academy's Birthday." *Acadian* [Wolfville] 23 June 1938: 1.
William's Cincinnati Directory, City Guide and Business Mirror: Or, Cincinnati in 1856. Cincinnati: Williams, 1856.
Wilson, Isaiah W. *A Geography and History of the County of Digby.* Halifax: Halloway, 1900.
Wright, Esther. *The Loyalists of New Brunswick.* Fredericton: U of New Brunswick P, 1955.

H. General References: Manuscripts, Collections, and Public Records

Acadia University Records. Board of Governors Minutes. Vaughan Memorial Library Archives. Acadia University, Wolfville, NS.
———. *Catalogue of the Officers and Students of Acadia College, Nova Scotia* 1861–62, 1863–64, 1870–71. Vaughan Memorial Library Archives. Acadia University.
———. Horton Academy Documents. Vaughan Memorial Library Archives. Acadia University.
Andover Newton Theological School Records. Newton Theological Institution, Faculty Minutes 1851–52. Franklin Trask Library, Andover Newton Theological School, Newton Center, MA.
Brown University Records. Accounts of Students 1852–53. John Hay Library Archives. Brown University, Providence RI.
———. *Catalogue of the Officers and Students of Brown University, First Term* 1851–52, 1852–53, 1853–54. John Hay Library Archives. Brown University.
———. Commencement Programme 1854. John Hay Library Archives. Brown University.

_____. Faculty Records (Minutes) 1851–54. John Hay Library Archives. Brown University.

_____. Junior Burial Programme 1853. John Hay Library Archives. Brown University.

_____. Library Borrowing Book 1852–54. John Hay Library Archives. Brown University.

_____. Philermenian Society, Library Borrowing Book 1852–54. John Hay Library Archives. Brown University.

_____. Philermenian Society, Minutes 1852–54. John Hay Library Archives. Brown University.

_____. Record of Standing, Classes of 1852–67. John Hay Library Archives. Brown University.

_____. Register 1827–58. John Hay Library Archives. Brown University.

_____. Spring Exhibition Programme 1853. John Hay Library Archives. Brown University.

Burpee, Lawrence Johnston. "Appreciation." "James De Mille." Ts. Burpee Papers, Killam Library Archives. Dalhousie University.

_____. "Biographical." "James De Mille." Ts. Burpee Papers, Killam Library Archives. Dalhousie University.

_____. "Lecture." Ts. Burpee Papers, Killam Library Archives. Dalhousie University.

_____. "Notes." [Unnumbered and largely illegible ms.] Burpee Papers, Killam Library Archives. Dalhousie University.

Camp Hill Cemetery [Halifax]. Deed Record Books 1844–1950.

_____. List of Plots.

_____. Minutes of Cemetery Committee 1835–90.

_____. Register of Burials 1844–78.

_____. Register of Burials 1869–90.

Census 1871 [Halifax]. Census Returns 1825–1901, "Census of 1871 for the Province of Nova Scotia," district 196, City of West Halifax, sub-district A–1, ward W. Record group [page] 73, microfilm C-10550. Records of Statistics Canada. National Archives of Canada, Ottawa.

Census 1881 [Halifax]. Census Returns 1825–1901, "Census of 1871 for the Province of Nova Scotia," district 9, City of Halifax, sub-division 1, ward 1. Record group 31, ser. C.1 [page] 88, microfilm C-10550. Records of Statistics Canada. National Archives of Canada, Ottawa.

Crawley, Edmund A. Letterbook. Vaughan Memorial Library Archives, Acadia University.

SELECTED BIBLIOGRAPHY

Dalhousie Gazette 1869–1925. Killam Library Archives. Dalhousie University.
Dalhousie University Records. Board of Governors Correspondence. Killam Library Archives. Dalhousie University, Halifax, NS.
———. Board of Governors Minutes. Killam Library Archives. Dalhousie University.
———. *Calendar* 1865–85. Killam Library Archives. Dalhousie University.
———. *President's Report for the Year July 1st, 1914-June 30th, 1915*. Killam Library Archives. Dalhousie University.
———. *President's Report for the Year July 1st, 1924-June 30th, 1925*. Killam Library Archives. Dalhousie University.
———. Senate Minutes. Killam Library Archives. Dalhousie University.
———. *Statutes and Bye-Laws for the Regulation and Management of Dalhousie College* 1864. Killam Library Archives. Dalhousie University.
De Boer, Louis P. "The De Mil Family in Europe and America." General Section, New Brunswick Museum Archives. New Brunswick Museum, Saint John, NB.
De Mill, Alfred H. "De Mill Pedigree." De Mille Papers, Killam Library Archives. Dalhousie University.
———. Letter to Dr. John Pryor. 6 Mar. 1880. De Mille Papers, Killam Library Archives. Dalhousie University.
De Mill, Elisha Budd. Journal, 3 vols. De Mille Papers, Killam Library Archives. Dalhousie University.
De Mill, Elizabeth Tongue [Budd]. Letter to Alfred H. De Mill. 15 Sept. [1859?]. De Mille Papers, Killam Library Archives. Dalhousie University.
De Mill, Frederick E. Notebook. De Mille Papers, Killam Library Archives. Dalhousie University.
———. Scrapbook. De Mille Papers, Killam Library Archives. Dalhousie University.
De Mill, Nathan Smith. Letterbooks. 1835–51. New Brunswick Museum Archives. New Brunswick Museum, Saint John, NB.
De Mille, Mrs. James [Annie]. Letter to Harper Brothers. [July 1887?]. Harper Brothers Archives, Butler Library, Columbia University.
De Mille, Arthur C. Letters to Harper Brothers. 9 Apr., 18 May, and 29 July 1880. De Mille Papers, Killam Library Archives. Dalhousie University.
"De Mille, Professor James. List of His Works Made For the Leg[islative] Lib[rary]." Nova Scotia Historical Society Papers MG 20, Vol. 707.7. Public Archives of Nova Scotia, Halifax.
Demill, Richard Mead. "Family Record." De Mille Papers, Killam Library Archives. Dalhousie University.

Fernhill Cemetery [Saint John]. Records. Fernhill Cemetery Office, Saint John, NB.

Griffin-Allwood, Philip G. A. "The Excommunication of John Pryor." Essay 1, CH642, 1976. Acadia Divinity College Archives. Vaughan Library, Acadia University.

Ganong Ms. Collection. New Brunswick Museum Archives. New Brunswick Museum, Saint John, NB.

Gilbert Family Records. New Brunswick Museum Archives. New Brunswick Museum, Saint John, NB.

Halifax County. Death Records 1872.

Halifax County. Deeds Register vol. 205, 1876.

Hamilton, P. St. C. Letter to Miss Freida Creighton. 28 May 1910. Public Archives of Nova Scotia, Halifax.

Harper Brothers Archives. Special Manuscript Collection. Butler Library, Columbia University.

———. Letter ["per J. T. F."] to Mrs. De Mille. 1 Mar. 1889. De Mille Papers, Killam Library Archives. Dalhousie University.

Hazen Papers. New Brunswick Museum Archives. New Brunswick Museum, Saint John, NB.

Knowles, J.S. Letter to Frederick E. De Mill. 24 Apr. 1906. De Mille Papers, Killam Library Archives. Dalhousie University.

———. List. Saint John Regional Library, Saint John, NB. [Filed with following entry.]

———. "Professor James DeMill: His Life and Life-Work." Ts. De Mille File. Saint John Regional Library, Saint John, NB.

Lancaster. Assessment Books for the Parish of Lancaster, Saint John County 1856, 1866. New Brunswick Museum Archives. New Brunswick Museum, Saint John, NB.

MacMechan, Archibald. Research Notes on James De Mille. MacMechan Papers, Killam Library Archives. Dalhousie University.

Mitchell, Martha L. Letter to the author. 3 Feb. 1983, 2 May 1983.

Paul, Robert. Letter to the author. 22 Feb. 1983.

Raymond, Muriel De Mill [Alden]. "John De Mill, Loyalist, His Ancestry and Descendants." General Section, New Brunswick Museum Archives. New Brunswick Museum, Saint John, NB.

Saint John Abstainers Society. Record of Meetings of Saint John Abstainers Society 1833–39. New Brunswick Museum Archives. New Brunswick Museum, Saint John, NB.

SELECTED BIBLIOGRAPHY

Saint John. Marriage Registers. Province of New Brunswick, Department of Health and Welfare, Saint John Board of Health Marriage Registers 1810–87 vol. F 288. New Brunswick Provincial Archives, Fredericton, NB.

Saint John. Register of Voters 1785–1862. New Brunswick Museum Archives. New Brunswick Museum, Saint John, NB.

Saint John County. Probate Minute Books (1861–64) Vol. K. New Brunswick Provincial Archives, Fredericton, NB.

_____. Saint John County. [Property] Records.

St. Luke's Anglican Church [Halifax]. Church Records of St. Luke's Anglican Church, Halifax, Baptisms. Public Archives of Nova Scotia, Halifax.

Tilley Papers. Report of the Committee of the Legislature on Currency and Decimal Accounting 19 Mar. 1860. New Brunswick Museum Archives. New Brunwick Museum, Saint John, NB.

Trinity Anglican Church [Digby]. "Notitia Parochialis of Trinity Parish, Digby, Nova Scotia." By Roger Viets ["Rector of Digby and Missionary from the Venerable Society for the Propagation of the Gospel in Foreign Lands, beginning July 12, 1786"]. MG 4 23. Public Archives of Nova Scotia, Halifax.

_____. Marriage Records. Marriages Solemnized in the Parish of Trinity in the County of Annapolis in the Year 1828. Church Records on Microfilm Collection. Public Archives of Nova Scotia, Halifax.

Index

Acadia College 42–43, 54, 83
   and Horton Academy, confusion of 92
   First College Hall (picture) 94
   student life 42
Acadian Recorder, The 14, 218
Allibone's Critical Dictionary 188
Allison, *History of Nova Scotia* 111, 116, 140 n1
American Catalogue of Books 177, 194 n2
Atlantic, The 213

Bailey, *Psi Upsilon Legends and Lyrics* 173 n5
Bayshore (Saint John), De Mill house on (picture) 34, 35
Bevan, Allan, "James De Mille" 244
Beaver, The Gilded (ship) 13
Bill, The Rev. I.E. 80, 81–82, 133, 148 n41
   controversy over the *Christian Watchman* 108 n23
   on temperance 99, 108 n25
Blackwood's Magazine 77, 201
Blakeley, *Glimpses of Halifax* 110–11
Bronson, *History of Brown University* 57, 58–59, 65, 66–67, 72, 73, 78
Brown University
   academic programme 58
   buildings 63
   Commencement 1854 77–78
   De Mille's accounts at 65, 68, 75, 76

   domestic arrangements 65–66
   history 57
   library 63, 67
   Philermenian Society 66–67 (picture) 64
   register 32, 57
   student life 62–63, 65
Budd, Elisha 29, 30
Burns, "To a Mouse" 111–12
Burpee, Lawrence J. 24, 234
   lecture 24, 26, 30, 35
   notes 27, 33, 37
   "Biographical" 29, 30, 31 n7, 33, 43, 45
   "Appreciations" 29, 31 n7, 198, 220
Butler, *Erewhon* 233, 236
Byron, G.G., Lord 48, 158, 171
   Childe Harold 160

Cameron, "Valedictory" 137
Campbell, *Philosophy of Rhetoric* 73, 124, 156
Cannon Miller 24, 25, 27
   Mr. Miller of, and his son 46
Cavell, "Bakhtin Reads De Mille" 235
Charlotte Street (Saint John), De Mill house on 30, 35
Census 1871 118, 133
cholera 80, 99, 108 n25
Christian Messenger 143 n32
Christian Visitor 23, 26, 96, 99, 133
Christian Watchman 96–99, 133, 153, 159, 176, 178, 229

INDEX

Cogswell, "Literary Activity in the Maritime Provinces" 164, 240
Coleridge, *Rime of the Ancient Mariner, The* 166
Coldwell, "Vaughn Prize Essay" 14
Collins, Wilkie 14, 215, 219
Colonial Book Store 89–91, 92–96
  "second branch" 92
  sale of 96
Cranford (Gaskell) 29, 198
Crawley, Rev. Dr. E.A. 83, 84, 85
  Memorials 37
  portrait in B.O.W.C. series 182
  "The Rise and Progress of Higher Education" 39
Crockett, "As Writer" 183, 188, 206, 213, 218
Crowell, The Rev. Edwin 120, 122, 123, 124, 145 n21
currency, conversion rate of 107 n21

Dalhousie College
  "Act Respecting Dalhousie College, An" 113
  college building (picture) 112
  cheating scandal 129
  draconian curriculum 116
  early years 113
  foundation of 111
  power to grant degrees 147 n31
  reorganization 113–14
  Statutes and Bye-Laws 115
  student life 116–17
Dalhousie Gazette 14, 117, 123, 137
Davies, Introduction to *The Dodge Club* 204
De Boer, "The De Mil Family in Europe and America" 19
Demill, Richard Mead 19, 21
  "Family Record" 20, 30 n2
De Mill (family before the American Revolution) 19–22
De Mill (family in Saint John) 21, 22;

(pictures) 88, 104, 196, 212
De Mill, Alfred 13, 33, 35, 87, 89, 103, 118, 121, 214, 222, 229, 239
  "De Mill Pedigree" 22
  letter to Richard Mead Demill 21
De Mill, Alice Susanna 24, 30 n5, 33, 89, (picture) 212, 220
De Mill, Charles Frederick 32
De Mill, Elisha 32, 74, 80, (portrait) 98, 183
  death 103
  editor of the *Christian Watchman* 97
  education 37, 54
  friendship with James 83
  illness 97
  journal 45, 55 n8
  marriage (to Emma Pryor) 74, (to Elizabeth Seeley) 103
  ordination 73
  pastorates (Amherst) 73, (Marsh Bridge Church) 97
  (portrait) 98
De Mill, Elizabeth (James's sister) 24, 89
De Mill, Elizabeth Seely (Elisha's second wife) 103
De Mill, Elizabeth Tongue Budd (Nathan's wife, James's mother) 29–30
  letter to Alfred 89, 106 n10
  (portrait) 28
De Mill, Emma Pryor (Johnston) 82
De Mill, Emily 24, 89
De Mill, Frederick Edward 33, 36
  Notebook 33, 149 n48
  (picture) 88
  Scrapbook 159, 160
De Mill, John ("the Loyalist") 21, 22–23, 30 n3
De Mill, Nathan 23–27, 29, 33–35, 89–90, 91
  aversion to novels 29
  business in difficulties 86–87, 89
  final illness of 103

285

nicknamed "Cold Water De Mill" 27
obituary notice by James 23, 30 n4
purchase of ships 23, 86, 106 n8
temper 35
De Mill, William John 32, 43
De Mille, Alban Bertram 118, 144 n15
Literature in the Century 250
(picture, with Annie and Frank) 254
De Mille, Anne Elizabeth Pryor
(Annie) 82, 91–92, 107 n13, 153, 163
and manuscript of "Class Poem
1854" 173 n4
Behind the Veil 163
(picture, with Frank and Alban) 254
De Mille, Arthur C. 149 n46, (picture)
212, 214, 215
De Mille, Ethel Maud 118, 133, 144 n14
De Mille, Frank Wilfred 118, 144 n16
(picture, with Annie and Alban) 254
De Mille, James (life)
academic life at Brown 58, 59–62,
71–72
appearance 78 n2, 120
eyesight 43, 85, (wearing of glasses)
100, 146 n22
appointment to Acadia 95
appointment to Dalhousie 114–15,
118–19
birthdate 32
bookstore *see* Colonial Book Store
death 139, 145 n19
debts 93, 107 n20, 222
early schooling (Saint John) 35–36
father and 23, 35, 83, 84, 89, 103, 105
"Female Seminary" and 85
illness 43, 71
involvement in the Pryor scandal
129, 131, 132–33
known as "Jim" 78 n2
library borrowings at Brown 68,
71–72, 77
lost journal of 45
mother and 32–33

personality 100–01, 252–53, 255
as teacher 101–02, 122, 124, 137,
139
conversational ability 121
depression 134
friendship with Elisha 83, 103
memory 33, 75
propensity for puns 76, 158
remembered by colleagues and
students at Dalhousie 119–24
temper 33
purchase of house 118, 135
recreation 118, 120–21
religious side 41, 133, 147 n37, 148
n41, 149 n42
resignation from Acadia 105
salary at Dalhousie 115
salary at Acadia 95, 105
scholarship 122, 135
social life at Brown 71–72, 76, 77, 78
student at Acadia College 42
teaches Canadian History 126, 146
n28
De Mille, James (fiction, general)
compared to Collins and other
writers 219
first-person narrators 201
list of works by family 178
novels of sensation 215–16, 217–18
payment for writing 222
problematic titles 175, 176, 177–78,
214–15
satirical romances 206–07, 208, 211
short stories 175–77
speed of composition 220–21
"thorough hack, a" 14, 221
"trash" and "pot-boilers" 219–20,
226 n11
"various contributions to light
literature" 14
De Mille, James (fiction, individual
titles and series)
"America Dissected" 199, 201, 215

INDEX

American Baron, The 135, 201, 206, 207, 208, 209, 224 n5, (synopsis) 252
Among the Brigands 135, 177
Andy O'Hara 177, 178, 182, 194 n2
"Andy O'Hara" 194, n2
Arkansas Ranger, The 176
"Artist of Florence, The" 175
"Ashdod Webster and His Starring Tour" 135, 158, 199, 201, 215
"Australian Footman, The" 175
B.O.W.C. series, the 178
   acronym explained 178
   Canadianism of 252
   critical reception 187
   moral and practical didacticism in 179–82
   women characters 181
"B.O.W.C., The" 40, 135, 178–79, 181, 183
Babes in the Wood, The 135, 201, 206, 208
"Balloon Ascent, The" 175
"Bend or Break; A Story for Boys" 176
Boys of Grand Pré School, The 135, 179, 182
"Captive's Flight, The" 175
"Castle and Crucible, The" 175
Castle in Spain, A 135, 198, 201, 206, 208, 209–11, 250, 252
   date of publication 223 n1
"Circassian's Revenge, The" 175
Comedy of Terrors, A 135, 201, 206, 208
"Contrabandist, The" 175
Cord and Creese 14, 135, 164, 203, 214, 240, 252, 253
   critical reception 218
   link with *Behind the Veil* 164
   relative popularity of 226 n9
   synopsis 225 n7
   Thuggee cult in 217, 226 n8

"Corsair of Scio, The" 175
Cryptogram, The 214, 217, 240, 252
Dodge Club, The 52, 135, 162, 201, 203–06, 211, 218, 250, 252, 253–54
   and *The Dodge Club Abroad* 223 n3
   composition of 203
   critical reception of 206
"Earl's Daughter, The" 135
"Faith, Hope, and Love" 81
Fire in the Woods 135, 177, 179–81
Helena's Household 188, 189–94, 222, 229, 253
   composition of 189–90
   critical reaction to 191
   synopsis 195 n10
"Highwayman, The" 176
"Isles of Greece, The" 135, 214–15
John Wheeler's Two Uncles 134, 177–78
Lady of the Ice, The 135, 201–03, 213, 252
Lily and the Cross, The 135, 177, 185–87, (synopsis) 194 n6
Living Link, The 135, 214, 217, 253
"Loss of the Hector, The" 175, 176–77
Lost in the Fog 135, 177, 179, 180, 181, 187
Martyr of the Catacombs, The 50, 188–89
"Minnehaha Mines, The" 85, 135, 201, 203, 251
"Missionary's Son, The" 85, 177, 178, 182
Old Garth 214, 217, 240
Open Question, An 135, 214, 217, 243
Picked Up Adrift 135, 177, 179, 183
"Priestess of the Sun, The" 175
"Rose of Acadie, The" 175
"Rudolph the Burgess" 175
Seven Hills, The 135, 177, 184
Soldier and the Spy, The 134, 176

287

"Spanish Knight, The" 175
Strange Manuscript Found in a Copper Cylinder, A 14, 135, 157, 172, 228–49
  anonymous publication of 228, 231
  CEECT edition of *(see under Parks)*
  composition of 228–29
  critical views of 234–39
  discovery of manuscript 228
  illustration from first edition 230
  influences on 235, 237
  New Canadian Library Edition *(see under Watters)*
  publication history of 228
  reviews of 232–33
  synopsis 247 n10
"Traitor's Doom, The" 175
Treasure of the Seas, The 135, 177, 179
"Under a Spell" 214, 215
"Were Wolf, The" 175
Winged Lion, The 135, 177, 184, 185
Young Dodge Club series, the 183
  moral instruction in 184
  alcohol, reference to in 184
De Mille (prose other than fiction)
  "Acadia College" 99
  "Acadie, and the Birth-place of Evangeline" 73
  "Arabian Fiction" 72
  contributions to the *Christian Visitor* 81, 105 n1, 105 n2, 261
  contributions to the *Christian Watchman* 97–99, 257–60
  Early English Church, The 133, 135
  Elements of Rhetoric, The 135, 146 n26, 167
  "Encourage Your Minister" 81
  "Hebrew Poetry" 99
  "Horton Sketches" 40, 41
  "Imagination and Fancy Among the Arabs" 72

"Powers of Conscience Illustrated, The" 105 n.1
"Recollections of Rome" 97, 99
De Mille, James (verse, individual titles)
  "And Dost Thou Hope My Favour" 163
  Behind the Veil 158, 163–69, 251
    posthumous publication 153
    biblical allusion of title 174 n13
    date of composition 164
    link with *Cord and Creese* 164
    reception 163–64
    synopsis 164–65
  "Bray from A Dunkie, A" 159
  "Brunensian Hippodrome, The" 73, 158–59, 173 n5
  "Class Poem 1854" 60–61, 63, 69, 75, 76, 78, 155–58
    illustration from 154
    manuscript 158, 173 n4
  "Cook, The" 163
  "Death of Havelock, The" 160
  "Dies Irae" 160
  "Eggs Eggs Eggs" (see also "A Nightmare") 162
    illustrated manuscript of 200
  "Fenian Song, A" 159
  "Fisher, The" 163
  "Forlorn Stave, A" 173 n6
  "Gallant Highwayman, A" 163, 174 n10
  "Havelock's March" 160
  "Hearken to the Loud Resounding" 159
  "In Barbary" 163
  "Indian Names of Acadia, The" 163
  "In New Brunswick You'll Find It" 162
  "In That High Hall" 163
  "Jesus – After the Manner of Stabat Mater" 160
  "Lines. To Florence Huntingdon" 162

"Lord Hilbert" 159
"Maiden of Passamaquoddy, The" 162
"Maranon, The" 77, 159
"Mic-Mac Chief, The" 159
"Moses Et Ingens Dux" 159
"Nightmare, A" *see* "Eggs Eggs Eggs"
"New Brunswick Land Jobbing" 173 n6
"Oad Detaylin A Resint Visit Till the Club's Domain" 159
"Oad on the Late Struggle, A" 159
"Oad. Porthrayin the Tory Party" 159, 160
"Oad! To an Angle, A" 159
"Oaken Tree, The" 159
"Ode to the Great Confederation, A" 173 n6
"Oh Its Ferra Wet in Ta Highlands" 163
"Oh Meet Me by Moonlight" 163
"Oh the Chieftainis Gone" 163
"Oh the Fashions Are Queer" 163
"Oh What Is That Glides Softly" 163
"Phi Beta Kappa Poem" 153, 157, 158, 169–172
    De Mille's persona in 171
    link with *Strange Manuscript* 172
"Raggedy Gang, A" 163
"Recollections of Rome" 160
"Solemn Dirge, A" 173 n6
"Song [Ye whimpering coves]" 73, 159
"Sympathy" 162
"There Was a Captive in a Prison" 163
"Thoughts of Home" 174 n9
"Throned beside the Yellow Tiber" 161
"Thy Friend He Is False" 163
"3,000,000 bushels coal!" 174 n9

James De Mille (letters)
    to Alfred De Mill 33, 35, 86, 87, 89, 121
    to *Blackwood's Magazine* 201, 223 n2
    to Goforth 121
    to Harper Brothers 199
    to J.W. Johnston 131, 147 n35
    to Messrs Harnes 178, 194 n4, 223 n1
    to Miss Booth 221, 227 n12
    to Ralph — 92
De Mille, James, and Annie Pryor De Mille 91, 92, 93
De Mille, James, and Elisha, European tour 45–53
    language study in 45, 49–50, 53
De Mille, Louise Pryor 105, 109 n9, 115, 133, 181
De Mille, Noel James (James's grandson) 19
De Mille, William Budd (Willie) 93, 105, 133, 179, 229
De Quincey, "Dream upon the Universe" 167
Dickens, Charles 29, 33
    Pickwick Papers 72, 218
Double XXtra 159
Douglas, "James De Mille" 187, 189, 191, 206, 234

Eaton, Arthur W. H., *History of King's County* 182, 187
Eaton, Brenton H. 107 n21
    Reply of the Granville Street Baptist Church 129, 131, 132, 147 nn32–33
Edwards, "Preliminary Checklist" 185, 189, 204, 214
Elizabeth Bentley, The 25, 43, (picture) 44, 53
Evangeline (Longfellow) 33

Fillmore, Hazen S. 89, 90, 93
Flag of Our Union 175

Flew, "Immortality" 166
Fraser, Duncan 116, 144 n9

Gaskell, Elizabeth 29, 220
Gilbert, W.S. 158
Gleason's Pictorial Drawing-Room Companion 175
Godey's Lady's Book 176
Goforth, John 121, 146 n22
Goldsmith, Oliver 171
Grant, Dr. George M. 121, 122, 146 n23, 221
Granville Street Baptist Church 114, 129–31
Gray, "Elegy Written in a Country Churchyard" 174 n17
Griffin-Allwood, Philip, "Joseph Howe Is Their Devil" 131

Haggard, H. Rider 232, 237
Halifax 110–11, 114, 133
Halifax City Directory 118
Hamilton, letter 118, 144 n11
Harnes, Messrs (see under *Literary World*)
Harper Brothers 199, 214, 215, 221, 222, 228, 229, 231
Harper's Magazine 204, 206, 213, 218
Harper's Weekly 231
Harvey, *Introduction* 113, 140 n2, 191
Horton Collegiate Academy 36
  confusion with Acadia College 92, 107 n14
  depicted as Grand Pré School 182
  "female department" 89
  residence (picture) 38
  student life 39–41
Howe, Joseph 113, 140 n1
Hughes, Kenneth, "A Strange Manuscript" 236–37, 238

Indian trot, the 180
Innocents Abroad, The (Twain) 206

Johnson, Professor John 113, 119, 120, 121, 125, 141 n5
Johnston, H.W. 65, 78 n1, 122
Johnston, J.W. 78 n1
  Letter 133, 147 n32
  Memorial 131, 132, 147 n32, n35, n36

Kilian, "The Cheerful Inferno" 235
Kime, "The American Antecedents" 237
Knowles, J.S.
  "Professor James De Mille" 36
  letter to F.E. De Mill 36
  list of De Mille's works 176, 178, 189, 214
Koopman, H.L. 67, 71, 78 n2, 169

La Bossière, "The Mysterious End" 238–39
Lawson, Professor George 113, 115, 119, 120, 136, 139, 142 n7, 149 n43
Lawson, Caroline (Mrs.) 120, 121, 145 n20, 148 n40
Legislative Library of Nova Scotia, The 178, 214
Leinster Street Baptist Church (Saint John) 33, 91
Liechti, James 119, 144 n18, 163
Lighthall, *Songs of the Great Dominion* 163
Literary World 178, 187, 188, 189, 203, 204, 206
Logan, J.W. 142 n6
Longley, *Acadia University* 37, 54
Lyall, Professor James 113, 136–37, 119, 136, 139, 140 n3

Macdonald, Professor Charles 113, 115, 119, 139, 142 n6
MacLeod, "James De Mille" 37, 54, 149 n42
MacMechan 13, 14, 23, 45, 119, 133,

153, 163, 191, 194 n1, 206, 211–13, 214, 219–20
Mahon, "James De Mille" 206, 209, 213, 219
Manning Saunders, Rev. Edward 131, 134
McCulloch, Professor Thomas 113, 114, 119
McFarlane, *New Brunswick Bibliography* 214, 234
Morning News (Saint John) 96, 159, 173 n6
Murray, rev. of *Behind the Veil* 163

Newton Theological Institution 54
New York Ledger 176
Novascotian, The 118, 128, 140 n1
Nova Scotian Institute of Natural Science 134, 135, 149 n43

O'Callaghan, *Documentary History of New York* 19
Otto, *Idea of the Holy* 167
Oxley, J. MacDonald 140 n3, 141 n4, 142 n7

Parker, Dr. 129, 131
Parks, M.G.
   CEECT edition of *Strange Manuscript* 229
   Introduction 231, 235, 246 n3
   "Strange to Strangers Only" 229, 236
Patterson, *More Studies in Nova Scotian History* 120, 145 n19
Paul, Robert (letter to author) 133
Pierce, *An Outline* 191
Plato, *Apologia Socratis* ("Apology") 165
Pope, Alexander 171
   "The Gardens of Alcinous" 173 n7
"Professorial Who's Who, A" 140–43 *passim*, 144 n18
Providence Daily Journal 169

Pryor, John 84, 91–92, 182, 193, 214, 222, 228–29
   and Dalhousie Chair of Classics 114–15
   suspension from Granville Street Church 129–32, 147 n32, n33, n34
Pryor, Tom 92, 107 n17

Raymond, "John De Mill, Loyalist" 23, 29, 30, 32, 33, 35, 54 n1, 55 n3, 93, 105, 107 n18, 118
Rhodenizer, *Handbook of Canadian Literature* 191
Richter, Jean-Paul 163
   Campaner Tal 167
   "Traum Über Das All" 167
Ritchie, *Songs of the Maritimes* 163
Roberts, Charles G.D., rev. of *Behind the Veil* 164
Roberts, Richard, Introduction 188
Ross, The Rev. James 113, 115, 119, 136, 140 n3

Sabine, *American Loyalists* 72
Saint John
   fires 25–26, 36
   freemen of 23
   Grammar School 35, 36
   Mechanics Institute 139
Scott, H.P. "James De Mille" 14, 120, 189–90, 191, 195 n8, 213, 221, 222
Scott, Walter, *Ivanhoe* 242
Siddons, Mrs. Scott 253
Smeed, *Jean Paul's Dreams* 167
Smith, Dr. Nathan 22
Songs of the Great Dominion 163
South Park Street (Halifax), De Mille's house on 113
St. Luke's Church, Halifax 133
Stewart, "Canadian Literature" 206
Swift, Jonathan 171
   Gulliver's Travels 236

Tennyson, Alfred, Lord 163
    "In Memoriam" 167
    "Locksley Hall" 160
    "Oenone" 174 n18
Thomas, *Taber's Cyclopedic Medical Dictionary* 43

Vergulde Bever, De (see The Gilded Beaver)

Watters, R.E.
    Checklist of Canadian Literature 177, 188, 214, 241
    Introduction 241
    New Canadian Library edition of *Strange Manuscript* 234–35
Week, The 163, 233–34
West Columbia Mining and Manufacturing Company 83, 203
Whately, *Elements of Rhetoric* 124, 156
Whidden, "Horton Academy's Birthday" 39
Woodcock, George
    "Absence" 235
    "De Mille" 235–36

Young, Sir William 191

Permissions

The author gratefully acknowledges the permission and cooperation of the following individuals and institutions that provided the photographs and illustrations reproduced in this book: "James De Mille" courtesy Dalhousie University Archives, De Mille Collection; "Elizabeth Tongue (Budd) De Mill" courtesy Dalhousie University Archives, De Mille Collection; "The De Mill house on the Bay Shore" courtesy Dalhousie University Archives, De Mille Collection; "Horton Collegiate Academy Residence" courtesy Acadia University Archives; The *Elizabeth Bentley* courtesy Dalhousie University Archives, De Mille Collection; "Brown University in De Mille's time" courtesy Brown University Archives, John Hay Library; "Emily, [an unknown person], Alice (in front), Frederick, Eliza" courtesy Dalhousie University Archives, De Mille Collection; "Acadia, First College Hall" courtesy Acadia University Archives; "Elisha Budd De Mill" courtesy Dalhousie University Archives, De Mille Collection; "Frederick, Eliza, Emily, and Alice in the grounds of the house on the Bay Shore" courtesy Dalhousie University Archives, De Mille Collection; "Dalhousie College" courtesy William Inglis Morse Collection, Special Collections Department, Dalhousie University Library; "The Rev. Dr. John Pryor" courtesy Acadia University Archives; "De Mille's Grave in Camphill Cemetery" was taken by the author; "Illustrated manuscript page of 'Class Poem — 1854,' describing the Junior Burial" courtesy Brown University Archives, John Hay Library; "Eliza, Emily, Frederick, Mrs De Mill, Alice" courtesy Dalhousie University Archives, De Mille Collection; "Illustrated manuscript page of 'Eggs, Eggs, Eggs' " courtesy Dalhousie University Archives, De Mille Collection; "Arthur De Mille, James's youngest brother, and Alice" courtesy Dalhousie University Archives, De Mille Collection; "An engraving from the first edition of *A Strange Manuscript Found in A Copper Cylinder*" courtesy Harper & Row; "Annie De Mille at the wedding of her youngest son, Frank" courtesy Noel James De Mille.